Risk Rules

A Practical Guide to Structured Professional Judgment and Violence Prevention

Derek Eaves
Chris D Webster
Quazi Haque
Joanne Eaves-Thalken

Risk Rules: A Practical Guide to Structured Professional Judgment and violence prevention

© Pavilion Publishing and Media Ltd

The authors have asserted their rights in accordance with the Copyright, Designs and Patents Act (1988) to be identified as the author of this work.

Published by:
Pavilion Publishing and Media Ltd
Rayford House
School Road
Hove
East Sussex
BN3 5HX
Tel: 01273 434 943
Fax: 01273 227 308
Email: info@pavpub.com

Published 2019

A catalogue record for this book is available from the British Library.

ISBN: 978-1-912755-24-0

Pavilion Publishing and Media is a leading publisher of books, training materials and digital content in mental health, social care and allied fields. Pavilion and its imprints offer must-have knowledge and innovative learning solutions underpinned by sound research and professional values.

Editors: Derek Eaves, Chris Webster, Quazi Haque & Joanne Eaves-Thalken
Production editor: Mike Benge, Pavilion Publishing and Media Ltd.
Cover design: Emma Dawe, Pavilion Publishing and Media Ltd.
Page layout and typesetting: Emma Dawe, Pavilion Publishing and Media Ltd.
Printing: CMP Digital Print Solutions

Editors

Derek Eaves
Lately, Executive Commissioner, Forensic Psychiatric
Services Commission of British Columbia
University of British Columbia
Simon Fraser University.

Chris D Webster
Psychiatry, University of Toronto
Psychology, Simon Fraser University
Child and Youth Care, University of Victoria
Child Development Institute, Toronto

Quazi Haque
Royal College of Psychiatrists Forensic Quality
Network & Elysium Healthcare

Joanne Eaves-Thalken
Clinical Social Worker
Burnaby Mental Health and Substance Use
Fraser Health

Dedications

Eaves Eagles
(Liverpudlians)

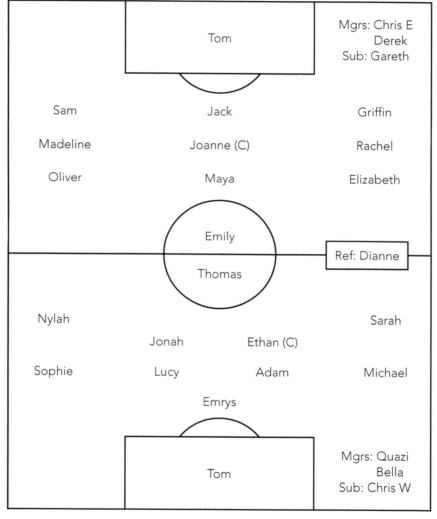

Tom

Mgrs: Chris E
Derek
Sub: Gareth

Sam   Jack   Griffin

Madeline   Joanne (C)   Rachel

Oliver   Maya   Elizabeth

Emily

Ref: Dianne

Thomas

Nylah   Sarah

Jonah   Ethan (C)

Sophie   Lucy   Adam   Michael

Emrys

Tom

Mgrs: Quazi
Bella
Sub: Chris W

Haque Academicals
(Scousers)

'The task of delivering better service delivery systems can never be complete, however, since it appears that as soon as one innovation is introduced, other issues and requirements arise... A comprehensive system of support should not only involve service agencies and government facilities, it should also address the social and security needs of clients. This may involve helping clients to establish an adequate social support network and ensuring they have adequate and appropriate housing. It is likely that gains in these areas may contribute to additional improvements in the conditions of multiproblem persons. Serious breakdowns can often be prevented if timely and appropriate interventions are available. Emergency services by trained personnel working with the police on the street, where most incidents occur, may result in a reduction in unnecessary hospitalization or incarcerations'

(Eaves,Tien & Wilson, 1997, p422)

Contents

Editors...iii

Dedications iv

Acknowledgements...3

Contributors 4

Foreword 5

Section 1: Fundamentals of practice............................7

Chapter 1: Risk rules – How Peter Scott and fellow luminaries shaped the foundations of modern risk assessment................9

Chapter 2: The law, the decision-maker, and the expert 27

Chapter 3: Mental disorders and violence...........................33

Chapter 4: Assessing psychopathic personality disorder – the client, the concept, the craft 39

Chapter 5: The increasingly recognised adverse role of trauma in forensic patients..49

Section 2: Foundational issues in violence risk assessment 57

Chapter 6: The ghost in the machine – the enduring presence of bias in forensic risk assessments.......................................59

Chapter 7: Why is it so difficult to achieve accuracy in predictions of violence? 65

Chapter 8: 'Actuarial' approaches to the prediction of violence – the violence risk appraisal guide – revised (VRAG-R) as an example.........79

Chapter 9: Violence risk assessment and management – from prediction to prevention 87

Section 3: SJP: The essentials...................................93

Chapter 10: On the absolute necessity of serial measurement...........95

Chapter 11: Structured Professional Judgment – an introduction to the HCR-20 V3 and related schemes 99

Chapter 12: Implementing SPJ schemes – getting from manual to day-to-day clinical practice 115

Chapter 13: From false starts to the real START – the practical integration of patients' strengths in clinical assessment and research work 127

Section 4: Specific applications of SPJ 133

Chapter 14: Principles for violence risk assessment with perpetrators of intimate partner violence 135

Chapter 15: SPJ and the elucidation of sexual violence risk 139

Chapter 16: Intellectual disability and violence
– minding the gaps 147

Chapter 17: Risk assessment and risk management
– in what ways must gender enter the fray 155

Chapter 18: Ethical and practical concerns regarding the current
status of risk assessment measures with Aboriginal offenders 167

Chapter 19: Assessing risk for group-based violence 173

Section 5: Treatment/transition issues.................................181

Chapter 20: Toward secure recovery in forensic care 183

Chapter 21: Patient involvement and shared decision-making
in risk assessment and management... 191

Chapter 22: Calming turbulent seas – The role of social
work and allied professions in practical risk assessment
and risk management 197

Section 6: Research and implementation 201

Chapter 23: Implementation – Thinking, planning and
integrating over the long term.. 203

Chapter 24: Risk in real time – Incorporating detailed
chronologies into risk assessment and management 213

Chapter 25: Early assessment of risks and their amelioration
by the Stop Now And Plan (SNAP) model – National and
international research.. 219

Chapter 26: The Cambridge Study in Delinquent Development 225

Chapter 27: In search of data that can inform clinical, policy
and legislative changes and public education in forensic mental
health: The National Trajectory Project.. 235

**Section 7: Ars Forensica – Applying mortar between
the scientific bricks 241**

Chapter 28: A framework for career development............................. 243

Chapter 29: Leading hands-on group discussions in forensic
mental health services – A poetic twist... 247

Chapter 30: Risk Rules – Seeing through brick walls faced
by clinicians, researchers and administrators 255

Afterword: Some thoughts on this volume and reflections
on the future 279

Acknowledgements

We, the editors, thank our contributors for applying themselves so diligently to the tasks we set them and for doing so with such good spirit. Christine Eaves and her family supported the project wholeheartedly from the beginning. Many readers will know of Derek's enthusiasm for soccer. We hope that they might perhaps enjoy our joke of laying out the dedication around a fictitious football match built around his family (and our own). Doubtless, our detractors will say that, instead of larking about in this way we should have spent that time improving the text. Our defense to such criticism would be that we did not have to worry much about how the book is organised, checked and presented. Darren Reed at Pavilion decided to take on the project, and having done so gave it a lot of attention from the very beginning of the project. Mike Benge joined him part way through and was always ready to offer prompt and constructive suggestions. We, the editors, and, it must be said, some of the contributors, seemed to have missed crucial grammar classes during their school days. Mike repaired the damage. Thanks are also due to our colleague Dr Stephen Hucker. Steve took a lively interest in the undertaking from the start and offered advice as we moved along.

An early version of the eventual book was presented in a March 2018 workshop to the Canadian Academy of Psychiatry and the Law in Victoria. We thank participants for their helpful suggestions. We are grateful to the Centre of Criminology and Sociolegal Studies at the University of Toronto for permission to reproduce Table 8.1 from a 1994 book called *The Violence Prediction Scheme* by Webster *et al*. Mr Justice Richard Schneider graciously gave permission to reproduce various excerpts from an occasional informal scientific newsletter distributed to members of the Ontario Review Board under the title 'Clinical Risk Assessment and Management (CRAM)'. The various issues (13 in all) were professionally prepared and distributed by Ms Marie Andryjowcz during 2016 and 2018. Two of the issues were supported by illustrations made by Ms Joy Santiago, who kindly gave permission for two of these to be included herein (Chapters 7 and 12). We also thank the American Psychological Association for granting permission to reproduce Table 8.2 from an article by Rice *et al* (2013) published in *Psychological Assessment*.

In London, we thank Ms Nicola Vance for her assistance in helping us with preparation of the manuscript, and for making sense of the numerous email exchanges between the editors. In Victoria, Chris thanks his grandson, Michael, for his hard work in getting the manuscript into shape. Michael brought exceptional technical skills to bear. As well, it was instructive to be able to sit side-by-side with someone who could peer into the murk and figure out what we were trying to say. We are fortunate that, given his adeptness with grammar, he did not skip his English classes as a schoolboy.

Contributors

Leena Augimeri, PhD. Child Development Institute; University of Toronto.

Hy Bloom, LLB, MD, FRCP(C). Faculties of Medicine & Law, University of Toronto; Psychiatry & Behavioural Neurosciences, McMaster University; Workplace.Calm, Inc.

Douglas P Boer, PhD. University of Canberra.

Johann Brink, MB ChB BA Hons FCPsych (SA) FRCPC. University of British Columbia.

Sumeeta Chatterjee, MD, FRCP(C). University of Toronto.

David Cooke, PhD, FRSE. University of Bergen.

Anne Crocker, PhD. Université de Montréal; Institut Philippe-Pinel de Montréal.

Kevin S Douglas, LLB, PhD. Simon Fraser University; Protect International Risk and Safety Services, Vancouver; Helse Bergen Competence Centre in Forensic Psychiatry, Bergen; University of Oslo.

Beate Eusterschulte, Dr. med. Vitos Klinik für Forensische Psychiatrie Haina.

David P Farrington, OBE, PhD. Cambridge University.

Stephen D Hart, PhD. Simon Fraser University; University of Bergen; Protect International Risk and Safety Services Inc.

Sheilagh Hodgins, PhD, FRSC. Université de Montréal; Karolinska Institutet.

Harry Kennedy, BSc, MB, MD, FRCPI, FRCPsych. Central Mental Hospital, Dublin; Trinity College, Dublin.

Randall Kropp, PhD, R.Psych. Forensic Psychiatric Services Commission of British Columbia; Simon Fraser University; Protect International Inc.

Caroline Logan, DPhil. Greater Manchester Mental Health NHS Foundation Trust; University of Manchester.

Mary-Lou Martin, RN MScN MEd. St. Joseph's Healthcare Hamilton; McMaster University.

Robert Menzies, PhD. Simon Fraser University.

Rüdiger Müller-Isberner, Dr. med. Vitos Klinik für Forensische Psychiatrie Haina.

Tonia Nicholls, PhD. University of British Columbia.

Stephanie R Penney, PhD. Centre for Addiction and Mental Health; University of Toronto.

John Petrila, JD, LLM. Meadows Mental Health Policy Institute.

Richard D Schneider, PhD, LL.B, LL.M, CPsych. University of Toronto, Faculty of Law, Department of Psychiatry, Faculty of Medicine.

Alexander IF Simpson, MBChB, BMedSci, FRANZCP. University of Toronto; Centre for Addiction and Mental Health.

Patricia Zapf, PhD. Palo Alto University.

Foreword

All societies struggle with assessing and managing risk in a variety of contexts. Various laws, methods and procedures have evolved for the consideration and management of risk in every country around the world. A variety of diverse professions have studied issues related to risk and have developed theories, methods and procedures for the assessment and management of risk within their particular contexts of interest. With respect to risk for violence, the process and the focus of risk assessment has evolved from the prediction of dangerousness, to an understanding of factors that, alone or in combination, increase or decrease the likelihood that someone will be violent, to consideration of how best to manage – or even prevent – violence and communicate most effectively regarding risk. This evolution in how we think about, assess and manage risk has occurred as a result of a diverse array of viewpoints, experiences, practices, successes and failures.

This practical guide to structured professional judgment (SPJ) and violence risk brings together the work of a veritable who's who of the international risk assessment field. The work of some of the field's top researchers, practitioners and scholars – from various countries and representing various disciplines – is presented in this guide. Together, the chapters in this guide represent the relevant base of research, policy and practice that set the foundation for best practices in the assessment and management of risk for violence.

The contributing authors are each well-known leaders in their respective areas of focus, representing a diverse accumulation of training, knowledge and experience. The resulting collection of chapters provides the reader with a practical guide replete with the collected wisdom of this group of international experts and leaders.

Organised into seven sections, the book provides a distillation of important fundamentals of practice, foundational issues in violence risk assessment, the essentials of the structured professional judgment approach, specific applications of the SPJ approach, treatment/transition issues, research and implementation considerations, and a holistic view toward developing knowledge and skill in the forensic mental health field.

The guide begins with a distillation of the fundamentals of practice, including discussions of how Peter Scott and fellow luminaries shaped the foundations of modern risk assessment (Chris Webster, Quazi Haque, Joanne Thalken-Eaves, Derek Eaves & Johann Brink); the law, the decision-maker, and the expert (Richard Schneider); mental disorder and violence

(Sheilagh Hodgins); the assessment of psychopathic personality (David Cooke); and the increasingly recognised role that trauma plays in one's development and functioning (Hy Bloom).

Foundational issues in violence risk assessment are discussed, including the presence of bias in forensic evaluation (Robert Menzies); the difficulties in achieving accuracy in violence predictions (Quazi Haque & Chris Webster); actuarial approaches to the assessment of violence (Quazi Haque & Chris Webster); and the evolution from prediction to prevention in violence risk assessment (Stephen Hart & Kevin Douglas).

The essentials of the SPJ approach to risk assessment are covered, including the necessity of serial measurement (Harry Kennedy); the HCR-20-V3 and related risk assessment schemes (Quazi Haque & Chris Webster); the implementation of SPJ in day-to-day practice (Chris Webster & Sumeeta Chatterjee); and the practical integration of patient strengths in clinical assessment and research (Mary-Lou Martin).

Specific applications of the SPJ approach are presented, including intimate partner violence (Randall Kropp); sexual violence (Caroline Logan); intellectual disability (Beate Eusterschulte); gender (Tonia Nicholls); culture (Douglas Boer); and group-based violence (Stephen Hart). Treatment and transition issues are elucidated through discussions of secure recovery in forensic care (Alexander Simpson); patient involvement and shared decision making (Quazi Haque); and the role of social work and allied professions in practical risk assessment and management (Joanne Eaves-Thalken).

Research and implementation issues (Rüdiger Müller-Isberner) are highlighted, including the incorporation of detailed chronologies into risk assessment and management (Stephanie Penney); early assessment of risks and their amelioration (Leena Augimeri); the Cambridge study in delinquent development (David Farrington); and conducting large scale research (Anne Crocker). Finally, a holistic view toward developing knowledge and skill in forensic mental health is presented from the perspective of the patient (Chris Webster) and the professional (Chris Webster and Quazi Haque) and a consideration of future priorities in the field of risk assessment (John Petrila).

This practical guide to structured professional judgment and violence risk is a must-own for anyone who is involved with the assessment and management of risk for violence. With a carefully curated selection of top international experts presenting concise coverage of the fundamentals of structured professional judgment and violence risk, it will quickly become an indispensible resource for any practitioner.

Patricia A Zapf, PhD

Section 1
Fundamentals
of practice

Chapter 1:
Risk rules – How Peter Scott and fellow luminaries shaped the foundations of modern risk assessment

By Chris Webster, Quazi Haque, Joanne Eaves-Thalken, Johann Brink & Derek Eaves

'Since the accuracy of prediction varies inversely with time, the maintenance of personal relationships and good communication seems the inescapable requirement in the management of potentially dangerous criminals.' (Scott, 1977, p127)

Much of day-to-day, world-wide practices in forensic mental health services depend on ideas propagated in the 70s and 80s by Saleem Shah (1978), John Monahan (1981) and Hank Steadman (Steadman & Cocozza, 1974). But if we, the authors of this introductory chapter, were asked to turn up from the era we have just mentioned, a *single* comprehensive, well-grounded article, we would, without hesitation, say there is none better than Scott's piece in the *British Journal of Psychiatry* (1977). In what follows we have borrowed Scott's words directly from his article.

The above setting quote speaks for itself. There are no simple, sure-fire methods for predicting violence into the future. This is especially the case for individuals at liberty in the general community (see Webster *et al*, 2014, p63) who point to studies demonstrating that prediction-outcome correlations are appreciably lower for released patients than those detained in hospitals).

What is remarkable about Scott's piece is the tone. He managed to incorporate all the major scientific facts available at the time he was writing, but retained throughout the article a strongly humanistic perspective. The patient, with all his or her faults, yet with full emphasis on his or her personal attributes, remains central in this account. And it does not stop there. From his broad experience, Scott understood how difficult can be the day-to-day work of those who provide care and treatment for patients in hospitals and the community. He also points out that line staff members have up-front knowledge about their clients which *must* form part of team discussions and be included in eventual reports.

In what follows, as a kind of exercise, we have selected quotations from the original Scott article as a 'lead' to each and every one of the remaining chapters in the book. The idea is not to show that Scott 'thought of everything' himself, and that therefore our readers have no need to go beyond this one article. Indeed, to the contrary, the point of our 'riffs' on Scott is to suggest how our present contributors have each, in their own ways, carried on from where Peter Scott left off.

Chapter 2: The law – Richard Schneider

> *'More difficult still is that factor which in a medical analogy would be called infectiousness, and which indicates the belief that others will be inclined to follow suit, to use this loophole in the law, to join the insurrection, to practice this clever form of deceit, or to gain ascendancy or preference in this new way.'* (p128)

Richard Schneider writes as a judge in charge of a tribunal which oversees a large group of patients previously determined by the courts to be Not Criminally Responsible by Reason of Mental Disorder (NCRMD) or Unfit to Stand Trial (UFST). Decisions made at Board hearings can be, and fairly often are, appealed to an appellate court. Yet his point is that the law needs, at least now and then, and at least in some instances, to be given a 'tweak'. The law is not static. Sometimes it needs to be challenged or changed, to be 'liberalised'. But sometimes, as in Scott's quotation above, the existing law needs to be defended when its actual purpose is being circumvented.

Chapter 3: Diagnostic entities – Sheilagh Hodgins

> *'...it is important to recognize that intercurrent states of anxiety and depression can exaggerate minor degrees of these traits which may then be mistaken for fully-fledged features of the personality and lead to over-pessimistic prediction.'* (p136)

In a book published by us in the Scott, Steadman, Shah, Monahan era (Webster *et al*, 1982), we presented data on how diagnoses were ascribed to patients at time of forensic psychiatric assessment (see, for example, Table

6.2, p146). What we the authors failed to take properly into account was the fact that our data were based on the *primary*, first-listed diagnoses. This was to overlook Scott's point about the fluidity of different mental or personality disorders within the same persons and how each can come into play over time and according to circumstance. In the quotation it is clear that Scott understood this actuality very clearly. More is said on the topic in Chapter 7 of this book. It is one reason why it is hard in practice to forecast violence.

Hodgins also makes the point that schizophrenia is the most common disorder amongst patients within forensic services across many countries, and highly prevalent in jails, yet poses great difficulties for courts and clinicians in terms of risk prediction.

Chapter 4: Discerning psychopathy – David Cooke

'We have to rely on a combination of **acumen, prediction and after-care**. *While this cannot be said to be reliable, it is pragmatic and certainly avoids or abbreviates many long terms of segregation, even though there may be occasional mistakes.* **If it is done it can be done better**. *What are the factors that can be looked for and fed to the diagnostic procedure, and from what different aspects should the problem be viewed?'* (p129)

David Cooke, a psychologist, could have been asked to write on the topic of using the general SPJ approach to assess the extent to which institutions, and the persons who work in them, can induce violent behaviour – a fact that Scott himself brought up. In fact he said: *'The incidence of violence amongst hospital patients or prisoners must not be too readily attributed to any psychiatric condition rather than to those grave frustrations which are common to closed institutions'* (p27). Readers should take note of David Cooke's work with Lorraine Johnstone in *Promoting Risk Intervention by Situational Management* (PRISM), 2008. It is a topic which ought to have been more fully covered in this text. Fortunately though, he has more than one string to his bow. In this text he deals with Scott's insistence on the need for 'clinical acumen'. He tells our readers how, practically, to gain information from and about persons under assessment. As Scott pointed out, there are ample reasons why some patients find it in their interest to provide information that is deceptive and misleading (see Scott, 2006, pp18–19). David Cooke suggests ways for clinicians to stay on course, with necessary inventiveness, as they conduct their assessment.

Chapter 5: Trauma – Hy Bloom

*'Excessive violence very **doubtfully warrants the importance assigned to it by judges and others who assess dangerousness** as a guide to sentencing. We forget that most murderers are amateurs and most victims healthy people with a firm hold on life, so that the killer is often horrified at the difficulty of killing and the awful sight and sounds involved, so that he strives in desperation or panic, to end the process quickly.'* (p131)

Many persons assigned by courts and other bodies for forensic mental health assessment have experienced extreme maltreatment, not just in their childhoods but in their adult lives as well. Peter Scott himself refers to the kinds of past traumas that can have adverse effects into the present. He says, for example: *'Battering parents are held, particularly in the American literature, to have experienced violence in their own childhoods, but there are many exceptions; clinical and ethological data suggest that other deprivations (of access to mother or play-fellows) may be equally important'* (p20). Hy Bloom, in his chapter, develops this angle. He points out that the authors of the HCR-20 V3 have devoted more attention to the topic of trauma than they gave in V2.

Chapter 6: Bias – Robert Menzies

'Because we all have experienced dangerous emotions there is the risk of projection and scapegoating.' (p127)

'For a start, it is healthy for the investigator to review his own role: has he been strictly neutral in his approach?' (p139)

Robert Menzies makes no case that mental health practitioners are necessarily able to leave their biases at home each morning as they proceed to work. Obviously, colleagues in the various mental health disciplines should approach their tasks with as neutral a 'mindset' – to use a currently popular term – as possible. He makes it clear just how easily and unwittingly many kinds of bias can enter the clinical process. This practical difficulty has long been acknowledged. One of the clearest examples was brought to attention by Stephen Pfohl (1978) who published transcripts of the often highly pejorative language used against patients as their cases were being reviewed by specially contrived tribunals. Bob Menzies draws on a rapidly expanding scientific literature on decision-making within sociology and social psychology. We may not be able, as we sit in clinical teams or review boards, to make fully disinterested decisions, but we can try to be as impartial as possible.

Writing for a general audience, Pontefract (2018), having reviewed recent thinking and research on decision-making, puts it well: *'... bad is much stronger than good. Our natural human tendency is to be more affected by things that are negative (or are potentially negative) than those that are positive'* (p56).

Chapter 7: Why predictions of violence fail – Quazi Haque and Chris Webster

'We strive after accurate prediction of dangerousness because this would quell our anxieties, enable us to draw clear lines between the dangerous and non-dangerous, and avoid the necessity of continuing contact with and concern for them. But no such magical process will be possible.' (p140)

Scott was right in his prediction. Forty years on, researchers and clinicians have hit on no 'magical process'. Yet *some* prediction power is possible in the aggregate. A 2011 review of 68 studies involving near 26,000 participants is instructive (Singh *et al*, 2011). These authors found median Areas Under the Curve (AUCs) were, in order, highest for the SVR-20 (0.78), SORAG – a specialised version of the VRAG for sex offending – (0.75), the VRAG itself (0.74), SAVRY (0.71), HCR-20 V2 (0.70), SARA (0.70), Static-99 – designed as an actuarial device for sex offending – (0.70), LSI-R (0.67) and PCL-R (0.66). When similar computations were performed on overall low/medium/high risk scores, the HCR-20 V2 came second in the 'horse race'. The SAVRY took over first place (0.76) and the VRAG, as before, came in third (0.66). The authors suggest that, generally, devices designed for specific populations (e.g. adolescents, sex offenders) tend to outperform (slightly) those developed as general risk assessment schemes.

A recent study has examined how well the HCR-20 V2 predicts success of Not Guilty by Reason of Insanity (NGRI) acquitees on release in the state of Oregon (Vitacco *et al*, 2018). The 238 patients on Conditional Release (CR) were followed from four to nine years. Most of the patients (66%) did *not* require re-hospitalisation during the study period. Overall the HCR-20 total scores were not related to failure on CR. In fact, only two items, both from the Risk Management Scale – Exposure to Destabilizers and Stress – were predictive. To the present authors, the fact that these items were predictive, especially over such a long period, is actually surprising. This is so in light of the many factors which work against achieving much in the way of precision.

Chapter 8: Actuarial predictions – Quazi Haque and Chris Webster

'Dangerous behaviour lies at the extreme of the aggression parameter, and most standardized tests tend to become unreliable at both their extremities, yet it is in just these areas that the most important decisions lie. Existing predictive scales tend to be over-inclusive; their results may be very useful for administrative purposes but are clinically unreliable...' (p128)

Some years ago we published a short book on the prediction of violence (Webster *et al*, 1994). The idea of the book was to bring the Violence Risk Assessment Guide (VRAG) to the fore, to put to practical use its painstakingly-gathered actuarial data on 618 men. We presented a bar-graph which showed the higher the VRAG score across nine increments (called 'bins'), the greater the likelihood of violence over the course of the subsequent years (Figure 4.1 p34). The figure is striking. It shows a perfectly-ordered rise in probability of violence from low left (Bin 1) to high right (Bin 9). But, impressive though this may appear at first blush, two problems arise. First, the VRAG scores, being normally distributed, there is a concentration of scores in the middle of the bin range (i.e. bins 3, 4, 5, 6 and 7). Simply put, knowing that the individual under consideration scored in the centre of the distribution does not advance the case in any particular practical way. It simply means that this person is like most other persons in the population under study. Knowing that a person is in bins 1 or 2 or 8 or 9 *may* be of some limited help in actual decision making but, as we have said, only relatively few cases are found in the extreme ends of the distribution (in this instance 82 and 38 cases respectively). Second, the authors suggest that once the VRAG score is ascertained, it may be possible to 'adjust' it on the basis of current or anticipated clinical considerations. The authors, though, limited such tampering by suggesting that this not be by more than 10 percent upward or downward. Given the benefit of years of hindsight, this was not a prescription that made much sense. The actuarial prediction is what it is. Although it is not uncommon to give some consideration in decision-making to actuarially-derived estimates of future probability, it is not – at least at the present state of the science – wise to place unverified limits on the weights to be allotted to such information.

Chapter 9: From prediction to prevention – Stephen Hart & Kevin Douglas

'Prediction studies should aim not to replace but to complement the clinical approach, and vice versa.

We cannot at present hope, by taking infinitely careful aim, to direct our dangerous patient to safety like an arrow to its target; rather, through effective supervision, we must accompany him, being prepared to adapt to his varying needs, whether encouraging independence, moderating activity or recalling him to start again from the beginning.' (p129)

A few months ago one of us (C.D.W.) had a slight disagreement with one of his fellow HCR-20 authors. My claim was that V2 of the HCR-20 was more oriented toward prediction than is its successor, V3. His argument was that *neither* version did or does give much weight to prediction, that both devices are concerned with the *prevention* of violence in the individual case. We would both agree, though, that V2 was limited in that it offered little or no guidance as to how to create treatment plans or possibly helpful interventions of one kind or another. It is this aspect which marks off V3 from its predecessor.

Chapter 10: Serial measurement – Harry Kennedy

'Much behaviour which at first sight seems insane, unadaptive, or inexplicable is seen to be rational when the longitudinal development of the incident is studied – the small steps by which it was reached…' (p130)

Scott's tenets may have applied to individual offenders, while Kennedy takes a similar scientific approach when considering how forensic services should evaluate different pillars of care provision. Kennedy and colleagues in Dublin have successfully employed a range of clinical assessments, SPJ devices and outcome measures to drive their care models. There is much to be impressed with by the continuing refinements of the programmes based on well-designed research and learning from international collaborations.

Chapter 11: Principles of SPJ – Quazi Haque and Chris Webster

'Before factors can be considered they must be gathered. It is patience, thoroughness and persistence in this process, rather than any diagnostic or interviewing brilliance, that produces results. In this sense the telephone, the written request for past records, and the checking of information against other informants, are the important diagnostic devices.' (p129)

As we have mentioned at various points in the text, and as Peter Scott insisted, there is need for guides in this area of professional work. As knowledge is accumulated from scientific studies and from professional practice, it needs to be codified to a degree. Moreover, such guides need to be revised at intervals. This is not only because new findings deserve to be incorporated but because words in everyday parlance charge their meanings, or drop out of use altogether (see Macfarlane & Morris, 2017).

There is, too, the not unimportant point that patients themselves should have a chance to know the basis on which they are being evaluated (and, actually, in many cases, use aspects of these SPJ devices to monitor their own progress).

Chapter 12: A conversation – Chris Webster and Sumeeta Chatterjee

Peter Scott called for *'an elementary practical guide to the more rational use of intuition.'* (p129)

The above sentence appeared close to the beginning of his article; the rest of the paper was given over to the elaboration of a guide. But by the time the end of the piece has been reached it has become evident to the reader that there is nothing particularly 'elementary' about assessing and managing risks. He does not conclude with some sort of a 'checklist' which will wrap up an evaluation with a bow. The whole article points to the complexities involved in this aspect of specialised clinical and research work. All the same, there has to be some way of transmitting hard-won knowledge from one generation to another. This is the point of the 'Imaginary Conversation' between a member of one generation to a member of another. It tries to deal with a serious topic in a way that is supposed to be good-spirited, and a little light-hearted.

Chapter 13: Assessing client strengths – Mary-Lou Martin

'Our disappointment may be alleviated if we accept that short-term assessment (which permits the scanning of the subject's present environment and associates, and his reactions to these) is likely to be much more reliable than long-term assessment, which, especially in the present setting of a mobile and changeable society, is likely to be totally beyond our reach.' (p140)

Peter Scott makes the point that 'youthful rebellion' does not necessarily indicate a poor prognosis. Persons in institutional care may have conflicts with staff. They may be troublesome. Yet, he would have it that '*aggressive behaviour which stems from strength and determination resolves itself, especially in the young*' (p21, emphasis added). Michelangelo is regarded as seeing every block of stone as having a statue inside and the task of the sculptor was to discover it. Similarly, we professionals need to find creative ways to help clients unearth and build up their strengths.

Chapter 14: Spousal assault – Randy Kropp

'*...the extremely common and potent provocation offered by a state of continued uncertainty; e.g. when a reluctant or frightened wife rejects but as it were leaves the door open and permits occasional contact; it is the vacillating rather than the abusing or aggressive wife who is most at risk.*' (p130)

'*Jealousy is sometimes frankly delusional or may be part of a psychosis, but pathological degrees of jealousy are not dependent on delusion (i.e. they are compatible with good insight).*' (p136)

Randy Kropp has been studying spousal assault for many years. The most recent work to come from his clinic is V³ of the *Spousal Assault Risk Assessment Guide* (SARA V³). Kropp and fellow colleagues share Scott's appreciation that spousal assault and other types of family violence need to be understood not just from the perspective of the perpetrator but also from the psychosocial adjustment and behaviours of the (potential) victim.

Chapter 15: Sex offending – Caroline Logan

'*Many dangerous offenders, believing that they cannot control their impulses, seek help from the police or from doctors. They must be taken seriously, for rejection of their angry dependency seems to facilitate the threatened crime. Some offenders, notably paedophiles, have a tendency to use psychiatric clinics as a sort of insurance policy against the next offence; their responsibility, if they wish to be at large, has to be made clear to them.*' (p131)

'*Once adolescence is passed, persistent failure to achieve a sexual partnership, despite attempts, with a history of at least one violent assault upon a female, is usually ominous.*' (p135)

Scott's concern is that certain high-risk sex offenders are able to move between health and correctional services without any real attention directed toward their behaviors and psychological problems. He makes the case that when treating such individuals, professionals should be clear about what are acceptable and unacceptable behaviours. Logan takes this further by demonstrating the value of developing SPJ-assisted risk formulations that are simple, jargon-free, and that make sense to the offender. This kind of approach seems necessary to help clients foster motivation to engage in what is often emotionally difficult treatment.

Chapter 16: Intellectual disability – Beate Eusterschulte

Peter Scott explains that Hefner and Boker (1973) '...*in a very large-scale German study, found that mental patients and "defectives" show no higher an incidence of violence than do mentally sound persons.*' (p137)

Eusterschulte challenges us to recognise the gaps and improve our knowledge in the field of intellectual disability and violence. We have moved on from using terminology such as 'defectives' that are enshrined in old mental health laws. Nonetheless, we can still do much better to develop diagnostic instruments and risk schemes sensitive to the needs and risks of those with mental impairment. The familiar HCR-20V3 may produce good enough predictive accuracy for certain cohorts of offenders with intellectual disability – but what is really required in the individual case is a basket of functional devices alongside the SPJ device(s) of choice, to help arrive at the best possible formulation and treatment plan.

Chapter 17: Gender – Tonia Nicholls

'*The general clinical experience is that women more rarely cross the threshold into dangerousness, but when they do, perhaps by substituting stealth for strength, they offer the same difficulties of prediction and treatment as do men.*' (p133)

Scott highlights that particular skills are required when assessing risk in women. Thanks to colleagues such as Nicholls, this area of practice has developed appreciably over recent years. Studies such as the National Trajectory Project (see Chapter 27, p235) demonstrate further that NCRMD women have a distinct clinical, criminological and psychosocial profile from their male counterparts. Gender-specific assessment, treatment and risk management in forensic services needs to expand further. The Early

Assessment Risk List -21 for Girls (EARL-21G) is a good example of how a gender specific risk assessment scheme can be linked successfully to the appropriate programme (Stop Now and Plan for Girls, see Chapter 25, p219), and the reader may also be interested in looking up the Female Additional Manual (FAM) (de Vogel *et al*, 2014) which can be used alongside the HCR-20V2 or HCR-20V3. The FAM contains nine specific risk factors for women as well as additional guidelines to five HCR-20 items. While such schemes continue to be refined and evaluated, the progress to greater client-centred risk assessment can only be seen as a positive step.

Chapter 18: Culture – Douglas Boer

'No doubt the contribution of new forms of standardized test is potentially great, but to date they are not clinically very helpful in the field.' (Scott, p135)

The RMGAO, on which Douglas Boer's piece is based, is not a psychological instrument or any other form of 'test'. None of the devices within the overall umbrella of SPJ decision-enhancing guides sets out to be 'standardised', where standardised means based on scores obtained from large numbers of persons. The guides are *structured*, not standardised. Yet the Scott quotation, slightly re-interpreted, remains apt. Boer makes the point that it is drastically unfair to apply a device like the HCR-20V3, holus bolus, to members of Aboriginal society. Yet he goes on to explain how it is that, working with Aboriginal colleagues, it remains possible to adapt and re-configure available schemes so that they become culturally informed. And he would argue that very *process* of re-shaping a scheme can be highly constructive for all concerned.

Chapter 19: Assessing risk for group-based violence – Stephen Hart

'Similarly, in social animals, much dangerousness depends upon disturbing the often precarious adjustment of other individuals, especially within a group; hence the importance of behavioural conventions or what are now called good manners, which in effect announce the individual's self-control and his concern for the feelings of others. The media of mass communication besides modifying attitudes to, and expectations of, violence, also change the boundaries of groups.' (p127)

'It is very difficult to generalize about the significance of offences committed in a group or alone. It will depend on whether the group is

a loosely structured one (as occurs in youthful affrays and pack rapes) or a highly organized group of professional criminals.' (p130)

Scott's observations about violence committed by groups is relevant when considering specific phases in the process of becoming a terrorist, or of specific roles in terrorist activity. Hart makes the point that structured professional judgment may be usefully applied to the risk assessment of terrorism. However, given that many know risk factors for common violence are in fact not risk factors for violent terrorism, the overall content of any instrument to assess the risk of terrorism will be very different from the substantive content of current instruments that address common violence. Group structure, ideologies, grievances and affiliations all change the boundaries and behaviors of groups.

Chapter 20: Recovery – Alexander Simpson

'Favourable response to after-care is seen when there is movement towards improvement rather than achievement...' (p138)

Scott's prescient observations are drawn from working in a south London forensic psychiatric facility and a busy Victorian remand prison. These are environments where principles of holistic care can be disintegrated by the need of staff and prisoners to just 'get through the day'. Similar pressures exist in the modern day as finite resources can impact on the care delivered to those suffering from severe mental illness and substance misuse disorders in prison and secure mental health services. Simpson's chapter describes how the principles of the recovery movement can be applied within the wider forensic system and have a positive influence on how patients move toward a great sense of self-management and fulfillment, even, or perhaps especially, at times when support in the community can be difficult to access.

Chapter 21: Partnerships with patients – Quazi Haque

'It is realized that it is an economy to aim straight for the personal contact, which has the advantage of serving a host of other useful functions simultaneously; it has the further advantage that it can be achieved by non-medical personnel provided they are well supported by a good system of communications. Involvement on a long-term basis and good communications are there the inescapable bases for assessment of dangerousness.' (p141)

The author of this chapter has spent many years implementing SPJ schemes within forensic, civil and correctional services. He observes that, with time, guides such as the HCR-20V2 or HCR-20V3 have been used differently. What may have been a 'done to' risk assessment has moved to a 'done with' (i.e. clinician with the patient) collaboration, and in some services has also included a 'done by' format. In such situations, risk assessments completed by the patient are part of a wider collaboration to achieve a comprehensive assessment of prior personal, health and criminogenic history, and an opportunity to engage in the task of formulation. Some readers may already be facilitating SPJ assisted treatment groups to support rehabilitation for their patients – this has been a welcome development for the SPJ approach.

Chapter 22: Calming turbulent seas – Joanne Eaves-Thalken

'After-care, and intermediate placements between secure hospital or prison, together with indeterminacy of detention, or partial indeterminacy offered by borstal sentences and various forms of parole and conditional discharge provide our only means of compensating for our inability to make accurate predictions of dangerousness. The after-care officer's onerous task is relieved if he is introduced to the offender at an early stage; if he is well briefed on his charge's characteristics, if his supervision is supplemented by periodic reassessments of the offender and discussion with the responsible medical officer, and if recall is undertaken quickly when the danger signals.' (p138)

A trip to the Manchester Art Gallery may lead one to the Joseph Mallord Turner exhibits. One of his lesser known paintings, 'Now for the Painter', depicts a scene at the port of Calais. It is a windy day and the seas are dangerously choppy. Passengers are trying to board a ship from a small boat. The 'painter' is a guide rope that the sailor tries to throw to secure the boat to help the travelers reach safety. This turbulent setting can be vividly applied to many clients seeking a safe transition from a secure psychiatric facility to life in the community. Finding suitable accommodation, a reasonable income, restoring relationships and re-learning basic activities of daily living can be easier with professional guidance, as described by Joanne Eaves-Thalken.

Chapter 23: Implementation – Rüdiger Müller-Isberner

'If it is done it can be done better.' (p129)

Vitos Haina Forensic Psychiatric Hospital in Germany consists of 350 patients and around 450 staff. Most patients suffer from severe mental illness or an ICD-10 diagnosis of mental retardation. All patients have committed at least one violent crime and have been sent to hospital under a criminal court order. Up until the mid-1990s, risk assessment was entirely based on clinical judgment with clinicians able to apply personally favoured methods case to case. The hospital leadership decided to try out a new scheme, the HCR-20 (Webster *et al*, 1995) as there was evidence that existing practices yielded estimations of the risk of violence that were no more accurate than chance. Dr Müller-Isberner provided medical leadership to the hospital across three decades which subsequently saw the implementation of three different versions of the HCR-20. Scott's observations in his 1977 paper are directed toward clinical assessment rather than implementation of risk assessment schemes. Nonetheless we believe he would have appreciated the efforts made by Vitos Haina to continuously evaluate and refine their risk approaches, while also using the latest evidence in the growing field of implementation science.

Chapter 24: Chronologies – Stephanie Penney

*'**The detail of the behaviour**, on the other hand, is so valuable that opinions should not be stated until the fullest possible information, including at least the witnesses' statements and the depositions, has been obtained. Such detail helps very much in the essential reconstruction of the equation: offender + victim + circumstance = the offence; each element of the equation is equally important.'* (p130)

Scott's paper and Penney's chapter really arrive at a similar underlying conclusion. Detailed chronologies are essential when re-constructing offending behavior. The task is better achieved through persistence, organisation and professional common sense when weighing up facts – sparkling élan is not a required attribute to do this well. The authors of chapter 8 on actuarial predictions, make the point that even the most algorithmic actuarial risk assessment tools require professional judgment when building up relevant chronologies to score mandated risk items.

Chapter 25: Children – Leena Augimeri

'If aggression appears early and is widely distributed – at home, at school and in the neighbourhood, and if it is present also in siblings and father, then it is likely to persist…' (p133)

'…untrusting and inquisitional punitive parents almost compel their children to lie.' (p135)

'Groups of immature offenders, once embarked upon aggressive activity can stimulate one another in circular fashion so that very great and quite unexpected and inappropriate degrees of destruction can be achieved within seconds. Common examples are the activities of 10- or 12-year-olds who have broken into a factory, or adolescents who indulge in the so-called pack-rapes. Fatigue, sleeplessness, low blood sugar, can all lead to irritability and a reduced tolerance to long continued stresses which are so commonly the background of violence.' (p132)

The Child Development Institute (CDI) in Toronto is more than 100 years old, established in 1909. It was started by a generous benefactor who supplied a home for children in need. In the mid-1970s it became a licensed children's mental health centre. In 1985 it began to develop a systematic programme for boys and girls under-12 in conflict with the law. This has now developed into a multi-faceted programme, Stop Now and Plan (SNAP), for children with serious behavioral problems, emotional dysregulations, poor self-control and limited problem solving skills. The programme was the arena within which two SPJ guides (the EARL-20B; Early Assessment Risk List -20 for boys and EARL-21G; Early Assessment Risk Assessment List -21 for Girls) were developed and integrated into the assessment and treatment pathway. Augimeri and her team have made great efforts to evaluate the outcomes of their treatment regularly, and the reader may glean ideas that will help evaluations in their own setting.

Chapter 26: Adolescents becoming adults – David Farrington

'It is a difficult area for those who sentence or who serve on parole boards; youth is intolerant of incarceration which, on its own, appears to have little or no reformative function, yet it is precisely this age group which is most likely to recidivate. In this respect it is very important not to fall into the common error of failing to differentiate between violent and non-violent offenders in respect of recidivism.' (p134)

The Cambridge Study in Delinquent Development is a classic longitudinal long-term survey of the development of offending and antisocial behavior in over 400 London males from childhood upwards. When first contacted in 1961-62, the boys were all living in South London. It does not take a leap of faith to imagine that some of these boys may have also been interviewed in their later years by Scott at Brixton prison. Farrington's study has been highly influential in supporting the case for early risk-focused prevention to not only reduce later offending, but to also break the cycle of intergenerational transmission of delinquency.

Chapter 27: Large-scale, cross-jurisdictional research – Anne Crocker

Peter Scott cited Steadman and Cocozza (1974) in reference to their ground-breaking American follow-up study of some 1,000 'Baxstrom' patients who had been detained on the ground of 'dangerousness' but who were released (or transferred to conditions of lessened security) by court order. Scott cites the authors themselves as saying: *'If we attempt to distinguish the potentially dangerous patient, we double our error by identifying as dangerous all of a group of patients when only one third of them will live up to their expectations'* (p129).

The National Trajectory Project, as described in this chapter, was organised across three provinces of Canada. A comprehensive review of 1,800 patient files and reconviction data reveal local differences in how provinces apply NCRMD (Not Criminally Responsible on Account of Mental Disorder) and possibly also challenge previous beliefs about patients subject to such legislation. Most people who were NCMRD-accused had not committed offences involving serious offences, were known to civil mental health services and subject to financial assistance. There are a wealth of findings from this study that will no doubt inform future policy.

Final thoughts

Scott's paper relies on: (1) knowledge of the literature; (2) extensive, direct clinical experience; and (3) his own research collected case-by-case as he conducted his own duties in assessment and treatment. Our closing chapters explore different routes for gaining knowledge as a professional or as a patient. Scott's third point deserves amplification. With a little organisation it is possible for clinicians, even harried ones, to collect from the very cases in front of them, data which may not only inform and improve their clinical judgments, but when published be of great value to colleagues they will never meet.

But the more general point is that Scott saw the necessity and value of large-scale research, the results of which can have very important policy implications.

References and further reading

Bloom H & Webster CD (2007) *Essential Writings in Violence Risk Assessment and Management*. Toronto: Centre for Addiction and Mental Health.

de Vogel V, de Vries Robbe M, van Kalmthout W & Place C (2014) *Female Additional Manual (FAM): Additional guidelines to the HCR-20v3 for assessing risk for violence in women*. English version. Utrecht, the Netherlands: Van der Hoeven Klieniek.

Johnstone L & Cooke D (2008) *PRISM: Promoting Risk Intervention by Situational Management: Structured professional guidelines for assessing situational risk factors for violence in institutions*. Glasgow: Northern Networking.

Kropp PR & Hart SD (2015) SARA-V3: *User Manual for Version 3 of the Spousal Assault Risk Assessment Guide*. Vancouver: Proactive Resolutions.

Macfarlane R & Morris J (2017) *The Lost Words: A Spell Book*. Toronto: Anansi.

Monahan J (1981) *Predicting Violent Behavior: An assessment of clinical techniques*. Sage, Beverly Hills, CA.

Pfohl SJ (1978) *Predicting Dangerousness: The social construction of psychiatric reality*. Lexington, MA: Lexington Books.

Pontefract D (2018) *Open to think: Slow down, think creatively, and make better decisions*. Vancouver, BC: Figure 1 Publishing.

Scott PD (1977) Assessing dangerousness in criminals. *British Journal of Psychiatry* **131** 127–142.

Shah SA (1978) Dangerousness: A paradigm for exploring some issues in law and psychology. *American Psychologist* **33** 224–238.

Singh JP, Grann M & Fazel S (2011) A comparative study of risk assessment tools: A systematic review and metaregression analysis of 68 studies involving 25,980 participants. *Clinical Pychology Review*. doi: 10.1016/j.cpr.2010.11.009.

Steadman HJ & Cocozza JJ (1974) *Careers of the Criminally Insane: Excessive social control of deviance*. Lexington, MA: Lexington Books.

Webster CD, Menzies RJ & Jackson MA (1982) *Clinical Assessment Before Trial: Legal issues and mental disorder*. Toronto, ON: Butterworths.

Webster CD, Harris GT, Rice ME, Cormier C & Quinsey VL (1994) *The Violence Prediction Scheme: assessing dangerousness in high risk men*. Toronto, Ontario: Centre of Criminology.

Webster CD, Eaves D, Douglas KS & Wintrup (1995) *The HCR-20 Scheme: The assessment of dangerousness and risk*. Vancouver: Simon Fraser University, and British Columbia Forensic Psychiatric Services Commission.

Webster CD, Haque Q & Hucker S (2014) *Violence Risk Assessment and Management: Advances through Structured Professional Judgment and Sequential Redirections*. Second Ed. Chichester: Wiley-Blackwell.

Vitacco MJ, Balduzzi E, Rideout K, Banfe S & Britton J (2018) Reconsidering risk assessment with insanity acquitees. *Law and Human Behavior* **42** 403–412.

Chapter 2:
The law, the decision-maker, and the expert

By Richard D Schneider

'It ain't no sin if you crack a few laws now and then, just so long as you don't break any.' – Mae West

The law

Borrowing from Harper Lee's *To Kill a Mockingbird* – should the weight of 'the law' necessarily be brought to bear upon the mischief in need of a remedy? Not from the perspective of Lee's character, Sheriff Heck Tate; contrary to the lawyerly reflexes of Atticus Finch. 'Diversions' may be appropriate. A legal response is often not the only response. Other courses might be more consistent with the public's interest. But when a legal response is required, the applicable law must be determined.

Mental health experts operating in a criminal law context are expected to know the relevant law. However, knowing the law is often more art than science. Law comes from statute produced by legislatures and parliaments, and 'case law' comes from the courts. When interpreting legislation, there must be a consideration of the object, context and purpose of the statute. There is rarely one 'plain meaning' that every objective viewer can agree upon. What is the 'mischief' parliament was trying to address? Has this changed since the statute came into force? How does all of that translate to the immediate factual situation? When considering case law, again, the question will be: to what extent do the facts in the precedent(s) mirror those of the immediate situation? At the end of the process it will inevitably be the case that there is a range of legally 'correct' answers to the question being posed.

Inherently, there is elasticity in 'the law'. The law is not static – it moves and grows with the times. Whole text books have been written on the topic of how to interpret the law! The law, as suggested above, is not as one might expect – a rigid set of rules to which the courts merely add colour. The law is more appropriately seen as an organism that is continuously developing, evolving and morphing in order to be responsive to changing societal demands. As well, different laws inter-mingle. And, as they do so, they cross-temper interpretations.

The decision maker

The science that drives our understanding of mental illness is also continuously evolving. Forensic mental health practitioners frequently act as decision-makers as they sit on tribunals. In this role there will often be room within the legally correct envelope to develop appropriate interpretational nuances and to 'nudge' the law in particular directions. The role of decision-maker will permit interpretation of the law and require an application of the law to the facts that have been determined as a result of hearing the evidence. Different 'facts', as found, will push different interpretations or slants on the law. The role of decision-maker on a tribunal is the same as that of a judge (with, perhaps, jurisdictional differences). The decision-maker does not just determine from the evidence what is to be accepted and therefore what is fact, they must also interpret the law and apply it to those facts. This connection is critical as courts of appeal continuously remind us, and there must be a clearly-articulated logical connection established between the facts and the legal determination (e.g. the accused is or is not a significant threat to the safety of the public). A simple regurgitation of the evidence followed by a legal conclusion is not acceptable. Further, the decision-maker must not substitute her own view of the science, interpretation of the evidence, and 'opinion' for that of the expert witness. Decisions have to be made on the basis of the evidence heard. It is not the role of the decision-maker to generate evidence.

The expert witness

Rather than a decision-maker sitting on a tribunal, a forensic practitioner might be participating in the legal arena as an expert witness. Here his role is obviously quite different than when acting as a decision-maker. If qualified by the court or tribunal as an expert[1], he will be asked to give opinion evidence to assist the trier of fact; a tribunal, a judge or a jury. Here, his involvement is limited to assisting with determinations of 'fact'. 'Forensic' anything is, of course, the interface of a particular discipline with the law, and all forensic practitioners and experts are expected to have a very good knowledge of the law as it interfaces with their principal discipline. While it is expected that the expert will have a good working knowledge of the relevant law, he is *not* there as a legal expert – he is a mental health expert. It is quite appropriate, if not obligatory, that the expert determine in advance from the referral source information about the precise legal question about which his opinion is being sought. Clarity with respect to the relevant law should be provided to the expert by the

---

1 'Expert' is a legal term of art. An initial hearing or *voir dire* may be held to determine whether 1) expert evidence is necessary in order for the tribunal to perform the task it must, and 2) the witness proposed is indeed qualified to give that evidence. Expert witnesses, unlike other witnesses (generally), are permitted to give opinion evidence.

referral source. It is imperative that the legal question at issue be clearly defined and articulated. The question, properly framed, sets the stage for the expert opinion. Expert opinions are not dispositive of the issues to be determined, but rather assist and inform the trier of fact with respect to those determinations. The expert provides opinions based upon facts; the court or tribunal will determine the answers to the legal questions.

The ultimate issue

Legal determinations to be made at the conclusion of a hearing are ultimately the task of the court or tribunal (hence the term 'ultimate issue'). And, while courts have become accustomed to, and perhaps too comfortable with, receiving opinions regarding the ultimate issue (for example, psychiatric experts on the issues of criminal responsibility or fitness to stand trial), that legal determination is really the role of the court. Unfortunately, there have too often been situations where competing experts were not disagreeing upon diagnoses, clinical formulations, or anything within the proper ambit of their 'expertise', but rather upon the ultimate issue: legal question(s). Determination of these legal questions is to be done by the court. While the courts and other tribunals have become comfortable with and routinely receive opinions regarding ultimate issues, these are legal determinations and the expert's view regarding whether or not a legal threshold has been met should be seen in that tempering light. While necessary in the resolution of determining certain facts[2], it is inappropriate for a mental health expert to be asked for an opinion on the ultimate issue. It puts the expert in a challenging and unfair position not consistent with their role in the fact-finding process.

So, while the expert will inevitably be asked, 'Is Mr. Smith fit to stand trial or not?', he should not shy away from a response which sets out the patient's present abilities, deficiencies, proclivities, etc. followed by, '...I leave it to the court to determine whether this translates into "unfit to stand trial" from a legal perspective'.

Similarly, when preparing reports for or testifying before a tribunal like a provincial or territorial review board, the board will want to know the probability of different types of behaviour occurring in what contexts within what windows of time[3]. It will be for the court or review board to determine whether the evidence proffered and accepted meets the legal test of, for example, 'significant threat to the safety of the public' – the ultimate issue at the disposition hearing of an accused found, in the Canadian context for example, to have been not criminally responsible (NCR) in respect of an

---

2   See for example: *R. v. Mohan* [1994] 2 S.C.R. 9
3   *Winko v. British Columbia (Forensic Psychiatric Institute)* [1999] S.C.J. No. 31 at esp. para 57.

otherwise criminal act(s). If the court or review board, in reviewing the evidence adduced, is unable to conclude that the accused constitutes a significant threat to the safety of the public, an absolute discharge is the necessary and appropriate disposition and jurisdiction is lost.

The court or review board will want to hear more than a recitation or cataloguing of observations and data from tests and actuarial instruments. Raw scores are very difficult for a court or tribunal to digest. The expert's job goes much further. The court or review board will rely upon the expert to integrate the available data so that an opinion may be provided as to the probability of what sort of behaviour occurring under what sorts of circumstances. There should be a clear explanation as to how the various pieces of information combine to produce the arrived-upon opinion. The expert should be prepared to concede that missing data or inaccuracies of one sort or another may militate toward their opinion moving 'north or south'.

Professional standards and best practices

Professional standards signal best practices and vice versa. The forensic practitioner must know the law and, obviously, stay current. The forensic mental health practitioner must also know the science and, obviously, remain up-to-date. The American Academy of Psychiatry and the Law has recently published a practice guideline that provides for consensus-based guidance, derived from available relevant literature which recommends the sort of information which should be amassed in performing different types of forensic psychiatric assessments (Graham *et al*, 2015).

Just as there is an 'envelope' from within which legally correct constructions may be extracted, there are also defensible 'scientific' explanations that may be arrived upon by connecting the clinical data (dots) in slightly different ways. It is best practice, when offering any opinion, to acknowledge that there are other ways to connect those same dots leading to different clinical opinions but that, for the reasons provided in detail, the explanation arrived upon is to be preferred. The expert should point to the weaknesses in their opinion as well as the opinions of the competing experts. Generally, as among competing explanations, the 'law of parsimony' should be invoked. That is, the explanation that incorporates the fewest unknowns is to be preferred over others. Or it may be that the expert acknowledges that there is not a lot to separate the strengths of different clinical views.

The forensic practitioner/expert does not 'win' or 'lose'. His job is to present opinions, when able, from an entirely disinterested perspective. Experts who adopt rigid positions are most often seen as less credible. The practitioner/expert should never take on the role of advocate or champion, rather their role is one of consultant/educator. The courts have recognised the perils of the biased 'expert' and will be quick to correct contamination of the sort that could affect their fact-finding objective[4]. As detailed in Chapter 6, Robert Menzies makes the strong point that biases are inevitable. Experts must acknowledge their own biases in order to suppress them when providing opinions to a decision-maker. And, as Atticus would admonish, the expert should not shy away from an unpopular cause.

Reference

Graham GD, Ash P, Bath EP, Buchanan A, Federoff P, Frierson RL, Harris VL, Hatters Friedman SJ, Hauser MJ, Knoll J, Norko M, Pinals D, Price M, Recupero P, Scott CL & Zonana HV (2015) AAPL Practice Guideline for the Forensic Assessment. *Journal of the American Academy of Psychiatry and the Law* **43** (2 supplement).

Further reading

The Mentally Disordered Accused (2nd Ed) (with Dr Hy Bloom) (Toronto: Irwin Law, 2017).

Forensic Psychiatry (with H Bloom) In: Pakosh C (Ed) *The Lawyer's Guide to the Forensic Sciences*. Irwin Law Inc., 2016.

Handbook of Forensic Mental Health Services (1st Edition), Edited by Ronald Roesch, Alana N. Cook, Routledge, 2017.

---

4   See for example: *Bailey v. Barbour* 2014 ONSC 3698.

Chapter 3:
Mental disorders and violence

By Sheilagh Hodgins

Mental disorders including schizophrenia, bipolar disorder, antisocial personality disorder (ASPD) and substance use disorders (SUDs) are each associated with elevated rates of violence relative to the general population. These disorders are moderately to highly heritable disorders, in which specific genetic variants increase sensitivity to negative environmental factors and lead to abnormal neural development. The same genetic variants, however, also increase sensitivity to positive environmental factors, such as warm supportive parenting and various treatments aimed at replacing unwanted behaviours with behaviours promoting health and happiness. Most patients in forensic psychiatric services present schizophrenia, almost one-half of prisoners present ASPD, and all present very high levels of chronic substance misuse.

Schizophrenia

Schizophrenia affects less than 1% of the population. In childhood and adolescence, individuals who will develop schizophrenia present cognitive deficits, motor abnormalities, psychotic-like experiences and internalising and externalising problems. Typically, the first acute episode of psychosis occurs in late adolescence or early adulthood and schizophrenia is diagnosed. By illness onset, wide-spread brain abnormalities are present. People with schizophrenia require antipsychotic medications to reduce delusions, hallucinations and agitation. When well-adjusted on these medications, they benefit from psychoeducation, cognitive rehabilitation, cognitive-behavioural programmes to increase social and interpersonal skills, and supported employment programmes.

Both before and after illness onset, individuals who subsequently develop schizophrenia are more likely than their healthy peers to engage in aggressive behaviour towards others. As they age, some incidents of aggressive behaviour lead to criminal prosecution. Since the early 1990s, research using health and criminal records of large population cohorts have robustly shown that people with schizophrenia, compared to the general population, are at increased risk for any type of crime, at even greater risk for violent crime, and at even higher risk for homicide. Importantly, the correlates of such aggressive behaviour and of violent crime are similar. During an acute episode when positive symptoms are elevated, large proportions of men and women with schizophrenia behave aggressively. But within days of taking antipsychotic medications, the aggressive behaviour disappears. Evidence from studies of health records of large numbers of persons with schizophrenia shows lower rates of violent crime when they take antipsychotic medication than when they do not. In countries where many persons with schizophrenia are sentenced to correctional facilities and parole, the lack of antipsychotic medication is linked to further violence.

Most people with schizophrenia who engage in aggressive behaviour and/ or violent crime do so prior to their first acute episode. Consequently, three to seven times more adolescents in the juvenile justice system and in substance abuse treatment programmes than in the general population are developing schizophrenia. Many first-episode schizophrenia clinics fail to assess histories of conduct problems, aggressive behaviour and other risk factors for future violence. Yet research has shown that at first episode two types of patients with schizophrenia who engage in violence are distinguishable.

One group – those who present the highest risk of violence – have had a history of antisocial and aggressive behaviour since childhood. Indeed, the prevalence of childhood conduct disorder is four times higher among men and 15 times higher among women who develop schizophrenia than in the general population. These individuals represent anywhere from 20% to 45% of men and women with schizophrenia. The number of conduct disorder symptoms that these individuals present in childhood is linearly, and positively, related to the number of violent crimes that they commit in adulthood. Further, these individuals respond less well than others with schizophrenia to antipsychotic medications and show additional, distinct neural abnormalities to those presented by others with schizophrenia.

At first episode, a second group of patients with schizophrenia present a recent history of aggressive behaviour that began as the illness onset. Little is known about these persons. Their aggressive behaviour may be a reaction to increasingly severe delusions and hallucinations, hostility and agitation, and/or intoxication. A small number of older, chronic patients with schizophrenia and no history of aggressive behaviour, suddenly become aggressive. Additionally, there is evidence that some persons with schizophrenia and no criminal history who threaten to hurt others are more likely than not to carry out their threats. In acute episodes when patients are not taking antipsychotic medication, violent behaviour may be linked to persecutory delusions accompanied by anger.

Antipsychotic medications and other treatments shown to be effective for schizophrenia are needed by all patients with schizophrenia. Additionally, those with a history of antisocial and aggressive behaviour since childhood require cognitive-behavioural programmes aimed at reducing these behaviours and promoting prosocial behaviour. Those with comorbid SUDs benefit from treatment programmes for SUDs that have been designed to be integrated with treatment for schizophrenia.

Bipolar disorder

This disorder includes episodes of major depression and mania and affects approximately 1% of the population. Although the first episode that fully meets diagnostic criteria does not usuallly occur until late adolescence or early adulthood, less acute episodes are present throughout childhood and early adolescence. Persons with bipolar disorder require medications to stabilise mood, and to prevent manic and depressive episodes. Bipolar disorder is associated with an increase in risk of violent crime compared to the general population, however it is far less of an increase than that associated with schizophrenia. In a study of a large population sample of persons with bipolar disorder, violent crime was less frequent during periods when they were taking mood stabilising medications than during periods with no medication. Further, violence by persons with bipolar disorder is almost always accompanied by intoxication.

Antisocial personality disorder

Cross-sectional studies estimate that antisocial personality disorder (ASPD) affects 5.5% of men and 2% of women, while prospective, longitudinal investigations of birth cohorts report higher prevalence and less difference in prevalence between men and women. ASPD indexes a stable pattern of conduct problems from early childhood through adult life and is more accurately referred to as conduct disorder/ASPD. Even as young children, individuals who will present conduct disorder/ASPD show moderately elevated levels of psychopathic traits. They have difficult relationships with parents and teachers, as they are persistently disobedient, and with peers who they bully and, in some cases, physically assault. They have great difficulty progressing in school. These features persist into adolescence when substance misuse and delinquency onset, and into adulthood when further criminality, typically non-violent, is observed. Additionally, approximately one-half of individuals with conduct disorder/ASPD present comorbid anxiety disorders, often from childhood onwards.

Persons with conduct disorder/ASPD place a considerable burden on society. Typically, they fail to contribute by their absence from the workforce, do not pay taxes, accept benefits to which they are not entitled, engage in illicit scams and cheat. They also contribute to creating another generation with similar problems by providing inappropriate and inadequate parenting to their children along with an adverse family environment.

It is possible to acquire diagnoses of conduct disorder and ASPD without showing any aggressive behaviour. The proportions of persons with this diagnosis who exhibit violent behaviour are not presently known. However, it is known that some proportion of men and women with conduct disorder/ASPD display early-onset aggressive behaviour that persists across the life-span. Yet males are much more likely than females to be convicted of violent crimes.

In most countries, ASPD is not diagnosed or treated. Given that the hallmark of this disorder is a failure to follow rules and laws and to conform to authority, engaging such individuals in treatment is a formidable challenge. Adults with conduct disorder/ASPD end up in the health system most often due to elevated rates of comorbid mental disorders such as anxiety or SUDs and physical disorders. They show reductions in antisocial and criminal behaviours following completion of offender rehabilitation programmes that are administered in some correctional facilities.

Common factors promoting violence

Several factors that promote violence characterise individuals who develop schizophrenia and as well those with conduct disorder/ASPD. (Little is known about the antecedents and correlates of violence among persons with bipolar disorder.) In childhood, persons who will develop schizophrenia and those who will develop conduct disorder/ASPD present lower than average IQ and they progress poorly at school. Additionally, they have difficulty establishing healthy, supportive relationships with adults and with their peers. They often misinterpret social situations because they are impaired in recognising emotions in the faces of others. Such impairment in face-emotion recognition persists across the life-span and it increases the risk of violence. Training programmes have been developed to address this impairment in children and in adults with schizophrenia and those with conduct disorder/ASPD.

Another factor promoting violence that is common to individuals who develop schizophrenia and to those with conduct disorder/ASPD is childhood maltreatment. Greater proportions of individuals with these disorders than the general population have experienced physical and/or sexual abuse in childhood. Maltreatment leads to changes in the activity of genes, causes abnormalities of neural structures and functioning and dysregulation of the stress response system, which may lead to hyper-sensitivity to threat that triggers emotionally charged aggressive behaviour and teaches children to behave aggressively. Individuals who have experienced maltreatment in childhood continue to experience more physical victimisation through adolescence and adulthood than the non-maltreated. Trying to resolve inter-personal conflicts by fighting increases the risk of physical victimisation. Among persons with schizophrenia, an experience of victimisation increases the risk of violence in the subsequent hours and days. Consequently, understanding patients' history of childhood maltreatment and repeatedly assessing current incidents of victimisation is necessary to prevent subsequent violence.

Another factor that promotes violence is SUDs. The younger the age at first substance use, the higher the likelihood of subsequent SUDs. Persons with schizophrenia and those with bipolar disorder show higher rates of SUDs than the general population, and almost all persons with conduct disorder/ASPD present at least one SUD. SUDs bring about further changes to an already abnormal brain and further increase the risk of violence conferred by the disorder. In all cases, reducing SUDs leads to reductions in violence. However, the presence of schizophrenia or bipolar disorder or conduct disorder/ASPD impedes participation in treatment programmes for SUDs and reduces the likelihood of a positive outcome. In Canada, two legal substances, alcohol and cannabis, are associated with an increased risk of violence. Cannabis use in early adolescence is associated with increased risks of dependence, use of other drugs, and with brain abnormalities indicative of reduced cortical control of behaviour, and lower IQ. Among individuals carrying genes promoting schizophrenia, cannabis use in adolescence adds further to the likelihood that schizophrenia will develop. In Canada, the average age of onset of cannabis use is 14 years.

People with schizophrenia, those with conduct disorder/ASPD, and some of those with bipolar disorder present low levels of psychosocial functioning and usually do not work. Such individuals frequently become homeless or live in high crime neighbourhoods where illicit drug use is common. These living situations increase the risk of victimization and SUDs.

Comorbidity

Studies that use structured, validated diagnostic interviews administered by clinicians specifically trained to use the instrument report higher rates of comorbid disorders than are observed in clinical services. Among persons with schizophrenia, SUD is the most common comorbid disorder that varies somewhat from place to place but is always considerably higher than in the general population where these individuals live. As noted above, anywhere from 20% to 45% of both men and women with schizophrenia present conduct disorder/ASPD. While rates of SUDs are high among persons with bipolar disorder, little is known about other comorbid disorders. Among people with conduct disorder/ASPD, and also incarcerated offenders with conduct disorder/ASPD, one-half present comorbid anxiety disorders and rates of depression are also high, as are suicide attempts. Almost all people with conduct disorder/ASPD present SUDs from early adolescence onwards.

Conclusion

Schizophrenia, bipolar disorder and conduct disorder/ASPD show elevated rates of violence relative to the general population. Importantly, despite the distinct differences in these mental disorders, several factors that promote violence are more common among those with than without these mental disorders. These factors include lower than average IQ, academic failure, difficulty in recognising emotions in the faces of others, absent and/or conflicted interpersonal relationships, childhood maltreatment followed by repeated physical victimisation, SUDs and poverty.

Further reading

Schizophrenia and violence

Hodgins S (2017) Aggressive behavior among persons with schizophrenia and those who are developing schizophrenia: attempting to understand the limited evidence on causality. *Schizophrenia Bulletin* **43** (5) 1021–1026.

Hodgins S & Klein S (2017) New clinically relevant findings about violence by people with schizophrenia. *Canadian Journal of Psychiatry* **62** (2) 86–93.

Hodgins S, Piatosa M & Schiffer B (2013) Violence among people with schizophrenia: phenotypes and neurobiology. In: K Miczek & A Meyer-Lindenberg (Eds.) *Neuroscience of Aggression*. Heidelberg: Springer-Verlag, 329–368.

Sariaslan A, Lichtenstein P, Larsson H & Fazel S (2016) Triggers for violent criminality in patients with psychotic disorders. *JAMA Psychiatry* **73** 796–803.

Bipolar disorder

Fazel S, Lichtenstein P, Grann M, Goodwin GM & Långström N (2010) Bipolar disorder and violent crime. *Archives of General Psychiatry* **67** (9) 931–938.

Medication and violent crime

Fazel S, Zetterqvist J, Larsson H, Långström N & Lichtenstein P (2014) Antipsychotics, mood stabilisers, and risk of violent crime. *The Lancet* **384** (9949) 1206–1214.

Antisocial personality disorder

Hodgins S, Checknita D, Lindner P, Schiffer B & De Brito S (2018) Antisocial Personality Disorder. In: A Beech, AJ Carter, R Mann & P Rotshtein (Eds) *Handbook of Forensic Neuroscience* (pp229–272). Oxford, UK: Wiley.

Chapter 4: Assessing psychopathic personality disorder – the client, the concept, the craft

By David J Cooke

Mr McPherson marched into the interview room. He glared through dark spectacles and, having put a large file and notebook on the table, stated decisively: 'I will be taking notes too, if that's alright with you, David?' We were meeting for the first time in a prison interview room so that we could prepare a detailed risk assessment. I started by explaining the process and his rights; Mr McPherson assured me that he would hide nothing; he wanted to clear up all the misunderstandings and misinformation that the court, the press and his victims had spread about him. Mr McPherson had just been convicted for the first time – in his early 60s. He had committed a series of serious sexual offences over a period of 40 years. He had sexually assaulted many vulnerable young women wherever he could find them – at his place of work and within his family home, his daughters and their friends.

I started gently, discussing his family of origin, his schooling, his employment history. Superficially he appeared to co-operate – he smiled and talked at length and with little hesitation – yet it soon became clear that his version of even neutral topics was implausible and inconsistent. He demonstrated a readiness and an ease with telling lies. These lies were clearly self-promoting and designed to impress – he had explanations that denied, minimised or externalised his culpability for all aspects of his offending. At subsequent interviews, when challenged with incontrovertible evidence, he displayed no embarrassment; he simply changed his account or denied that he had made the previous account. When challenged more rigorously he became threatening in his bearing.

Throughout all our interviews he was difficult to keep on track; he talked at length and then slid off the topic onto his preferred subjects, the core themes of his narrative being how superior he was to those around him – and so misunderstood. When discussing family and friends there was little evidence of an emotional connection; when discussing his victims his tone was derogatory and blaming. He did not show any evidence that he understood the effect of his behaviour on others. Ultimately, I formed the clinical opinion that Mr McPherson had appreciable personality pathology. In terms of interpersonal style he was garrulous, insincere, manipulative, deceitful and domineering. In terms of his attachments to significant others he was uncommitted, detached and uncaring. In terms of emotional functioning he lacked anxiety, emotional depth and remorse. In terms of his self-perception he was self-centred, self-aggrandising, self-justifying and had a sense of invulnerability. In brief, he suffered from Psychopathic Personality Disorder (PPD).

Psychopathic personality disorder: an elusive concept

PPD is a particular form of personality disorder. Personality disorders are forms of mental disorder that are chronic in nature, starting in adolescence or early adulthood. They are evident in how an individual thinks, feels, behaves and, in particular, they are evident from chronic disturbance in the individual's relations with self and others. These chronic difficulties lead, in turn, to subjective distress and/or a failure to appropriately fulfil social roles and responsibilities. PPD is a particularly virulent form of personality disorder that has long been recognised even in pre-clinical writing, and has been long associated with criminal behaviour in general, and violent behaviour in particular.

PPD thus has forensic mental health relevance. People who suffer from this disorder can place significant demands on forensic mental health services. They can be hard to assess, monitor and manage; they often fail to benefit from standard treatment protocols; they may pose an elevated risk of engaging in criminal behaviour, substance misuse and suicidal behaviour; frequently they have difficulty maintaining close, confiding relationships; they have a tendency to die at a younger age than their peers.

It is important to emphasise that PPD can be a dangerous concept (Scott, 1977, and Chapter 1, this volume). Evidence about PPD within courts and other tribunals may be more prejudicial than probative; the predictive utility of procedures used to measure the concept is frequently overstated (Edens *et al*, 2018). Test scores can have a profound effect on how a defendant is viewed and treated within legal and clinical contexts: in certain jurisdictions those found guilty and diagnosed as psychopathic have a greater likelihood of suffering capital punishment; the diagnosis is often used to justify exclusion from treatment. Nevertheless, the concept of PPD – and particularly one measure of it, the Psychopathy Checklist-Revised (PCL-R) (Hare, 1991) – remains a widely used concept in forensic practice.

Psychopathic personality disorder: mapping the concept

While PPD has been long been recognised and described, its fundamental nature remains a source of controversy (Hart & Cook, 2012). Psychology lacks the articulated theories, methods and measurement technology that are available to the more established sciences. As a consequence it can be difficult to discriminate between facts and artefacts or amongst flawed data, real and illusory phenomena – and the connections amongst the phenomena of concern. Tautology is an ever-present danger: why has Mr McPherson committed these many crimes? It is because he suffers from PPD. How do you know he suffers from PPD? Because he has committed these many crimes.

In the absence of a clear map it is difficult to navigate with confidence amongst the many and diverse phenomena that have been said to be expressions of PPD. Cook and Campbell (1979) argued that the foundation of any psychological research is the careful explication of the concept to be studied: '*...the careful pre-experimental explication of constructs so that the definitions are clear and in conformity with public understanding of the words being used*' (p60).

Given the absence of consensus about the nature of psychopathy, my colleagues and I endeavoured to explicate the concept of PPD (Cooke *et al*, 2012). Rather than adopt a top-down approach relying on the particular view of a single authority (e.g. Cleckley, 1976), we espoused a bottom-up approach. We adopted a multi-method, multi-source approach to the identification of the key elements of PPD. First, we carried out detailed reviews of the relevant clinical and research literatures. Second, we interviewed a cohort of subject matter experts, asking them to describe, in their own words, the symptoms that they had observed in patients who they considered suffered from PPD.

The challenge was how to dissect and then integrate all this information in a meaningful way. We adopted the lexical hypothesis. This hypothesis proposes that salient individual differences in personality are encoded in everyday, non-technical language in adjectives or adjectival phrases. In broad terms, the more synonymous adjectives there are for a personality trait the greater salience of that trait. Our endeavour was to provide a comprehensive description of PPD yet one which was comprehensible using non-specialist language rather than terms-of-art. To ensure comprehensiveness, we tried to ensure that our model reflected the consensus of the major sources reviewed rather than complete unanimity.

We built a concept map that we named the Comprehensive Assessment of Psychopathic Personality (CAPP). Concept maps provide a means to lay out knowledge about a particular topic in a simple graphical form. The concept map is hierarchical in nature. Thirty-three symptoms compose the bottom level of description. These symptoms are designed to be atomistic – to describe basic features of personality functioning rather than complex blends of symptoms (Cooke *et al*, 2012). Each symptom is described by a trait-descriptive adjective or adjectival phrase. Linguistic terms are by their nature fuzzy so, in order to clarify the meaning of any particular symptom, we 'triangulated' each symptom with three synonymous adjectives or adjectival phrases. For example, the symptom antagonistic was triangulated and defined by the adjectives *contemptuous, disagreeable* and *hostile*.

Moving up a level in the hierarchy we realised that the 33 symptoms could be distributed rationally into six domains that represent basic functional domains of personality: *attachment, behavioural, cognitive, dominance, emotional* and *self*. Adding this level to the concept map provides additional context for interpreting the meaning of symptoms and thereby further reduces ambiguity. *Attachment* symptoms focus on interpersonal affiliations, for example the failure to form close, stable emotional bonds with others, and problems with intimacy with others. *Behavioural* symptoms reflect difficulties in organising goal-directed activities such as being disruptive and aggressive. *Cognitive* symptoms reflect mental inflexibility and include being intolerant, distractible and suspicious. *Dominance* symptoms reflect difficulties in interpersonal agency, for example being excessively assertive, domineering and antagonistic. *Emotional* symptoms reflect affective difficulties including the tendency to experience shallow and labile emotions. *Self* symptoms entail difficulties with identity and individuality, for example having a sense of uniqueness and being self-centred and self-aggrandising.

One advantage of the lexical approach is that the CAPP concept map can be readily translated; at the time of writing there are at least 25 language versions. These translations have permitted tests of the content validity of the concept map through prototypicallity studies (Cooke, 2018). Diagnostic categories such as PPD are fuzzy – or Roschian – concepts that are best conceptualised in terms of a prototype, or best exemplar. Symptoms that are central to the definition of the concepts i.e. those with high prototypicallity, should be present in the majority of category members, the less typical features being present in only a minority of members. Prototypicallity studies have been carried out in a range of languages (e.g. English, Spanish, Swedish, Norwegian, German, French, Persian and Korean). There is a high degree of consistency across languages regarding which symptoms are considered to be central to PPD (i.e. *lacks remorse, un-empathic, self-centred, manipulative, lacks emotional depth*) and which symptoms are considered to be of least importance (i.e. *unstable self-concept, lacks concentration, lacks pleasure*). It would appear that not all symptoms are equally diagnostic.

The craft of assessment

While the CAPP model may provide a detailed description of PPD, it can only demonstrate clinical utility when it captures useful information about an individual. Effective evaluation requires a clear, coherent and implementable assessment strategy, a strategy that allows the people being assessed to reveal themselves in such a way that a skilled assessor can collect relevant information. The key element of the assessment craft is managing the interplay between the assessor and the assessee to generate information. This is a particular challenge where there is a high-stakes forensic decision that will be influenced by the outcome of the assessment. Clients who suffer from PPD are likely to attempt to dominate any interaction and use subtle tactics throughout the interview to either conceal or distort information relevant to the assessment.

Having a *structured* approach has many advantages, not least that it can direct the types of enquiries required and assist the detection and management of evasive responding. A seven-step approach to assessment has benefits – preparation, initial contact, interviews, monitor, challenge, reflect and communicate (see Cooke & Logan (2018) for a detailed account). Each step is informed by what is known about PD in general, and PPD in particular.

Step one: preparation

Preparation is essential prior to the first interview, and indeed prior to subsequent interviews. Conducting a thorough file review not only provides information about how the assessee behaves across time and across settings, but it also aids the identification of inconsistencies, gaps or conflicts in the evidence base. Such inconsistencies need to be explored in the interviews; one must consider whether inconsistencies are the result of poor assessment, poor record keeping, or deliberate deception. The careful evaluation of files should also provide material which can be used for challenges. In complex cases it is sensible to review the files between interviews in order to detect new inconsistencies or gaps. A brief written plan will help focus and clarify your overall strategy.

Step two: initial contact

The assessment begins from the first contact; first impressions can be very informative. PPD is an unusual mental disorder in that a dominant and self-confident personality style is a prevalent feature. Right from the off the assessee – like Mr McPherson – may endeavour to achieve dominance. Most of us, when we meet a new professional, are somewhat hesitant or deferential. An individual with PPD, with their inflated, arrogant self-image and their lack of anxiety, may behave differently. They may assert dominance and control by invading a person's interpersonal space, by staring, by squeezing your hand relentlessly, or by calling you by your first name without being asked to do so.

Step three: the interviews

Multiple interviews are generally required. Assessing PPD is a complex task that requires a life-history perspective and consideration of many domains. The person being assessed may not be open in their account and may be downright hostile. Having more than one interview has a number of advantages. First, more interviews provide more opportunities to sample the features of PPD. Second, multiple interviews can help when it comes to detecting deception. To lie effectively one must remember previous accounts.

The initial stages of the interview are about rapport building. You might inform the assessee that you not only wish to know about their problems or vulnerabilities but also about their strengths. This has the benefit of being true, but it may also encourage those who are inclined to brag to do so.

Interactions should be as unforced and natural as possible. As an interviewer you should talk much less than the assessee; good listening skills in which an open, respectful and non-judgmental approach are displayed will foster effective information gathering. Careful listening and observation can yield good clues about deceptive responding; attention has to be paid to both the content and form of responses.

Step four: monitor

An interview is a complex process. As an interviewer you are formulating your questions, you are listening to and recording responses, and critically, you are monitoring and observing behaviours and emotional expressions. You only have limited attentional resources, thus at times it makes sense to focus your attention primarily on the affective component rather than the content of their response. A salient feature of PPD is limited, restricted, inappropriate or short-lived emotions; there may only be a few occurrences of short-lived emotions and it is important that you detect these.

Monitoring interpersonal style is also important to detect and record attempts to breach professional or personal boundaries. Does the assessee engage in intrusive gestures, inappropriate touching, requests for inappropriate information, stare, split etc? You may become aware of attempts to control the interview.

Step five: challenge

In any assessment interview it is likely that you will have to challenge the account of the assesse. Challenging is necessary, not only to check out inconsistencies in accounts across interviews, or inconsistencies between the assessee's account and the collateral information, but also to determine the speed and nature of their response to challenges. Individuals who are pathologically dominant are prone to respond badly to challenges. When it is clear that you have spotted their lies, are they embarrassed or, like Mr McPherson, do they create further implausible accounts with apparent ease? Challenging should be carried out with care and with the usual security precautions in place for a forensic interview. Different levels of challenge are discussed elsewhere (Cooke & Logan, 2018).

Step six: reflection

A sequence of interviews with someone suffering from PPD provides a complex set of information to assimilate. It is a series of interpersonal interactions and, as such, results in complex transference and counter-transference reactions. It is important to be conscious of our personal biases (Robert Menzies, Chapter 6, this volume) and remember that we can all be fooled. This is where reflection is so important. Often the process of unconscious incubation leads to clarity. Reflect before committing your assessment to paper – frequently being forced to put your assessment on paper increases clarity of diagnostic formulation.

Step seven: communication

Having determined that the person being assessed suffers from PPD, the key question is how to communicate that information. Using traditional assessment methods clinicians have often applied a numerical value – and an arbitrary cut-off – in an attempt to communicate the presence of PPD. This approach is limited. First, reducing many hours of file review, interviews and diagnostic formulation into a single number is wasteful and perhaps even unethical (see Chapter 7). Second, numerical values obscure the rich variations in the complex pattern of traits that underpin the emergent concept of PPD. Within forensic mental health practice the primary reason for considering PPD is in relation to violence risk formulation; that is, the clinician has to consider to what extent the features of PPD contribute, in combination with other risk factors, to our understanding of whether the individual is likely to engage in violence. Individuals are violent for different reasons: any one individual may be violent for different reasons on different occasions. Those suffering from PPD may be violent, for example, because of their feelings of superiority over others, because they perceive others as having maleficent intent towards them, because they lack the affective responses that inhibit violent behaviour, or because they are reckless and do not consider the consequences of their violence. It is only through understanding the unique manner in which the traits of PPD are present in any individual that a coherent risk formulation can be achieved.

Assessing individuals like Mr McPherson is one of the major challenges of forensic practice; it requires time, skill and care. However, concluding that someone suffers from PPD is a serious matter with profound implications for the sufferer and his family – it is a 'sticky label' that is hard to remove. Ethical practice requires thoroughness and care.

In conclusion, despite the central role that PPD has played in clinical forensic practice, it remains a concept that is subject to controversy (Hart & Cook, 2012). Key questions remain: what are the central features of the disorder? Is criminal behaviour a cardinal diagnostic feature or a consequence of core traits? Which traits, or combination of traits, put individuals at risk of being violent? How do gender, culture, age, comorbid disorders etc. affect the expression of the PPD? Is it responsive to treatment and management? And there are many more.

PPD remains elusive. As clinicians and researchers we should remain humble about our understanding of this concept that pervades and persists in forensic clinical practice. Individuals are active, reactive, interactive and adaptive organisms; traits of PPD combine in complex and mysterious ways; their interplay may be synergistic – amounting to more than the sum of their individual parts – resulting in an emergent concept that we tentatively describe as PPD. While concept maps such as the CAPP might provide initial, speculative guidance on the road to understanding, the field requires the refinement of constructs, the development of multi-modal measurement procedures to capture both the complexity and intricacy of symptoms. Additionally, clarity will be promoted through the adoption of analytic methods that better reflect the complex interplay amongst symptoms.

Guiding principle

When it comes to PPD, I think that the quote attributed to Aristotle – probably apocryphally – is apposite: 'The more you know, the more you don't know'.

References

Cleckley H (1976) *The mask of sanity* (Vol. 5). St Louis: Mosby.

Cook TD & Campbell DT (1979) *Quasi-experimentation, design and analysis issues for field settings*. Chicago: Rand McNally College Publishing Company.

Cooke DJ (2018) Psychopathic personality disorder: capturing an elusive concept. *European Journal of Analytic Philosophy* **14** (1) 15–32.

Cooke DJ, Hart SD, Logan C & Michie C (2012) Explicating the construct of psychopathy: development and validation of a conceptual model, the Comprehensive Assessment of Psychopathic Personality (CAPP). *International Journal of Forensic Mental Health* **11** (4) 242–252.

Cooke DJ & Logan C (2018) Capturing Psychopathic Personality: Penetrating the mask of sanity through clinical interview. In: CJ Patrick (Ed.) *The Handbook of Psychopathy* (2 ed). London: Guildford Press.

Edens JF, Petrila JP & Kelley SE (2018) Legal and ethical issues in the assessment and treatment of psychopathy. In: CJ Patrick (Ed.) Handbook of Psychopathy. New York: The Guilford Press.

Hare RD (1991) *The Hare Psychopathy Checklist – Revised.* Toronto, Ontario: Multi-Health Systems.

Hart SD & Cook AN (2012) Current issues in the assessment and diagnosis of psychopathy (psychopathic personality disorder). *Neuropsychiatry* **2** (6) 497–508.

Scott PD (1977) Assessing dangerousness in criminals. *British Journal of Psychiatry.* **131** 127–142.

Chapter 5:
The increasingly recognised adverse role of trauma in forensic patients

By Hy Bloom

'...when a stone is dropped into a pond, the water continues quivering even after the stone has sunk to the bottom.' (Arthur Golden, Memoirs of a Geisha, 1997, p265)

Childhood victimisation is pervasive in the general population, and is blind to race, culture, gender, class or geographical location. Particularly high rates of victimisation are seen in special populations such as psychiatric and forensic patients (Spitzer *et al*, 2006), and offenders (especially in sexual and violent offenders). Trauma, in fact, envelops the lives of many forensic psychiatric patients, and many, if not most, were born into it.

Early victimisation has profound negative implications for development, and is often associated with enduring difficulties later in life. Sequelae include a wide array of potential psychiatric conditions and psychopathology, for example post-traumatic stress disorder (PTSD), depression, anxiety disorders, dissociative disorders, substance abuse, psychosomatic conditions, maladaptive personality traits (e.g. antisocial, borderline), self-injurious behavior, psychosexual disorders and psychosexual adjustment problems, and paraphilic behavior.

Early trauma also leads to psychosocial adjustment difficulties that include problems with trust and intimacy, delinquency, crime, deviancy and violence, poor psychosocial adjustment, learned helplessness, educational and vocational underachievement, attachment problems with one's own children, poor interpersonal and social relations, problems with authority and control, and vulnerability to poly-victimisation.

Trauma is highly infiltrative. In its psychological wake, many previously high functioning and hitherto well-adjusted individuals may suffer a diminution in their capacity to function in day-to-day life. Trauma also affects enjoyment of the most fundamental elements of life – eating, sleeping, sustaining attention, relating to others, and experiencing pleasure – and it changes one's outlook on life and one's-self (ie. confidence and self-esteem). Early maltreatment, resulting in shame, self-condemnation, and a pervasively negative world view, may set the tone for how things will play out later in life. Individuals whose genetic and environmental susceptibility to major mental disorder is complicated by early trauma often fare worse. A confluence of psychopathology, paired with the many personal, social and relational deficits individuals in this group may experience, often portends a perfect storm of conditions to result in a criminal and/or forensic course. The well-known battle cry for early intervention was never more valuable than for this population.

Associations have also been found between psychological trauma and physical illness, accelerated biological aging (Han et al, 2018) and risk of premature death (Walker et al, 2015). Recent prospective studies drawing on large cohorts have shown a connection between PTSD and cardiovascular disorders (Koenen et al, 2017), and PTSD and autoimmune disorders like thyroiditis, inflammatory bowel disease, rheumatoid arthritis, lupus and multiple sclerosis (O'Donovan et al, 2015; Roberts et al, 2017). These potential physical sequelae, particularly the cardiovascular consequences, should reasonably engender exponential alarm in clinicians treating traumatised forensic patients with psychotic disorders with atypical antipsychotic medications. This group of medications has become notorious in its own right for causing/contributing to so-called 'metabolic syndrome' – a condition characterised by susceptibility to Type 2 Diabetes, varying degrees of weight gain, dyslipidemia and hypertension. The unfortunate combination of the effects of trauma, medication and lifestyle associated with chronic psychotic disorders not only diminishes quality of life, but can significantly foreshorten it as well.

Stigma and ensuing self-stigmatisation are also problems – at times to a debilitating degree – for individuals with mental health problems, those caught up in the criminal justice system, and for individuals who have suffered childhood victimisation. Designated systemically and publicly as *mentally disordered offenders*, stigma is multilayered in forensic patients.

A number of studies have convincingly demonstrated a significant association between childhood physical and psychological abuse and neglect (Spitzer et al, 2006), sexual victimisation (Glasser et al, 2001) and a forensic trajectory.

The points noted below are particularly instructive for this traumatised patient population:

- ■ Childhood trauma 'exerts a powerful environmental influence on the expression of psychosis' (Larkin & Read, 2008), affects amenability and resistance to treatment (Hassan & DeLuca, 2015), and is associated with poorer functioning in young people with psychosis, compared to non-abused controls (Schäfer & Fisher, 2011). Greater childhood emotional trauma is found in the backgrounds of patients who develop bipolar disorder (Watson *et al*, 2014). Affective instability, which is associated with poorer outcomes in persons with mood disorders, is greater in patients who have experienced childhood trauma (Marwaha *et al*, 2016). The earlier the child is exposed to sexual and physical abuse, the greater and more longstanding the risk of depression (McCutcheon *et al*, 2009).

- Amongst various types of trauma, emotional trauma in particular is associated with the development of maladaptive personality traits (deCarvalho *et al*, 2015), and earlier onset in those who go on to develop antisocial personality disorder (ASPD) and violence (Bruce & Laporte, 2015). Each additional adverse experience increases a youth's risk of becoming a chronic and serious violent offender (Fox *et al*, 2015).

- Childhood trauma is associated with higher levels of substance abuse; drugs and alcohol are used to quell PTSD symptoms (Müller *et al*, 2015).

- The relationship between trauma, PTSD and violence has been known for some time through study of military populations (see for example, MacManus *et al*, 2013). Recent research has particularised subcomponents of trauma, namely anger dysregulation and self-medication with alcohol, as having an even greater noxious effect on bringing about violence in the general population (let alone the forensic psychiatric population) afflicted with PTSD (Blakey *et al*, 2018). Given the extent to which alcohol abuse and anger problems are issues in forensic patients, it would be reasonable for the treatment teams to pay even greater attention to these symptoms.

Against this background, some psychiatric patients, particularly those with comorbid substance use disorders, go on to commit marked violence themselves, and some end up in the forensic system. Although they may be the perpetrators, their acts are almost always committed during times when they are experiencing any one or more of acute paranoid delusions, disorganisation and affectively charged states. When the psychosis lifts, and some measure of reality rears its head, the person may be traumatised by what he or she did and its effects on others. Parenthetically, one cannot but wonder whether the emotional deficits experienced by many forensic patients, particularly those with schizophrenia, paradoxically protects them from experiencing the full traumatic weight of the tragic acts they commit.

- Although a patient's psychiatric and other records may reflect that he or she was a victim of childhood trauma, the treatment focus in forensic psychiatric facilities is often on the elimination/amelioration of symptoms of major mental illness, dealing with substance abuse, and reigning in problematic behavior and risk factors for violence and self-destructive behaviour. In such patients, and for whatever reasons, surveillance and intervention have already come up short earlier in life. Failure to address early life trauma in concerted treatment more proximal to detection (let alone occurrence) can impede progress and promote a worse course.

■ Many clinicians who care for forensic patients have observed a worsening in their patients' mental state before and after annual review board (and potentially indeterminate) hearings. Rehashing the event that led to the not criminally responsible (NCR) finding can re-traumatise the patient (and obviously the victim) and result in some regression of the patient's clinical progress. In this regard, it would be reasonable, notwithstanding the clearly legal agenda inherent in review board proceedings, to consider the potential value of infusing review board hearings with as much therapeutic ambience as the legal framework can muster.

In the last 30 years or so, clinicians, researchers and the public at large have become increasingly aware of the prevalence and virulence of early life victimisation, the many ways in which trauma degrades psychological and emotional well-being, and that it often leads to self-destructive and aggressive behavior. In certain populations, for example forensic patients, trauma often worsens the course of mental illness, impedes progress and recovery, and ultimately contributes to risk.

With this unfortunate reality in mind, the authors of the HCR-20 V3 (Douglas *et al*, 2013), altered the content of Item H8 to focus exclusively on 'History of Problems with Traumatic Experiences'. Item H8 in the previous version had been entitled 'Early Maladjustment'. The authors' rationale for the change is stated as follows: 'This risk factor describes a history of experiencing harmful or traumatic events at any point during the lifespan that disrupt normative development, attachment processes, or learning of prosocial attitudes and problem solving skills' (p81).

Infinitely complicating matters is the fact that forensic psychiatric and correctional facilities are often dangerous places to be. Traumatic events earlier in life 'are further compounded by experiences in criminal justice settings, where people are again exposed to violent and traumatic events' (Kapoor *et al*, 2018, p105).

This discussion would no doubt lack balance and appear unduly pessimistic and defeatist if not for the countervailing force of resilience. In this regard, Alexander (1996) aptly questioned 'why some individuals display psychopathology after trauma and others do not... [and] why some cases of PTSD become chronic and other are short-lived' (p2).

Needless to say, the issue of who will suffer symptoms or end up with a diagnosis of PTSD is inextricably tied to a person's genetics, early life experience within his/her family of origin, temperament and personality, intellect, support network and history of exposure to other adverse life events. Predisposition certainly increases risk of developing PTSD, but susceptibility is not a precondition, especially when the traumatic event is severe.

Resilience is defined as a psychobiological capacity individuals possess to varying degrees which allows them to adapt to adverse life events (Shrivastava & Desousa, 2016). While some degree of capacity for resilience may be biological/genetic (i.e. hard-wired), there is evidence that resilience is modifiable and can be fostered (Charney, 2004; Rutter, 2012).

Research into resilience is a byproduct of our expanding knowledge of the many facets of mental disorder. This is certainly no surprise and is consistent with the medical model. Identifying, isolating and fleshing out the cause(s) of a condition and susceptibility to it inevitably leads to theories about prevention, modulation of the expression of the condition, and to diminishing its effects (symptoms, morbidity and mortality) through treatment. Alexander presciently flagged this notion more than 20 years ago when he stated that a 'much-prized dividend [of looking at these factors] would also be the identification of methods of effective psychoprophylaxis' (p3).

As noted, resilience is not immutable, and can be cultivated and/or bolstered in individuals who have been dealt the bad hand of having too little, or who have had some of theirs stripped away by a harsh and trauma-filled life.

The final point to make is that better outcomes are likely when clinicians working in forensic contexts recognise that many of their patients have suffered severe trauma, and take deliberate and concerted steps to address it. Clinicians who work in the field appreciate that shortages in financial and human resources, and insufficient staff training on point, markedly limit service availability in institutional settings. Increasing recognition of the depth and scope of the problem of trauma in this patient population and its implications for perpetuating serious mental illness and associated impairment, and for further violence, may be a timely impetus for an expanded and more specific service. Shortages of resources (and potentially in expertise) may also allow for greater opportunities to link these patients to community-based mental health practitioners as adjuncts to institutional-based care, and to build bridges for subsequent follow-up in the community once the patient is sufficiently derestricted to access these services in the community, or is discharged from the forensic/correctional system outrightly.

References and further reading

Alexander DA (1996) Trauma research: a new era. *Journal of Psychosomatic Research* **41** (1) 1–5.

Blakey SM, Love H, Lindquist L, Beckham JC & Elbogen EB (2018). Disentangling the link between posttraumatic violent behaviour: Findings from a nationally representative sample. *Journal of Consulting and Clinical Psychology* **86** (2) 169–178.

Bruce M & Laporte D (2015) Childhood trauma, antisocial personality typologies and recent violence among males with severe mental illness: Exploring an explanatory pathway. *Schizophrenia Research* **162** 285–290.

Charney DS (2004) Psychobiological mechanisms of resilience and vulnerability: implications for adaptation to extreme stress. *American Journal of Psychiatry* **161** (2) 195–216.

deCarvalho HW, Pereira R, Frozi J, Bisol LW, Ottoni GL & Lara DR (2015) Childhood trauma is associated with maladaptive personality traits. *Child Abuse & Neglect* **44** 18–25.

Douglas KS, Hart SD, Webster CD & Belfrage H (2013) HCR-20 V3: Assessing Risk for Violence, User Guide. Burnaby, BC: Mental Health, Law, and Policy Institute, Simon Fraser University.

Fox BH, Perez N, Cass E, Baglivio MT & Epps N (2015) Trauma changes everything: Examining the relationship between adverse childhood experiences and serious, violent and chronic juvenile offenders. *Child Abuse & Neglect* **46** 163–173.

Glasser M, Kolvin I, Campbell D, Leitch I & Farrelly S (2001) Cycle of child sexual abuse: links between being a victim and becoming a perpetrator. *British Journal of Psychiatry* **179** 482–494.

Golden A (1997) *Memoirs of a Geisha*. New York: Alfred A Knopf.

Han LKM, Aghajani M, Clark SL, Chan RF, Hattab MW, Shabalin AA, Zhao M, Kumar G, Xie LY, Jansen R, Milaneschi Y, Dean B, Aberg KA, van den Oord EJCG & Penninx BWJH (2018) Epigenic aging in major depressive disorder. *American Journal of Psychiatry* **175** (8) 774–782.

Hassan AN & De Luca V (2015) The effect of lifetime adversities on resistance to antipsychotic treatment in schizophrenic patients. *Schizophrenia Research* **161** 496–500.

Kapoor R, Dike CC & Norko MA (2018) Psychiatric treatment in forensic hospital and correctional settings. *Psychiatric Annals* **48** (2) 102–108.

Koenen KC, Ratanatharathorn A, Ng L, McLaughlin KA, Bromet EJ, Stein DJ, Karam EG, Ruscio AM, Benjet C, Scott K and Atwoli L (2017) Posttraumatic stress disorder in the world mental health surveys. *Psychological medicine* **47** (13) 2260-2274.

Larkin W & Read J (2008) Childhood trauma and psychosis: evidence, pathways, and implications. *Journal of Postgraduate Medicine* **54** (4) 287–293.

Marwaha S, Gordon-Smith K, Broome M, Briley PM, Perry A, Forty L, Craddock N, Jones I & Jones L (2016) Affective instability, childhood trauma and major affective disorders. *Journal of Affective Disorders* **190** 764–771.

McCutcheon VV, Heath AC, Nelson EC, Bucholz KK, Madden PAF & Martin NG (2009) Accumulation of trauma over time and risk for depression in a twin sample. *Psychological Medicine* **39** 431–444.

McManus D, Dean K, Jones M, Rona RJ, Greenberg N, Hull L, Fahy T, Wessely S & Fear NT (2013) Violent offending by UK military personnel deployed to Iraq and Afghanistan: a data linkage cohort study. *The Lancet* **381** 907–917.

Müller M, Vandeleur C, Rodgers S, Rössler W, Castelao E, Preisig M & Ajdacic-Gross V (2015) Childhood adversities as specific contributors to the co-occurrence of posttraumatic stress and alcohol use disorders. *Psychiatry Research* **228** 251–256.

O'Donovan A, Cohen BE, Seal KH, Bertenthal D, Margaretten M, Nishimi K & Neylan TC (2015) Elevated risk for autoimmune disorders in iraq and afghanistan veterans with posttraumatic stress disorder. *Biological Psychiatry* **77** 365–374.

Roberts AL, Malspeis S, Kubzansky LD, Feldman CH, Chang SC, Koenen KC & Costenbader KH (2017) Association of trauma and posttraumatic stress disorder with incident systemic lupus erythematosus in a longitudinal cohort of women. *Arthritis & Rheumatology* **69** 2162–2169.

Schäfer I & Fisher HL (2011) Childhood trauma and psychosis – what is the evidence? *Dialogues in Clinical Neuroscience* **13** (3) 360–365.

Shrivastava A & Desousa A (2016) Resilience: a psychobiological construct for psychiatric disorders. *Indian journal of psychiatry* **58** (1) 38.

Spitzer C, Chevalier C, Gillner M, Harald JF & Barnow (2006) Complex posttraumatic stress disorder and child maltreatment in forensic inpatients. *The Journal of Forensic Psychiatry & Psychology* **17** (2) 204–216.

Walker ER, McGee RE & Druss BG (2015) Mortality in mental disorders and global disease burden implications: a systematic review and meta-analysis. *JAMA Psychiatry* **72** (4) 334–341.

Watson S, Gallagher P, Dougall D, Porter R, Moncrieff J, Ferrier IN & Young AH (2014) Childhood trauma in bipolar disorder. *Australian & New Zealand Journal of Psychiatry* **48** (6) 564–570.

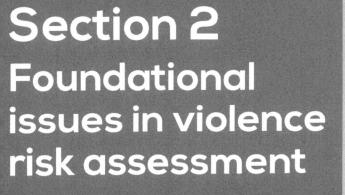

Section 2
Foundational issues in violence risk assessment

Chapter 6:
The ghost in the machine – the enduring presence of bias in forensic risk assessments

By Robert Menzies

'Everything that can be counted does not necessarily count; everything that counts cannot necessarily be counted.' – Albert Einstein

'Don't become a mere recorder of facts, but try to penetrate the mystery of their origin.' – Ivan Pavlov

By way of setting the stage for this review, it may be instructive to begin by citing the *Oxford English Dictionary's* (2017) three main definitions of 'bias', namely:

- 'Inclination or prejudice for or against one person or group, especially in a way considered to be unfair.'

- 'A concentration on or interest in one particular area or subject.'

- 'A systematic distortion of a statistical result due to a factor not allowed for in its derivation.'

Consistent with these OED definitions, proponents of the risk assessment paradigm generally conceive bias as a contaminant and threat to scientific best practices in the forensic system. This characterisation, in turn, yields two key understandings:

- According to such a view, bias constitutes an unwelcome incursion of human subjectivity and erroneous thinking into a process that should rather be governed by the Baconian application of methodical, rigorous, replicable, value-free and precise ideas and practices to the mapping and interpretation of the empirical world.

- When it comes to forensic decisions about violence, such factors as the socio-demographic attributes of clinicians, their professional education, affiliations, experiences, beliefs and predilections – in tandem with the widely-shared but often misdirecting mental heuristics to which all human judgment is routinely subject (Kahneman *et al*, 1982) – are viewed as vectors of bias that must be neutralised before risk assessment can attain the heights of diagnostic precision enjoyed by assorted other disciplines and pursuits.

Working largely from these premises, in recent years researchers and commentators as diverse as Baird (2009), Douglas *et al* (2017), Martinez (2014), McGarraugh (2013), McKiernan (2012), Mossman (2006), Murray and Thomson (2010), Neal and Grisso (2014), and Zapf and Dror (2017) have yielded a wealth of material addressing the subject of bias in both general forensic decision-making and instrument-based actuarial risk assessment. By way of illustration:

- In their selective review of the prevailing literature, Neal and Grisso (2014, p201) chronicle the two main trajectories of inquiry on human cognition and decision-making under uncertainty – the 'heuristics and biases' (HB) tradition, and the 'naturalistic decision making' (NDM) tradition – and they proceed to mobilise these two bodies of work to consider how bias adversely influences forensic activities.

- Also writing from the USA context, Zapf and Dror (2017) enumerate seven factors 'that might interfere with accurate observations and objective inferences in forensic conclusions' – to wit, 'cognitive architecture and the brain, training and motivation, organisational factors, base rate expectations, irrelevant case information, reference materials, and case evidence'.

- Scottish researchers Murray and Thomson (2010) point to illusory correlations, context effects, attribution effects, selective perception, confirmation bias, learnability and hindsight bias, confidence, under-use of base rate data, and the undermining presence of representativeness, availability, anchoring and adjustment heuristics (Kahneman *et al*, 1982) as the principal reasons why risk assessments go awry.

- In Canada, McKiernan (2012) quotes forensic materials engineer Paul Okrutny in identifying four key sources of bias that potentially disrupt professional decisions in legal and clinical settings:
  - 'Anchoring bias' ('someone gives you an idea or a concept, and then you begin thinking based on that anchor they've provided').
  - 'Bandwagon effect' ('the probability of any person doing something increases based on the number of people already doing it').
  - 'Confirmation bias' ('you tend to confirm your initial instinct by looking for information that confirms it')

- 'Noble cause bias' ('when people are trying to do something for the greater good').

Additionally, observers have noted the presence of wider structural arrangements, power imbalances, cultural exigencies and professional interests that may conspire to undermine the validity of violence risk assessments in complicated ways:

- While the Federal Court's finding for the complainant was ultimately reversed at the appeals level, the widely-publicised British Columbia prisoner's rights case of *Canada v. Ewert* (2016) raised the concern that judgments informed by commonly used risk assessment instruments like the PCL-R, V-RAG, SORAG, Static 99 and VRSSO may be invalid when applied to people of Aboriginal heritage – and that their use under such circumstances may therefore abrogate human rights protections against cultural and racial discrimination (Shepherd & Lewis-Fernandez, 2016).

- US researchers have reported that African-American prisoners are susceptible to higher rankings on forensic risk scales than their Caucasian counterparts, with implications paralleling those relevant to the evaluation of indigenous subjects (Angwin *et al*, 2016; but see Herriott, 2012).

- Similarly, Canadian feminist scholars and activists have challenged the applicability of risk assessment instruments and procedures to women inmates of correctional systems (Hannah-Moffat, 2009; Pate, 2002).

- Comprehensive meta-analytic research by Singh and colleagues in Britain and Norway has identified a phenomenon that they term 'assessor bias' in the validation of actuarial judgments about risk, raising the awkward prospect that the reported accuracy of assessment instruments may hinge, at least in part, on who precisely is involved in the validation of these tools – with studies conducted by instrument creators yielding higher overall levels of accuracy than those undertaken by disinterested third parties (Singh *et al*, 2013).

Taken together, these writings suggest that the broad circulation and widespread use of actuarial and other standardised risk assessment procedures have by no means heralded the banishment of bias from – nor even necessarily its reduction within – the domains of law and mental health.

Aspirations of scientific rigour and impartiality aside, the human factor continues to pervade every phase of forensic risk assessment, from the initial drafting and validation of evaluation instruments to the formulation of professional decisions, to the ultimate disposition of patient/offenders.

Moreover, the ostensive dichotomy between clinical and actuarial decision-making in psycho-legal settings – and along with it the very possibility of a fully depersonalised, bias-free, objective risk assessment enterprise – relies on an idealised conception of knowledge production that is belied by the messy, value-steeped, culturally rich, ideologically saturated, and at least partially improvisational nature of *all* human scientific activity. In practice:

■ Bias is *not* an external contaminant that undermines otherwise perfectible judgments yet can somehow get neutralised through the sober application of scientific methodologies.

■ Bias is rather an immanent and inescapable element of all decision-making in the world of forensic practice, as in life.

■ While the presence of bias can demonstrably be associated with (un)reliability, in contrast, bias is neither interchangeable nor even necessarily correlated with (in)validity. Research efforts directed at improving assessment precision (i.e. increasing the proportion of assessment 'hits' relative to false positives and negatives) through the reduction of bias are therefore misplaced. Not only is the presence of bias an irreducible feature of all decisions clinical and actuarial, within and beyond the forensic arena, but there is no reason to believe that the act of 'debiasing' risk assessments (Neal & Grisso, 2014 p207) would systematically lead to either a heightening or a decline in classification validity levels – any more so than the utopian advent of an error-free assessment tool would have the effect of eliminating bias from the decision-making equation. Indeed, a certain dosage of bias – informed, one hastens to add, by self-awareness, full disclosure, and freedom from discriminatory intent and outcome – may paradoxically prove itself a necessary precondition for a successful assault on the error term of forensic risk assessments.

Taking these concerns into account, the mandate of researchers and clinicians should not be to pursue a banishment of bias from forensic assessments of risk, whether such assessments be clinical, actuarial or some combination of the two. To the contrary, a genuinely ethical, professionally sound, conceptually rigorous and methodologically robust forensic evaluation process demands, above all:

■ Honestly and reflectively mapping the biases that are endemic to one's theories, instruments, methods and outcomes.

■ Making these biases manifest to all participants in the process.

■ Accepting the resulting uncertainty of one's choices and their effects on individuals and organisations.

■ Acknowledging the potentially unsettling (and, one hopes, humility-inducing) implications of the above for the value and validity of one's judgments.

■ Tempering one's assertions and prescriptions – and, perhaps most critically, one's choice to become involved at all – accordingly.

References

Angwin J, Larson J, Mattu S & Kirchner L (2016) *Machine bias: There's software used across the country to predict future criminals. And it's biased against blacks* [online]. Available at: https://www.propublica.org/article/machine-bias-risk-assessments-in-criminal-sentencing (accessed December 2018)

Baird C (2009) *A question of evidence: A critique of risk assessment models used in the justice system* [online]. National Council on Crime and Delinquency. Available at: http://www.nccdglobal.org/sites/default/files/publication_pdf/special-report-evidence.pdf (accessed December 2018).

Canada v. Ewert, 2016 FCA 203 (CANLII). Available at: http://decisions.fct-cf.gc.ca/fca-caf/decisions/en/168972/1/document.do (accessed December 2018).

Douglas T, Pugh J, Singh I, Savulescu J & Fazel S (2017) Risk assessment tools in criminal justice and forensic psychiatry: the need for better data. *European Psychiatry 42* 134–137.

Hannah-Moffat K (2009) Gridlock or mutability: Reconsidering 'gender' and risk assessment. *Criminology and Public Policy* 8 1 201–219.

Herriott BL (2012) Assessing risk of violence in Caucasian and African American male forensic patients. Ph.D. dissertation. Department of Psychology, Indiana State University.

Kahneman D, Slovic P & Tversky A (1982) *Judgment Under Uncertainty: Heuristics and Biases*. Cambridge, NY: Cambridge University Press.

Martinez MA (2014) Good habits start early: identifying and managing potential bias in forensic evaluations as an early career forensic psychologist. *American Psychology – Law Society News*.

McGarraugh P (2013) Up or out: why 'sufficiently reliable' statistical risk assessment is appropriate at sentencing and inappropriate at parole. *Minnesota Law Review* 97 1079–1113.

McKiernan M (2012) *Getting beyond bias. Legal report: Forensics* [online]. Canadian Lawyer. Available at: http://www.canadianlawyermag.com/4419/Getting-beyond-bias.html (accessed December 2018).

Mossman D (2006) Critique of pure risk assessment or, Kant meets Tarasoff. *University of Cincinnati Law Review* 75 2 523–609.

Murray J & Mary ET (2010) Applying decision making theory to clinical judgments in violence risk assessment. *Europe's Journal of Psychology* 6 2 150–171.

Neal TMS & Grisso T (2014) The cognitive underpinnings of bias in forensic mental health evaluations. *Psychology, Public Policy, and Law* 20 2 200–211.

Oxford English Dictionary – English (2017) https://en.oxforddictionaries.com/definition/bias (accessed December 2018).

Pate K (2002) The risky business of risk assessment. *Hecate: A Woman's Interdisciplinary Journal* 28 1 166–190.

Shepherd SM & Lewis-Fernandez R (2016) Forensic risk assessment and cultural diversity: contemporary challenges and future directions. *Psychology, Public Policy, and Law* 22 4 427–438.

Singh JP, Grann M & Fazel S (2013). Authorship bias in violence risk assessment? A systematic review and meta-analysis. *PLoS One* 8 9 (e72484): https://doi.org/10.1371/journal.pone.0072484

Zapf PA & Dror IE (2017) Understanding and mitigating bias in forensic evaluation: lessons from forensic science. *International Journal of Forensic Mental Health* 16 3 227–238.

Chapter 7:
Why is it so difficult to achieve accuracy in predictions of violence?

By Quazi Haque and Chris Webster

Over 20 years ago, on the basis of a long-term follow-up study of nearly 600 forensic patients, it was found that the prediction-outcome correlation failed to break a 0.40 'barrier' (where 0 = no correspondence, +1.0 = perfect positive correlation, and -1.0 = prefect negative correspondence (Menzies & Webster, 1995)). (Readers will note that high levels of negative correlation would be just as practically useful as high positive scores – only requiring that the decision be adjusted accordingly!) The same authors did not then argue that forensic mental health professionals should give up offering advice about risks to law-enforcement officials, courts and decision-making bodies. The finding, nonetheless, raises two vital questions: (1) why is the prediction-outcome correlation ceiling set so relatively low? (e.g. Ramesh *et al*, 2018) (2) what steps could be taken to enhance prediction accuracy?

This sketch by Joy Santiago depicts a group of clinicians 'scratching their heads' as they try to reach a collective decision. Maybe they are trying to figure the likelihood that a particular client who, if released by the community, might perpetrate an act of

violence over the course of the coming six months. Before you continue, we invite you, dear reader, to scratch your own head. Maybe you should avail yourself of pen and paper and write down, in shorthand form, as many possible reasons why predictions of future risk may fail. How is it that, when data are massed, prediction-outcome correlations rarely exceed +0.40?

Item 1: societal shifting

All of the major long-term follow-up studies in forensic mental health (e.g. Hodgins & Janson, 2002; Steadman & Cocozza, 1974; Monahan *et al*, 2001; Menzies & Webster, 1993; Michael *et al*, 2013) have to deal with the fact that laws and customs change as time progresses. The notion of cyberbullying, for example, was unknown a couple of decades ago[5]. Now whole books are devoted to the topic (Cassidy *et al*, 2018). As well, the *scale* on which violence can be inflicted in civil society has increased. Certain members of the public have come to the realisation that they can turn ordinary rifles into automatic weapons, which is not particularly difficult to do given a few instructions from the internet and the availability of an elementary machine-shop. An incidental point is that, in the immediate aftermaths of such calamities, there is a tendency to attribute the cause – without much, if any, evidence – to the perpetrator being mentally ill. Such careless attributions increase stigma and make it easy for commentators to reach for such facile explanations. This conflating of mental disorder and violence will likely affect not just members of the ordinary public, but even professional mental health workers. Even if only to a slight degree, this will affect their ability to make accurate forecasts.

Item 2: police screening

Police officers on the beat have wide discretion as to whether or not to apprehend individuals who are behaving oddly or unacceptably in the community. Although this discretion does not apply if the matter involves serious injury or death at the scene, such extreme instances are relatively infrequent. Often, too, the on-the-spot decision has to be made not only in terms of what lies before him or her at the particular time, but in light of competing calls to attend other, and possibly more important, investigations. A good deal depends, too, on the amount of education the officer has or has not received on the topic of mental disorder[6], as well as his or her past experiences in taking persons to psychiatric emergency services. Some officers will have found that, once

---

5   Peter Scott did, though, in his 1977 article, refer to blackmail, which he observed to be 'on the borderline of dangerousness' (p9). In general, Scott considered, 'psychological damage is very real and is frequently noted as a result of aggressions' (p9). If Scott is correct, and the current authors would side with him, it is worth noting that it creates a difficulty in terms of prediction-outcome correlations. Psychological damage is not as easy to assess and quantify as physical damage.

6   We are reminded of a *New Yorker* cartoon in which the police officer is on the phone to HQ. He has handcuffed a suspect to a railing and is telling the dispatcher that he has got the right man – that his prisoner has a schizoaffective disorder with pronounced paranoid tendencies (or some such). The joke is, of course, that the officer could in no way be expected to have such a degree of sophisticated psychiatric knowledge. More usual reports received from on-the-beat officers would be something like: 'Nuts – needs to see shrink'.

they have delivered the person, at no small cost in terms of time, the seemingly ill individual is released by the hospital authorities forthwith. This naturally discourages some officers from making future efforts to drive to the hospital. These and other 'front end' difficulties are discussed at length by Webster *et al* (1982, p21, note 8 and pp43–45).

Item 3: lax lawyering

Many criminal lawyers specialise in helping the mentally disordered. Naturally, they know 'how the systems work' and can offer their clients sound advice as to whether or not to pursue some form of insanity plea[7]. They know what consequences will follow their client if directed either to hospital or to prison. But not all lawyers, especially in remote areas, will have this degree of understanding. There is the point, too, that even highly experienced lawyers practicing in their specialised field of the criminal law can be beguiled into thinking, for example, that highly effective, sure-fire treatments have become available to alleviate particular kinds of mental and personality disorder. An example of this occurred in Ontario, Canada, in the 1960s, where it was touted that the staff at the Oak Ridge Division of the Penetanguishene Mental Health Centre could pretty much 'cure' psychopaths[8]. This resulted in large numbers of such persons being 'diverted' by the courts to that facility as not guilty by reason of insanity (see Fine, 2017).

Item 4: courtroom theatricalising

It is instructive to visit courtrooms in which insanity and the 'dangerousness' of offenders are being heard[9]. There will sometimes be much glaring by the prosecutor, even the throwing down of pencils. Defense counsel have their own fund of antics. A lot depends, also, apparently, on the 'warmth' of the expert witness and even whether the expert is male or female (Neal *et al*, 2012). This is only to say that what goes on in the courtroom, the 'performances' put on by the 'leading actors', affects, to a degree, who is and who is not accepted into the forensic mental health

---

7   It goes without saying that in many cases counsel need not apply much cognitive effort. If the offence was extremely serious and if the accused displayed uncontestable signs of mental illness, there is only one course and it is easily set.

8   Space precludes a detailed account here. But the point made in the text can be strengthened by referring to the fact that in the 1960s in Ontario, the courts allowed themselves to find an appreciable number of men to be NCRMD with undoubted psychopathic personalities. This created many subsequent difficulties (see *The Globe and Mail*, Thursday, June 8th, 2017, page A1 and A14).

9   A similar tour of a wing in which convicted persons with mental disorder are housed will cause wonderment as to why at least some of these persons were not sent to a hospital in the first place.

system[10]. It needs also to be mentioned that in these kinds of courtroom shenanigans (or as a result of behind-the-scenes discussions) the nature of the charge may be altered. A sexual assault occurrence, for example, may in the end be dealt with as simple assault (and recorded as such).

Item 5: hobbled psychiatric assessing

The point to be stressed here is not that forensic mental health professionals are willfully uninformed about the persons they are obliged to evaluate. It is simply that, oftentimes, crucial information is lacking – at least at the time of assessment. It takes time to retrieve criminal justice, mental health, immigration and other such records. We have referred to this process previously as 'bureaucratic glaciality' (Padgett & Webster, 2005). In some instances, such records will never be studied. They no longer exist, as in the case of refugees escaping from war-torn lands. As well, even in stable countries, administrators must order the destruction of old records to make room for new ones.

Item 6: decision-maker biasing

As Robert Menzies explains at some length in Chapter 6, people, including 'experts', tend to make strong judgments on the basis of slight information. When the patient appears at a decision-making tribunal, he or she – whether the panel members realise it or not – is being 're-judged' in that setting. The patient may or may not be called upon to testify. But that does not mean that the panel members will not be taking into account the person's physical size, gender, mode of dress, presence of distinguishing characteristics, and so on. We know that readily apparent facial features affect decision-making in regard to 'dangerousness' (Esses & Webster, 1988). Judgments of psychopathy, for example, tend to be based on 'thin slices of behavior' (Fowler *et al*, 2009). And it turns out that people make intuitive judgments of trustworthiness on the basis of facial appearance (Porter *et al*, 2008).

---

10 No matter how long the follow-up period, it seems it can never be long enough. In the Menzies and Webster undertaking it was set at six years following initial assessment in Toronto. As part of the data collection process, the second author visited the officers of the British Columbia Review Board in New Westminster. His search turned up a man, part of the original sample, who had recently murdered an acquaintance in a pub. He had used a broken beer bottle. Extensive notes about the incident were taken. On return to the office in Toronto, Chris looked up the record. The man had been deemed relatively low-risk for future violent offending against others. So, in terms of the follow-up the prediction was correct. The man had *not* committed, so far as was known at any rate, violence over the six-year period. Yet further perusal of the file showed that the murder had occurred *outside the time frame* (by a matter of weeks). So 'in reality' the prediction was wrong, but according to the predetermined research protocol, it was right.

Item 7: prediction-outcome research lacking

John Monahan, in his 1981 short book on violence prediction, hammered home the point that predictions will always be far from perfect so long as there is a lack of clarity about what factors are being measured and how they are defined in the first place, and similarly, all too often, key factors and events may not get 'captured' during follow-up investigations. Researchers, no matter how hard they try, face practical limitations in what kinds of data they can accumulate.

In an ideal clinical-research world, the patient, on being inducted into a forensic mental health service – be it outpatient or inpatient – automatically becomes a member of a master research project. This means that his or her progress will be monitored and recorded over some set period of time. This is of course presuming the ethical issues underlying the project have been resolved. The advantage of such a research plan is three fold: (1) the patient can likely not only *benefit* from being included in the research but may in fact be able to 'give back' – in the sense that his or her experience within the project may benefit others; (2) when individual and pooled data are consolidated the results can be relayed to the members of the assessment team – only in this way can professional practice stand a chance of being improved; (3) the eventual pooled data, possibly combined from other jurisdictions, can be examined to see if systems-wide changes are needed to policy and procedures.

Some of these points are considered in Chapters 23-27. It goes without saying that without such a research plan, persons, once discharged, become 'lost'. How these losses might have contributed to Correlation Degradation will never be known. Many years ago it was pointed out by Ziskin and Faust (1988) that making forensic and correctional mental health risk assessments and subsequently not completing follow-along studies is akin to playing golf while blind-folded. Their metaphor remains apt. It is hard to see how improvements in prediction accuracy can occur in the absence of such information. While it is true that it takes much effort and many resources to complete such studies, it is essential that they be conducted.

Item 8: diagnostic slipping

The ascription of up-to-date diagnoses is very important for clinical and research purposes. Most studies link diagnostic categories to eventual outcome. Ideally, in such studies such diagnoses are arrived at via the use of special schedules and procedures (e.g. Michel *et al*, 2013). While such elegance and precision can often be achieved in research work, it is not always present in routine mental health work. Not infrequently, diagnoses are 'carried forward' from one year to the next, from one 'attending psychiatrist' to the next, and so on. Not only this, but there is perhaps insufficient realisation that in cases where multiple diagnoses are assigned, there will often be 'interaction effects' among disorders within the week, within the day, within the hour. Eventual statistical analyses performed 'when all the data are in' can be based on an unduly 'static' view of diagnostic entities. Correlating inaccurate, simplified, diagnoses with outcome measures will degrade prediction-outcome correlations[11].

Item 9: complexities in coding

There are always difficulties in translating standard criminal-legal categories demanded by the courts into numerical forms required by social science researchers. 'Seriousness' has to get quantified. This can be done, if not exactly, then to an extent (see, for example, Cormier, 1994). But some crimes pretty much defy capture. Consider, for example, the notion of *folie à deux*. In such instances the violence arises not so much *within a person* but is shared *between persons*. Sometimes these instances occur suddenly and under circumstances that could not be anticipated even by the perpetrators. These occurrences may happen below the level of consciousness of either person. A brilliant example of this is to be found in Alice Munro's 'Child's Play' (see Webster & Béslisle, 2015). This kind of 'interactive aggression' is hard to code. The struggle to pin it down, though, is not an easy one to win. When such complicated forms of aggression are involved, it is likely to impede the accuracy of prediction.

Item 10: inept interviewing (and compiling)

It is helpful when researchers and clinicians point to the fact that, in their study, this or that assessment scheme was used. And, of course, we argue that it is all the better if that scheme belongs to the family of *structured* devices in which items are fully and carefully defined. But, this much said, as emphasised in most SPJ manuals, it is *essential* that the evaluator be clinically experienced and skilled (see, for example, V3 of the HCR-20, p38). Inexperience on the part of the assessor will likely reduce prediction accuracy in the individual case and in the aggregate. David Cooke, Chapter 4, this volume, would agree.

Item 11: deficient risk assessment training

Pilots being trained for their high-risk responsibilities are not allowed into the skies without an experienced colleague in the other seat. More especially, a great deal of their training takes place on the ground, with the aid of carefully

---

11   One of the present authors (C.D.W), in his own early work, had a regrettable tendency to over-ascribe importance to 'primary diagnoses' (cf., Webster *et al*, 1982). Of course, as pointed out by Douglas Boer in Chapter 18, it can become grossly unfair to subject persons from 'special populations' to assessment schemes in which their cultural considerations are not taken into account. If such persons are subsequently included in prediction-outcome correlation studies, coefficients will almost certainly be degraded.

constructed flight simulators. The materials presented to them via screens arise from actual incidents in which failures or near-failures occurred. In other words they are trained and tested against known outcomes. In the area of forensic and correctional mental health there is no lack of known outcomes. The media pounce, as it should, on the 'cases gone awry'. There are also inquests and inquiries (see Maden, 2007, for a compelling account of 'institutional failures'). But so far as we are aware, little of this knowledge and experience finds its way into training programmes for nurses, psychiatrists, psychologists, social workers, recreationalists, occupational therapists, educators and others. There is, though, a notable article by Teo *et al* (2012) which shows that the accuracy of psychiatric residents' assessments of risk *can* be improved by providing well-structured training programs.

Item 12: non-optimal device selecting

Recently one of us (C.D.W.) was asked by some kind colleagues to 'sit in' on a V3 assessment the staff had completed. The inducement was strengthened by a free lunch. Under discussion was the case of a 19 year-old who had committed some kind of not-very-serious offense. After going through all V3 items it was necessary for the 'outsider' to offer an opinion. The opinion, politely and deferential expressed, was that the whole assessment could likely have been accomplished better via the START: AV (Vilgoen *et al*, 2014) than V3. It was immediately pointed out that the young man was 19, not 18, and that the 'cut off' for V3 is 18. Yet it was necessary to point out that the V3 manual is explicit in saying that:

> '...it may make more sense in certain cases not to use HCR-20 V3 with a 19 or 20-year-old (a person living at home and dependent on parents, for instance). It will be up to the evaluator to judge whether HCR-20 V3 or another instrument is most appropriate in these cases on the cusp. In some such cases it may be beneficial to use **both** HCR-20 V3 and an instrument developed for use with adolescents such as the Structured Assessment of Violent Risk in Youth...' (p35, emphasis added)

It is to be hoped that the colleagues present for the discussion swallowed the 'correction' along with their lunches.

The example above is, though, instructive. With the development, post-Scott, of so many risk assessment devices over recent years, it takes some appreciable skill to know which schemes to apply to which circumstances. This issue has been taken up to very good effect by Fazel & Wolf (2018). These authors point out that there are now available more than 200 risk assessment schemes in criminal justice and forensic psychiatry. Moreover, the use of some of these is mandated. Fazel and Wolf offer 10 factors to determine the quality of a particular risk assessment device. These are paraphrased below:

1. Has the scheme been validated externally?
2. Has the validation exercise been conducted with a population that corresponds to the area of interest?[12]
3. Is there a sound method of validation? Is it replicable?
4. Do high scores on the scheme correspond to high outcome scores?
5. Is it sufficiently easy to use?
6. Does it perform properly in routine clinical practice (rather than just in study samples)?
7. Is it based on a reasonably contained number of prediction variables?
8. Is there a scheme for weighting items?
9. Have the originators 'cherry-picked' the optimal follow-up period from a range of alternative ones used by them to justify their scheme?
10. Have the originators split the original sample into randomly-chosen sub-groups to determine their scheme's internal validity?

Item 13: unrealistic result expecting

We have repeatedly stressed that the purpose of SPJ schemes is *prevention* of violence in the individual case, not *prediction* (see especially, Steve Hart's Chapter 9). Yet it is perfectly reasonable to determine the extent to which scores on the HCR-20 V3 correspond with subsequent violence and related outcomes. Such a study was recently performed by Vitaco *et al*, 2018. These authors followed 238 persons under Conditional Release (CD) from the Psychiatric Secure Review Board in Oregon. The clients had been assessed by Version 2 of the HCR-20 (Webster *et al*, 1997). The follow-up lasted between four and nine years. The outcome was measured by revocation of the CD. The authors were disappointed that only two items from the V2 correlated with revocation (both items were from the Risk Management Scale – Exposure to Destabilizers and Stress). To the present authors of this chapter, the surprise is that, after such a long follow-up interval, *any* items correlated – since the originators of the V2 scheme never anticipated it having such 'long legs' into the future. There is, as well, the fact that revocation of CD is one thing, actual violence is another. Revocation in the Vitaco *et al* study could occur for 'mental health deterioration leading to dangerousness, absconding, or major violation of rules (e.g., drug or alcohol use)' (p406).

---

12 Of course, as pointed out by Douglas Boer in Chapter 18, it can become grossly unfair to subject persons from 'special populations' to assessment schemes in which their cultural considerations are not taken into account. If such persons *are* subsequently included in prediction-outcome correlation studies, coefficients will almost certainly be degraded.

It makes sense that prediction accuracy is apt to be greater when tested with schemes specifically designed for the short haul rather than the long one. This is confirmed by Ramesh *et al* (2018). These authors, using very large samples, found that schemes intended for the near future achieved median AUCs of 0.83. In contrast, those with longer windows had an appreciably lower median AUC at 0.68. The more general point to be taken from this is that accuracy of predictions will depend on the prediction instruments selected; poor results can be expected if schemes intended for the short range are applied to the long term, and vice-versa. Furthermore, generally, results can be best if a *specific* device can be used where appropriate (e.g. SARA, SVR-20).

Item 14: hospitals as violence-inducing

It is not easy to exist peacefully in many psychiatric hospital units. These are busy places and many a patient ends up on the receiving end of unwanted, unexpected aggression. When these incidents have died down, it is often hard to pin-point who was the perpetrator and who was the victim. As well, staff sometimes have to seclude persons or indeed force medications on them to protect themselves and co-patients. These 'last ditch' methods can work against mental stability, leaving a patient, at the extreme, with attitudes and behaviors more violent than those he or she possessed at admission. The reality of these effects, clearly noted by Peter Scott, is that they can work against prediction accuracy. He called attention to the '…grave frustrations which are common to closed institutions' (Scott, 1977, p21). So it is that a prediction of low potential for violence over the long-term – one made at time of admission – may be upset by the iatrogenic effects of the hospital itself (or by unforeseeable events occurring while at liberty in the community).

Item 15: inadequate treating

Readers do not have to look far to find published examples of good-quality, well-researched, treatment programmes (e.g. Cullin *et al*, 2012). But, on a day-to-day basis, it can be surprising how little actually gets done on a routine basis either in hospital or the community. There can be a near absence of programmes. In some jurisdictions there is a tendency to avoid or defer treatment efforts for those who suffer from a major mental disorder *and* substance abuse. The patient is expected to deal with the problems, in sequence. Only when the addiction or dependence is overcome will the mental illness be tackled, or vice versa. There can, too, be a tendency to invest considerable staff energy toward patients whose problems seem easily 'fixable' and to set aside those whose problems are more extreme. Finally, it should be noted that, even in well-developed treatment programmes (e.g. Cullen *et al*, 2012) there can be high drop-out rates. This state of affairs may diminish the strength of prediction-outcome correlations.

Item 16: unduly cautious tribunal decision-making

Persons deemed not guilty by reason of insanity or incompetent (unfit) to stand trial are, in most jurisdictions, given periodic reviews by courts or tribunals. In these proceedings there is opportunity for court officers or the various parties to question the need for continued detention. But sometimes the hospital detention drags on, seemingly unnecessarily, year after year. So it is that some patients are not given as much opportunity to reoffend as they would have had if they had been released to the community. And if they are in the community they may be under unnecessarily restrictive conditions. This can obviously work against achieving high prediction-outcome of violence. In one sense the boards are doing a 'good job' of holding down rates of violence. This could be construed as a 'fine thing' (though it raises important legal and ethical issues). But from a researcher's point of view it can be unhelpful and lead to Correlation Degradation (i.e. the person is unduly restrained for violence which had been predicted previously).

Item 17: ineffectual transitioning

Ideally, when persons are discharged from hospital to community services, their care and treatment requirements are conveyed very explicitly to the receiving outpatient programmes. No doubt this is the usual case. But sometimes 'failure' in the community is more or less assured because the housing, financial and other resources were never put properly or fully into place. Such lacks may have a great deal to do with setting the scene for new violence. Indeed in some instances it is perpetrated by the individual precisely to regain admission to the hospital. When this happens it may get scored as a 'violent incident' from a research point of view. Yet, as noted, the contrived, self-sabotaging act may have more connection with absence of support than intended or misplaced aggression. These matters are dealt with at some length by Mary-Lou Martin (2014).

Item 18: strong treatment responding

Frequently, persons appear at assessment having committed horrendous crimes while in an indisputable state of psychosis, possibly fueled by abuse of alcohol or substances. A good example might be Randy Starr (2002) who killed his mother while grossly disturbed. Yet Randy, like others, made an excellent response to treatment. He did exceptionally well in hospital and was released to the community in record time. He obtained work and married successfully. Yet chances are that an assessment performed right after the index offence, and taking his criminal history into account, would *not* have offered a very positive prognosis. In other words, he would have been swimming against the actuarial or any other kind of data tide. In this way he would play a role in decreasing accuracy of prediction.

Item 19: false precision claiming

The advertisements on TV tell us that by using toothpaste A rather than toothpaste B, we can count on a 72% increase in the whiteness of our snappers. Such a daily treatment, or so the manufacturers would have us believe, will enable us to near-blind our family and friends (and attract many a lover). But as a viewer of the advertisement, it is hard to know where the seemingly exact 72% came from. Why not 71% or 73%? Perhaps not to same extent, but it is sometimes possible to be beguiled by reading some papers in the research literature. These describe prediction-outcome accuracy to the second decimal place. Is it the case that mental health scientists have reached such degrees of precision?

In a similar way, consider how it can be that in psychiatric reports to decision-making tribunals there can, in the boiler plate, be mention that a certain actuarial measure correlates *strongly* with eventual outcome. Such an assertion would be most likely incorrect. The whole point of this chapter is based on the idea that prediction-outcome correlations scarcely ever exceed a +0.40 prediction-outcome correlation. This being so, those members of the tribunal who do *not* have a detailed knowledge of the language of r's, AUCs, standard errors, standard deviations and the like, may be inclined to ascribe more importance than they should to the results from the particular risk assessment device referred to in the report. It is not easy to convey statistical meanings in everyday words.

Item 20: insular follow-up data retrieving

It is extremely difficult to undertake searches of criminal justice records. Research protocols must pass ethical scrutiny. Pledges must be given about the de-identification of data and so on. Even when the access is formally and finally granted and the records are in hand, the amount of information they contain can be very thin. It may not go beyond the listing of a conviction. Charges may be excluded. From the offense it may be impossible to guess 'what actually happened' – to determine whether in actual fact the person under consideration was as much a victim as a perpetrator. Even more problematic is the fact that, to get a fuller picture of events transpiring during the follow-up period, it is necessary to search records obtained from sources other than criminal justice. This warning crops up in the piece by Leena Augimeri (Chapter 25). She points out how much Christopher Koegl gained by searching, in one of the Child Development Institute Studies, health records as well as criminal justice ones. Much violent behavior is dealt with in the emergency departments of hospitals so the research network needs to be cast as wide as possible. As well, if at all possible, the paper record should ideally be supplemented through interviews with patients, former patients and collaterals (see especially, ACT IV, in Chapter 12 by Chris Webster and Sumeeta Chatterjee, and Chapter 26 by David Farrington).

Appendix: The Correlation Degradation Worksheet-20 (CDW-20)

Item	The Problems	Yes	No
1	Societal Shifting		
2	Police Screening		
3	Lax Lawyering		
4	Courtroom Theatricalising		
5	Hobbled Psychiatric Assessing		
6	Decision-Maker Biasing		
7	Prediction-Outcome Research Lacking		
8	Diagnostic Slipping		
9	Complexities in Coding		
10	Inept Interview (and Compiling)		
11	Deficient Risk Assessment Training		
12	Non-Optimal Device Selecting		
13	Unrealistic Result Expecting		
14	Hospitals as Violence-Inducing		
15	Inadequate Treating		
16	Unduly Cautious Tribunal Decision-Making		
17	Ineffectual Transitioning		
18	Strong Treatment Responding		
19	False Precision Claiming		
20	Insular Data Retrieving at Follow-Up		

References and further reading

Borum R, Bartel P & Forth A (2006) *Manual for the Structured Assessment of Violence Risk in Youth (SAVRY)*. Oddessa, Florida: Psychological Assessment Resources.

Cassidy W, Faucher C & Jackson MA (Eds) (2018) *Cyberbullying at University in International Contexts*. New York: Routledge.

Cormier C (1994) *Offender Psycho-Social Assessment Manual Correctional Model*. Penetanguishene, Ontario: Ontario Mental Health Centre.

Cullen AE, Clarke AY, Kuipers E, Hodgins S, Dean K, & Fahy T (2012). A multi-site randomized controlled trial of a cognitive skills programme for male mentally disordered offenders: social-cognitive outcomes. *Psychological Medicine* **42**, 557–569.

Esses VM & Webster CD (1988) Physical attractiveness, dangerousness, and the Canadian criminal code. *Journal of Applied Social Psychology* **18** (12) 1017–1031.

Fazel S & Wolf A (2018) Selection a risk assessment toll to use in practice: a 10-point guide. *Evidence Based Mental Health* **21** (2) 41–43 doi: 10.1136/eb-2017-102861.

Fine S (2017) Doctors tortured patients at Ontario mental health centre, judge rules. *Globe and Mail* **8 June**. Available at: https://www.theglobeandmail.com/news/national/doctors-at-ontario-mental-health-facility-tortured-patients-court-finds/article35246519/ (accessed December 2018).

Fowler KA, Lilienfield SO & Patrick CJ (2009) Detecting psychopathy from thin slices of behaviour. *Psychological Assessment* **21** 68–78.

Fukui S, Goscha R, Rapp C, Mabry A, Liddy P & Marty D (2012) Strengths model case management fidelity scores and client outcomes. *Psychiatric Services* **63** 708–710.

Hodgins S & Janson C-G (2002) *Criminality and violence among the mentally disordered: The Stockholm Metropolitan Project*. Cambridge: Cambridge University Press

Maden A (2007) *Treating Violence: A Guide to Risk Management in Mental Health*. Oxford, England: Oxford University Press.

Martin M-L (2014) Transitions. In: CD Webster, Q Haque & SJ Hucker (eds) *Violence Risk Assessment and Management: Advances through structured professional judgment and sequential redirections, Second Edition*, pp98–105. Chichester, UK: Wiley-Blackwell.

Menzies RJ & Webster CD (1995) The construction of validation of risk assessments in a six year follow-up of forensic patients: a tridimensional analysis. *Journal of Consulting and Clinical Psychology* **63** 766–778.

Michel SF, Riaz M, Webster CD, Hart SD, Levander S, Müller-Isburner R, Tiihonen J, Repo-Tiihonen E, Tuninger E & Hodgins A (2013) Using the HCR-20 to predict aggressive behaviour among men with schizophrenia living in the community: accuracy of predictions, general and forensic settings, and dynamic risk factors. *International Journal of Forensic Mental Health* **12** 1–13.

Monahan J (1981) *Predicting Violent Behavior: An assessment of clinical techniques*. Beverly Hills, CA: Sage.

Monahan J, Steadman HJ, Silver E et al (2001) *Rethinking Risk Assessment: The MacArthur Study of Mental Disorder and Violence*. Oxford, England: Oxford University Press.

Neal TMS, Guadagno RE, Eno CA & Brodsky SL (2012) Warm and competence on the witness stand: implications for the credibility of male and female expert witnesses. *Journal of the American Academy of Psychiatry and the Law* **40** 488–497.

Padget R, Webster CD & Robb MK (2005) Unavailable essential archival data: major limitations in the conduct of clinical practice and research in violence risk assessment. *Canadian Journal of Psychiatry* **50** 937–940.

Porter S, England L, Juodis M, ten Brinke L & Wilson K (2008) Is the face a window to the soul? investigation of the accuracy of intuitive judgments of the trustworthiness of human faces. *Canadian Journal of Behavioural Science* **40** 171–177.

Ramesh T, Igoumenou A, Montes MV & Fazel F (2018) Use of risk assessment instruments to predict violence in forensic psychiatric hospitals: a systematic review and meta-analysis. *European Psychiatry* **52** 47–53.

Scott PD (1977) Assessing dangerousness in criminals. *British Journal of Psychiatry* **131** 127–142.

Starr R (2002) A successful reintegration into the community: one NGRI acquitee's story. *Federal Probation* **66** 59–63.

Steadman HJ & Cocozza JJ (1974) *Careers of the criminally insane: Excessive social control of deviance*. Lexington Books, Lexington, MA.

Teo AR, Holley SR, Leary M & McNeil DE (2012) The relationship between level of training and accuracy of violence risk assessment. *Psychiatric Services* **63** 1089–1094.

Vilgoen JL, Nicholls TL, Cruise KR, Desmarais SL & Webster CD (2014) *Short-term assessment of risk and treatability: Adolescent Version User Guide (START: AV)*. Burnaby, Canada: Mental Health Law and Policy Institute.

Vitaco MJ, Balduzzi E, Rideout K, Banfe S & Britton J (2018) Reconsidering risk assessment with insanity acquittees. *Law and Human Behavior* **42** 403–412

Webster CD, Béslisle E (2015) How literature can add value to structured professional judgments of violence risk: An illustrative rare risk example inspired by Alice Munro's Child's Play. *Archives of Forensic Psychology* **1** 14–26.

Webster CD, Menzies RJ & Jackson MA (1982) *Clinical Assessment Before Trial: Legal Issues and Mental Disorder*. Toronto, ON: Butterworths.

Webster CD, Douglas KS, Eaves D & Hart SD (1997) *HCR-20: Assessing risk for violence, Version 2*. Burnaby, BC, Canada: Law, Mental Health and Policy Institute, Simon Fraser University.

Ziskin J & Faust D (1988) *Coping with psychiatric and psychological testimony* (4th ed). Los Angeles: Law & Psychology Press.

Chapter 8:
'Actuarial' approaches to the prediction of violence – the violence risk appraisal guide – revised (VRAG-R) as an example

By Quazi Haque and Chris Webster

The word 'actuarial' in the title of this chapter is placed in inverted commas to reflect the fact that true actuarial prediction tends to be based on thousands of massed cases, not the few hundred typically found in the arena of law and mental health. In this domain, a total sample of 1,000 cases is considered an accomplishment (e.g. Monahan *et al*, 2001, nearly 1,000 cases drawn from three separate American cities). Actuaries working for life insurance and related businesses crunch large numbers. The data they require are fairly simple to gather (e.g. age, gender[13] at birth, date of death, presence or absence of easily identifiable medical conditions). It is easier to predict mortality than some complicated behavior which may or may not subsequently have been 'constructed' to be violent (by witnesses, by police, by courts, by mental health clinicians, by researchers, and so on).

When epidemiological researchers predict death on the basis of a few simple pre-existing medical conditions they can achieve Areas Under the Curve (AUCs) of around 0.90 (where 0.50 is chance and 1.0 is perfect correspondence). If prediction estimates are imprecise and if outcome measures are imprecise, it will *always* be difficult to achieve AUC values much beyond 0.75 or so. The point, then, is to get prediction-outcome AUC values that are truly convincing (i.e. in the 0.85 range), and to achieve this it would be necessary that the sample size be very large and that the prediction and outcome scores be well defined and amenable to unambiguous coding.

---

13 Even this piece of seemingly straightforward data can occasionally be hard to code due to gender reassignments.

Researchers in this area rely mainly on two different measures of correlation. One is the AUC just mentioned. The other, more traditional, is usually referred to as r (the Pearson correlation coefficient). It has limits of 0 (no correspondence) and +1.0 (perfect correspondence). In fact it is possible for perfect negative correlations of -1.0. Using the r framework, as discussed in the previous chapter, it was argued 30 years ago that the statistical prediction between mental disorder and violence will, under usual conditions, never exceed +0.40 (Menzies & Webster, 1985). This observation was drawn in part from a study of theirs based on 248 patients from six different cities across Canada and followed subsequently for 18 months (see Webster *et al*, 1982).

By massing data across as many cases as can be arranged it is often possible to discern points of systemic failure in which stage or stages of a release programme, failure is most apt to occur (e.g. Müller-Isberner *et al*, 2007). The availability of such data can have major procedural implications. At the most basic level, this kind of aggregated information can help policy makers and legislators decide whether or not it is necessary to rebuild an existing hospital or create a new one, whether changes to the criminal law provisions are due, and so on. When such studies include 'follow-along' months or years after initial assessments the efforts to conduct them is likely never wasted (e.g. Webster & Chatterjee in Chapter 12). The recent published research of Anne Crocker and colleagues is outlined in Chapter 27. The value of this work in part is due to the fact that it crosses jurisdictional boundaries. Policy and procedures found to be effective in one state or province may deserve a trial in a sister jurisdiction.

The VRAG in its initial form

The original Violence Risk Appraisal Guide (VRAG), then called the RAG (Risk Assessment Guide), was first published in 1993 by Grant Harris, Marnie Rice and Vernon Quinsey. It was based on patients detained under the Ontario Review Board, actually the then Lieutenant Governor's Review Board. The information the study yielded was considered important at the time and it remains important to this day. What the investigation showed was that 12 variables, when coded according to the RAG manual, could 'predict' violence. These variables, ordered in terms of predictive strength, are displayed in Table 8.1. In this study, original charge did not correlate with outcome (p = -0.01). When data were pooled across a subsample, a low but significant correlation was achieved (+ 0.16). This was based on the assessment work of three psychiatrists pooled. What was interesting, though, was the range of the correlations. Two colleagues performed at a chance level (+0.05, +0.17). The third achieved a significant correlation of +0.35.

Table 8.1: Correlations (r) between original RAG items and outcome at 7-year follow up

The Original 12 RAG items correlated with outcome (r) at seven-year follow-up (left column). Present day status of the items (right column).

Variables	r	Status*
Psychopathy Checklist Score	0.34	M
Elementary School Maladjustment	0.31	R
DSM-III Diagnosis of Personality Disorder	0.26	D
Age at Index Offence	-0.26	R
Separated from Parents under Age 16	0.25	R
Failure on Prior Conditional Release	0.24	R
Non-violent Offence History	0.20	R
Never Married	0.18	R
DSM-III Diagnosis of Schizophrenia	-0.17	D
Victim Injury	-0.16	D
Alcohol Abuse	0.13	M
Female Victim Index Offence	-0.11	D

*Note: six variables were retained into the VRAG-R (2013). They are marked R. Two items were modified (M). Four items were deleted (D).

(Table adapted with permission from Webster et al, 1994, p31. Present-day status of the items is shown in the right-hand column. Six variables were retained into the VRAG-R (2013). They are marked R. Two items were modified (M). Four items were dropped (D).)

The Current VRAG-R (2013)[14]

Modified items

Readers might wish to note that, in all likelihood, items in schemes like the VRAG-R will *always* be in need of periodic refinement since society itself is in a constant state of flux – in ways which, ultimately, might lead to increases in violence, or in ways which might induce decreases in prevalence. Two items were reworked:

Psychopathy – Hare PCL-R Score. At first blush, this change is hard to understand since in the original 1993 study it was the very best

---

14 Readers will note that one of the aims of the 2013 study was to collapse the VRAG with another device of the authors' making – The Sex Offender Risk Assessment Guide, SORAG.

predictor item – at +0.34. Yet the originators of the new VRAG-R had to acknowledge that some users found it time consuming and cumbersome to have to administer a whole separate scheme (one which demanded that clinical assessors receive proper training and experience with the device). So in the VRAG-R, this item is replaced with a simpler-to-score item called 'Antisociality'[15]. It should be added that the substance of the new item covers much the same ground as the Hare PCL-R. Indeed, it is derived from 5 Hare PCL-R items. Poor Behavioral Controls, Early Behavior Problems, Juvenile Delinquency, Revocation of Conditional Release, and Criminal Versatility.

Alcohol Abuse History – This item is now broadened to take drug-abuse history into account. Drug abuse worldwide has become much more common than it was in 1993. The item is now named 'Substance Abuse'.

Dropped items

Any Female Victim in the Index Offense – This original VRAG item is dropped because it failed to correlate in the 2013 study with later violent sex offending.

Injury to Victim in the Index Offense – Dropped for the same reason as Any Female Victim.

Schizophrenia – This item is now dropped because it requires 'diagnostic criteria'.

Personality Disorder – This item is now dropped for the same reason as Schizophrenia.

New items added

- Conduct Disorder Score.

- Violent Criminal History.

- Sex Offending.

- Number of Prior Admissions to Correctional Institutions.

Performance of the new VRAG-R

From Table 8.2, an adaption of Table 5, p958 of the Rice *et al* (2013) article, it is possible to discern the performance of the VRAG-R.

---

15 The VRAG-R authors do concede that the Hare PCL-R might be '...important in decision making about therapy for and clinical management of violent offenders...' (p960).

Table 8.2: Correlations between VRAG scores and outcome at mean of 21-year follow-up.

	Whole Sample (n=1,261)	Validation Sample (n=300)
Antisociality	.38	.34
Admission to Corrections	.31	.30
Failure on Conditional Release	.30	.33
Elementary School Adjustment	.30	.31
Conduct Disorder Score	.30	.31
Nonviolent Criminal History	.29	.29
Age at Index Offense	.27	.23
Violent Criminal History	.24	.23
Substance Abuse	.22	.14
Sex Offending	.19	.22
Lived with Both Parents	.18	.16
Marital Status	.12	.14

(Adapted from Rice *et al*, 2013)

Commentary on the VRAG-R

The authors of this large-scale project conducted over so many years deserve commendation for keeping it up-to-date through extending their original sample, and by refining their prediction and outcome measures. They themselves point to the fact that researchers should feel bound to conduct such exercises from time to time.

One may ask, when all the tinkering is done, has there been a notable improvement in prediction accuracy? The answer to this seems to be 'no'. The overall AUC in the original VRAG construction sample was 0.75; the approximate estimate for the VRAG-R was essentially the same at +0.76 (p959). Yet it was by no means a mistake to undertake this study. It shows, for example, that when schizophrenia and personality disorder are taken out of the equation it makes no difference to overall prediction-outcome scores.

Readers will observe, though, that 'mental disorder' (MD) and 'personality disorder' (PD) are no longer situated within the VRAG-R. This means, since MD and PD usually are law-defined, highly-relevant factors in forensic psychiatric decision making, care must be taken when matching the results of such assessments to prevailing legal statutes and to current clinical practice.

Rice *et al* would have it that, with the progress they and others have shown over recent years in 'actuarial prediction', it ought to be possible to dispense with clinical opinion altogether. They admit that the VRAG-R scheme is 'not perfect' and they acknowledge '...that some commentators have simply declared that existing actuarial systems are not good enough to be used to make important decisions...'. And they go on to add that 'this leaves practitioners and criminal justice professionals, when decisions must be made, with no better method to use instead' (p961). Their *hope*, then, is that 'Further research will eventually yield larger predictive effects for violent recidivism using as yet untested variables and their interactions' (p961). They propose that, in the meantime, 'the VRAG-R is among the methods of choice to make long-term appraisals of risk in forensic populations' (p961).

How much help does a VRAG-R score provide in decision making?

The answer to this is: it depends. As readers may know, VRAG scores in the previous and new schemes are divided into nine 'Bins'. It is easy to show, both in the original and the new scheme, that *on average* the higher the Bin score the greater is the chance, statistically, that an individual will recidivate. A person with a VRAG-R score in Bin 1 has a +0.08 chance of recidivating after five years (and a .17 chance after 15 years). A person with a VRAG-R score in Bin 9 will have a +0.80 chance of recidivating after five years (and +0.91 after 15 years). A person in Bin 5 will have a +0.25 chance of recidivating in five years and a +0.54 chance at 15 years. The average level of risk rises in an orderly way as Bins increase from 1 through 9. But, because the VRAG-R scores are 'normally distributed' there are relatively few cases in Bins 1-3, relatively more in Bins 4-6, and, again, relatively few in Bins 6-9. So knowing that the particular patient is rated by VRAG-R as being in Bin 5 (i.e. exactly in the middle of the distribution) is not necessarily of much practical use to clinical or tribunal decision makers. In the Rice *et al* (2013) study, 20% of the whole 1,256 population (252 cases) fell into Bin 5. How helpful is this information when trying to make a decision in an individual case?

With the above reservations stated, it seems that, if a 'Bin 9 person' is being considered for a full discharge, it may be wise to take pause and to include some further consideration of this fact. This, of course, is not to say that the eventual decision should be more-or-less *automatically* influenced by Bin score; only that it should be taken into account – and discussed along with other considerations. Similarly, the tribunal or court might be prompted to wonder why a person with a VRAG-R Bin 1 score continues to be detained. Of course, there may be many sound reasons for such continued confinement within the hospital or sustaining supervision in the community, but the low score might itself prompt productive discussion (i.e. to explore what conceivable conditions might need to be established to allow for safe discharge).

What is the value of clinical opinion in the predictions of future violence?

The way Rice *et al* (2013) read the literature, there is no value. They say, quite explicitly, 'permission to countervail actuarial scores based on clinical judgment[16] is likely to lead to *decreased* accuracy overall...' (p961, emphasis added). In other words, clinical opinion decreases predictive accuracy. While it is the case that individual clinicians *do* vary considerably in their ability to predict future violence (see previous chapter), it would, it seems, be more profitable to figure out why some colleagues make relatively accurate predictions (or relatively inaccurate ones), and to learn from them.

References and further reading

Harris G, Rice M & Quinsey V (1993) Violent recidivism of mentally disordered offenders: the development of a statistical prediction instrument. *Criminal Justice and Behavior* **20** 315–335.

Menzies RJ, Webster CD & Sepejak DS (1985) Hitting the forensic sound barrier: Predictions of dangerousness in a pre-trial clinic. In: CD Webster, MH Ben-Aron & SJ Hucker (Eds) *Dangerousness: Probability and prediction, psychiatry and public policy*. New York: Cambridge University Press.

Monahan J, Steadman HJ, Silver E & Banks SM (2001) Rethinking Risk Assessment: The MacArthur Study of Mental Disorder and Violence. Oxford, England: Oxford University Press.

Müller-Isberner R, Webster CD & Gretenkord L (2007) Measuring progress in hospital order treatment: relationships between levels of security and C and R scores of the HCR-20. *International Journal of Forensic Mental Health* **6** (2) 113–121.

Rice ME, Harris GT & Lang C (2013) Validation of and revision to the VRAG and SORAG: The Violence Risk Appraisal Guide-Revised (VRAG-R). *Psychological Assessment* **25** 951–965.

Harris GT, Rice ME, Quinsey VL & Cormier CA (2015) *Violent offenders: Appraising and managing risk* (3rd Ed). Washington, D.C: American Psychological Association.

Webster CD, Harris GT, Rice ME, Cormier C & Quinsey V (1994) *The Violence Prediction Scheme: Assessing Dangerousness in High Risk Men*. Toronto, Canada: Centre of Criminology, University of Toronto.

Webster CD, Menzies RJ, Butler BT & Turner RE (1982) Appendix G. In: CD Webstee, RJ Menzies & MA Jackson (1982) *Clinical Assessment Before Trial: Legal issues and mental disorder* (pp259–283). Toronto, Canada: Butterworths.

---

16 The authors say, 'Blending the empirical strength of actuarial techniques with mostly unevaluated management items reducing [sic] predictive accuracy without conferring benefit' (p961).

Chapter 9: Violence risk assessment and management – from prediction to prevention

By Stephen D Hart and Kevin S Douglas

'The best way to predict the future is to invent it.' – Alan Curtis Kay (1940 –)

Background

In the 1990s, within the span of just a few short years, the process of violence risk assessment and management underwent major evolutionary changes. The first evolution was from 'unstructured clinical judgment' (UCJ), which is decision making unconstrained by any rules or guidelines, to 'actuarial decision making' (ADM), which is decision making constrained entirely by fixed and explicit rules. This shift can be dated to 1993 and the publication of the *Violence Risk Assessment Guide* (Harris *et al*, 1993), subsequently renamed the *Violence Risk Assessment Guide*, the first of the modern actuarial risk assessment instruments for assessing violence risk (Menzies *et al*, 1995).

The second evolution was from ADM to 'structured professional judgment' (SPJ), which is decision making systematised by evidence-based practice guidelines (Hart *et al*, 2016). This shift can be dated to late 1994 or early 1995, with the publication of the *Manual for the Spousal Assault Risk Assessment Guide* (Kropp *et al*, 1994) and the *HCR-20 Scheme* (Webster *et al*, 1994), the first SPJ guidelines. Importantly, the primary goal of violence risk assessment evolved in parallel with its process, from 'identification of dangerousness' to 'violence prediction to violence prevention'.

Dissatisfaction with UCJ was multifarious, widespread, intense and longstanding by the early 1990s for reasons discussed at length by many – perhaps most comprehensively and cogently by Monahan (1981/1995). In contrast, dissatisfaction with ADM, was spurred in part by more recent recognition of the limitations of prediction.

Some of those limitations had been discussed with respect to criminal behavior more generally with great regularity since the 1950s, although the wise cautions and recommendations offered by so many authors (see, for example, the excellent summaries by Gottfredson and Gottfredson (1988) and Gottfredson and Moriarty (2006)) appear to have been widely ignored. But additional limitations related to uncertainty and complexity have been explored in many areas of science, especially since the 1980s. The application of these general limitations to the problem of violence risk makes it clear that developing statistically-based prediction models that are accurate at the individual level is difficult, and may even be impossible. This is particularly true in the absence of clear definitions of key concepts, well-specified etiological theories, and an experience pool that is deep and systematic – three problems that plague the study of violence (see discussions by Hart, 1998; 2004/2011; Hart & Cooke, 2013; Hart *et al*, 2016).

Interest in SPJ, as an alternative to ADM, was spurred on by the recognition that it is not sufficient for professionals to simply identify people who are most likely to commit violence; professionals must also determine how to stop those people from committing violence (Hart *et al*, 2016). Violence prevention is achieved through planning, that is, prioritisation of actions for a given case to maximize the chances of successful outcome in the face of complexity and uncertainty. To assist planning, contemporary SPJ guidelines incorporate two important analytical processes: formulation (also known as case conceptualisation) based on an action theory framework; and development of case management strategies and tactics based on scenario planning methods (Hart *et al*, 2016; see also Hart & Logan, 2011).

Action theory-based formulation

The most important use of formulation is in the identification of strategic objectives for risk management. If we understand *why* someone committed violence in the past, and by extension might do so in the future, then we can target the factors most relevant to violence risk for intervention, and even the optimal order or sequencing in which they should be targeted[17]. In SPJ guidelines for comprehensive assessment of violence risk, the strategic objectives identified through the process of formulation are typically divided into four major categories:

■ 'Monitoring' strategies are intended to provide feedback about the status of critical risk factors and the effectiveness of the management plans.

---

17 In contrast, actuarial risk assessment instruments focus on the identification of risk level – that is, how 'risky' someone is. Risk level may be a crude indication of how much intervention someone requires, but it doesn't tell you why intervention is required or what intervention should target.

- 'Supervision' strategies are intended to make it more difficult for people to commit violence by restricting their rights and freedoms (e.g. of residence, association, movement, activity, and so forth).

- 'Treatment' strategies are intended to remediate deficits in people's psychological or social functioning that may be functionally related to risk.

- 'Victim safety planning' strategies are intended to enhance the internal and external security resources of identifiable potential targets of violence, helping them to better avoid or withstand violence.

- The strategies in each of these categories should be targeted at critical risk factors (i.e. those that figure prominently in formulating of violence risk). Each critical risk factor should be addressed by one or more strategies, and each strategy should address one or more critical risk factors.

Techniques for the formulation of violence risk can be grouped loosely into two categories: atheoretical and theoretical. Atheoretical techniques do not make assumptions about causal mechanisms underlying violence or the causal roles played by risk factors. Evaluators let the meaning emerge from their analysis of the case, rather than imposing meaning on the case. This may be done using techniques such as graphing (e.g. trying to represent the association among clusters of risk factors using arrows) or root cause analysis (in which proximal causes are traced back to distal causes). Theoretical techniques analyse cases using a particular conceptual model or lens. The model we use for SPJ guidelines is based on Action Theory.

According to Action Theory, violence – like all other voluntary behavior – is the result of a decision-making process that involves movement from goal to intent to action. Action Theory assumes people are rational agents, but rational in the sense of being thoughtful rather than logically coherent. Indeed, Action Theory assumes that people's decision making is influenced by a range of factors, often resulting in bad choices (i.e. those with maladaptive outcomes) or choices made badly (i.e. in a disorganised manner). The foundations of Action Theory are well accepted in fields such as philosophy, law, economics and cognitive neuroscience. In psychology and criminology they underlie specific models such as the Theories of Reasoned Action and Planned Behavior, Control Theory, Strain Theory, Situational Action Theory, Routine Activity Theory, and I3 Theory.

Viewed through the lens of Action Theory, formulation involves identifying risk factors that motivate, disinhibit or destabilise decisions about violence. Motivators increase the likelihood that people will perceive violence as a viable response in a given situation or, alternatively, increase the perceived potential benefits of violence. Disinhibitors decrease the likelihood that people will inhibit thoughts of violence as a viable response in a given situation or, alternatively, decrease the perceived potential costs of violence. Destabilisers disrupt, disturb or disorganise decisions about violence, making it difficult for people to accurately perceive and reason about situational cues, consider alternatives, or weigh potential costs and benefits.

Scenario-based management plans

The identification of strategic objectives is necessary but not sufficient for good planning. Planners also need to determine how to achieve those objectives. They must consider the specific tactics and logistics that will be required to deliver optimally effective services in light of people's strengths, vulnerabilities and living situations. Making decisions of this sort is based on an understanding of the sort of violence people might commit – *what* they might do, rather than *why* they might do it. Put simply, planning is pointless until we have figured out what we are trying to prevent.

Scenario-based planning was developed for use under conditions of unbounded uncertainty, those in which 'unknown unknowns' abound (Chermack, 2004; for a gentle introduction, see Orndoff, 2002). It assumes that scenarios – brief accounts of possible futures that are deemed plausible in light of knowledge and experience – are essential to developing sensible and detailed plans to achieve desired outcomes and avoid undesired outcomes. It is common in scenario planning to develop a reasonably brief set of scenarios, as few as two or three and as many as five or six, that represent the range of plausible outcomes. They should include both 'best case' and 'worst-case' scenarios.

We have recommended that evaluators consider at least four scenarios of future violence:

- 'Repeat' scenarios are those in which people commit any of the kinds of violence they perpetrated in the past.

- 'Escalation' scenarios are those in which people's violence escalates in severity, up to lethal or life-threatening harm (so-called 'worst-case' scenarios).

- 'Twist' scenarios are those in which people's violence changes in nature – for example, their motivation, modus operandi or victim selection changes.

- Finally, 'desistence' scenarios are those in which people stop perpetrating violence ('best-case scenarios'). Desistence scenarios are in many respects the most important, as the ultimate goal of violence risk assessment is the prevention of violence; the other scenarios are reasonably foreseeable obstacles that must be avoided to achieve desistence.

Each scenario must be detailed so its plausibility can be evaluated. We must consider what kind of violence we are concerned people may commit – what will they do, to whom, and why? What might be the psychological or physical harm suffered by others? Where and when are they likely to perpetrate such violence? Is the risk acute in nature, limited to certain times or situations, or is it chronic? How certain or confident are you that this kind of violence might actually occur? Asking and trying to answer questions like these allows us to use narrative cognition to evaluate the plausibility of the scenario in light of what we know about violence and people in general, and more specifically about the people we are evaluating and their history of violence. We must remember that all scenarios, as stories of a future that has not yet and may never occur, are fictional. The goal is not to predict what *will* happen, but rather to consider systematically what *might* happen.

Conclusion

Accurate prediction of earthquakes, typhoons or viral epidemics is difficult or even impossible. Furthermore, in and of itself, accurate prediction is of little or no use in prevention or mitigation of harm stemming from such disasters. Yet it is still entirely possible to take effective steps to prevent or mitigate harm (e.g. development of building codes, evaluation plans, vaccination programmes) even in the absence of accurate prediction. The same holds true when dealing with the risk of violence posed by people. The SPJ approach to violence risk assessment increasingly focuses on the application of well-established planning methodologies to the development of individualised management plans, thus avoiding simplistic management plans based on risk level ('do nothing' versus 'do lots').

References and further reading

Chermack TJ (2004) Improving decision-making with scenario planning. *Futures* **36** (3) 295–309.

Gottfredson SD & Gottfredson DM (1988) Violence prediction methods: statistical and clinical strategies. *Violence and Victims* **3** 303–324.

Gottfredson SD & Moriarty LJ (2006) Statistical risk assessment: old problems and new applications. *Crime & Delinquency* **52** 178–200.

Harris GT, Rice ME & Quinsey VL (1993) Violent recidivism of mentally disordered offenders: The development of a statistical prediction instrument. *Criminal Justice and Behavior* **20** 315-335.

Hart SD (1998) The role of psychopathy in assessing risk for violence: Conceptual and methodological issues. *Legal and Criminological Psychology* **3** 121–137.

Hart SD (2011) Complexity, uncertainty, and the reconceptualization of violence risk assessment. In: R Abrunhosa (Ed) *Victims and Offenders: Chapters on psychology and law* (pp57–69). Brussels: Politeia. (Original work published in 2004.)

Hart SD & Cooke DJ (2013) Another look at the (im-)precision of individual risk estimates made using actuarial risk assessment instruments. *Behavioral Sciences and the Law* **31** 81–102.

Hart SD, Douglas KS & Guy LS (2016) The structured professional judgment approach to violence risk assessment: Origins, nature, and advances. In: L Craig & M Rettenberger (Volume Eds) and D Boer (Series Ed) *The Wiley Handbook on the Theories, Assessment, Treatment of Sexual Offending: Volume II. Assessment* (pp643–666). Oxford, UK: Wiley.

Hart SD & Logan C (2011) Formulation of violence risk using evidence-based assessments: the structured professional judgment approach. In: P Sturmey & M McMurran (Eds) *Forensic Case Formulation* (pp83–106). Chichester, UK: Wiley-Blackwell.

Kropp PR, Hart SD, Webster CD & Eaves D (1994) *Manual for the Spousal Assault Risk Assessment Guide*. Vancouver, Canada: British Columbia Institute on Family Violence.

Menzies R, Webster CD & Hart SD (1995) Observations on the rise of risk in psychology and law. In B Wolfe (Ed) *Proceedings of the Fifth Symposium on Violence and Aggression* (pp91–107). Saskatoon, Canada: University Extension Press, University of Saskatchewan.

Monahan J (1995) *The Clinical Prediction of Violent Behavior*. Northvale, NJ: Jason Aronson. (Original work published in 1981.)

Orndoff K (2002) Strategic tool for RIM professionals. *Information Management Journal* **36** (6) 65–71.

Webster CD, Harris GT, Rice MT, Cormier C & Quinsey VL (1994) *The Violence Prediction Scheme: Assessing dangerousness in high risk men*. Toronto, Canada: University of Toronto, Centre of Criminology.

Section 3
SJP: The essentials

Chapter 10:
On the absolute necessity of serial measurement

By Harry Kennedy

'If you don't measure it, you won't see it; if you can't measure it,
either you haven't tried hard enough, or it isn't real; if it isn't
moving, measure it once; if it's moving, measure it regularly'
(Webster C: personal communication, 2018)

Structured evaluation schemes are finding their way into undergraduate
and postgraduate training. This represents a real advance in how clinicians
acquire expertise, just as the introduction of structured professional judgment
lifted risk assessment out of the medieval world of scholastic authority and
traditional custom and practice, a crude skill without craft, evidence or
innovation. The methods of the early structured evaluation schemes have
been applied in ever widening areas – triage, waiting list management,
assessment of functional mental capacity, progress in treatment and recovery,
even proportionality of interventions for violence and aggression. Things
can be measured that are not usually thought of as quantities or sizes or
amounts. Clinicians can measure various met and unmet clinical needs in
ways that allow them to be aggregated and compared. It is even possible to
quantify quality of life and the atmosphere in a ward.

The study of the ecology of risk and violence, interventions and recovery has
awaited the very recent emergence of conceptual frameworks and related
tools to measure human action, interaction and milieu in therapeutic security.

But being able to use a handbook and having knowledge of the primary
reliability and validity studies is not enough to make use of any such
instrument, judgment support framework or scheme. 'Service' replication
studies of validation statistics are never as good as research studies by the
original authors (Fazel *et al*, 2012; Singh *et al*, 2013), though that is not
an indictment. Validation is also required for the setting (country, clinical
group) where the scheme will be used and for the outcome (Fazel *et al*,
2012; Singh *et al*, 2013). Most importantly, a measure is only useful if it is
relevant to the care and treatment of the patient, and relevant to the model
of care in which the patient is engaged (ACI, 2013).

Having introduced a new measure or scheme as part of the over-arching model of care, how can a clinical manager influence clinicians to improve the reliability, consistency and effectiveness of decisions about each patient, without trivialising the nature of expertise and clinical judgment? (O'Neil, 2002; Collins & Evans, 2007).

Thinking of structured professional judgment instruments as 'schemes' is a key to using them well. The model of care (ACI, 2013) or process within which the new instrument is used should have consistent elements, while consistent use is an ethical obligation (Daniels & Sabin, 2002).

Training and use should be multi-disciplinary (Thornicroft & Tansella, 1999) – though the evidence for measureable benefits from this is thin. See, for example, the gap between research and service statistics for reliability and validity (Singh *et al*, 2013). The reason everyone should be trained and involved is to ensure a shared understanding of the language and purpose of the new skill or measure. This should include patients and decision makers, managers and members of tribunals and review boards (Webster & Hucker, 2003; Crocker *et al*, 2014).

There should be a system for quality control – fidelity to the handbook, regularly monitored inter-rater reliability – and a system for consistent decision making – governance structures. Perhaps in the near future, some key outcome measures, as distinct from judgment support frameworks, will be administered by psychometricians who are part of a laboratory system of high-quality, high-reliability data management – also an inherent part of the over-arching model of care.

The patient should be involved in the process. This is thought to enhance engagement and ultimately respects the patient's role in their own recovery. But there is evidence that in some settings co-production can impair predictive accuracy and reliability (Troquete *et al*, 2013).

Reliable opinions are only as good as the measurements, observations and facts they are based on. Serial measurement of change is the most valuable clinical intervention there is. It is a powerful aid to achieving insight and a persuasive piece of 'proof by demonstration' – a form of scientific method more commonly seen in the humanities and fine arts (Hockney, 2001).

The periodic reports to independent tribunals, review boards and leave committees should not be accepted as complete until serial measurements have been tabulated; no opinion on these matters should be accepted unless grounded in serial measurements of relevant change.

Summary

■ When new evaluation schemes are introduced into service, it is vital that they be tested in situ. It must not be assumed that the purported reliability and validity, as espoused by the authors, will necessarily 'carry over' to the local service.

■ Aside from ensuring validity and other scientific dictates, a process has to unfold. Colleagues in the different disciplines, with their particular argots, have to learn together how to use the new scheme to best advantage and with acceptable degrees of consistency.

■ How teams function as they take on the challenge of faithful implementation of a new device or health technology is little understood at present.

■ Reliable opinions are only as good as the measurements, observations and 'facts' that they are based on. Serial measurement of change is the most valuable clinical intervention there is.

■ The periodic reports to independent tribunals, review boards, parole authorities and the like, should not be accepted as complete until serial measurements have been tabulated.

■ No opinion should be accepted until grounded in serial measurement of relevant change

References

Fazel S, Singh JP, Doll H, Grann M (2012) Use of risk assessment instruments to predict violence and antisocial behaviour in 73 samples involving 24 827 people: systematic review and meta-analysis. *BMJ* **345** doi: https://doi.org/10.1136/bmj.e4692.

Hockney D (2001) *Secret Knowledge: Rediscovering the lost techniques of the old masters*. London: Thames and Hudson.

Singh JP, Desmarais SL & Van Dorn RA (2013) Measurement of predictive validity in violence risk assessment studies: a second-order systematic review. *Behavioural Science and the Law* **31** 55–73.

Agency for Clinical Innovation (2013) *Understanding the process to develop a Model of Care An ACI Framework. Version 1.0, May 2013*. ACI: New South Wales Australia.

O'Neill O (2002) *A Question of Trust: The BBC Reith lectures*. Cambridge: Cambridge University Press.

Collins H & Evans R (2007) *Rethinking Expertise*. London: University of Chicago Press.

Daniels N & Sabin JE (2002) *Setting Limits Fairly: Can we learn to share medical resources?* Oxford: Oxford University Press.

Thornicroft F & Tansella M (1999) *The Mental Health Matrix: A manual to improve services*. Cambridge: Cambridge University Press.

Webster CD & Hucker SJ (2003) *Release Decision Making*. Hamilton: St Joseph's Healthcare.

Crocker AG, Nicholls TL, Charette Y, Seto MC (2014) Dynamic and static factors associated with discharge dispositions: the national trajectory project of individuals found not criminally responsible on account of mental disorder (NCRMD) in Canada. *Behavioural Science and the Law* **32** 577–595

Troqete NA, Van den Brink RH, Beintema H, Mulder T, Van Os TW, Shoevers RA & Wiersma D (2013). Risk assessment and shared care planning in out-patient forensic psychiatry: cluster randomised controlled trial. *British Journal of Psychiatry* **202** 365–71.

Chapter 11: Structured Professional Judgment – an introduction to the HCR-20 V3 and related schemes

By Quazi Haque and Chris Webster

The idea of SPJ is very straight-forward. It centres on isolating and applying variables which *might* be applied sensibly to a person who *could* be at risk for carrying out some kind of violence or antisociality in the future. The variables are of two kinds: those that could, conceivably, *increase* the risk of some form of violence and those that could *decrease* the likelihood of occurrence of such violent acts. In the present context it needs to be made clear that SPJ guides are for use by properly trained professional mental health and correctional professionals.

The important characteristic of SPJ devices is that they offer carefully considered definitions of the various items contained within the particular schemes. The descriptions of items tend to be amalgamated from the experiences of practicing clinicians as well as from the published results of scientific studies. Over the past two decades or more, these definitions have often been sharpened by the process of back-and-forth language translations of many of the various schemes. The approach is well described by Heilbrun *et al* (2010).

How information from SPJ devices can be used in an actuarial way for important research and calibration purposes

SPJ devices can be used in an actuarial manner by converting, say, in HCR-20 V3 terms, Low, Moderate, or High overall ratings to numerical form (i.e. 0, 1, 2) and matching these numbers to information obtained at subsequent follow-up, similarly converted to numerical form. This is *not*, however, the main purpose for which SPJ schemes are designed. That main purpose is to help guide clinical assessors to reach conclusions, in individual cases, that will help connect patients to conditions which are as least restricting as possible given the parallel importance that criminal, mental health and related laws attach to public safety.

It is necessary to point out that, as well as providing a protocol for evaluating risks and risk management practices in individual persons, those who develop SPJ schemes *must* be able to produce data to show that the schemes possesses *reliability* and *validity*. By reliability we mean that one rater using the scheme will obtain the same or highly similar ratings as another colleague (without consultation between them). By validity we mean that the scheme must be shown to measure what it purports to measure (e.g. future violence). Lacking these two essential characteristics, any SPJ device will gain little recognition in scientific circles. So, in a way, any SPJ schemes must be tested in an actuarial way. But, to repeat, this is not their primary purpose. An SPJ scheme, properly developed and tested, must be demonstrated to possess validity. Yet unrealistically high prediction-outcome correlations cannot be expected (see Chapter 7).

How specific items in SPJ schemes are derived

As already noted, the descriptions of individual items tend to be amalgamated from the experience of practising clinicians as well as from the gradual accumulation of scientific information. Because of the ever-changing nature of both scientific and ordinary day-to-day word meanings, items in the various schemes must be revised and re-tested from time to time (with items being added, dropped or re-cast). As well, naturally, the guides have to take account of results from scientific studies as they accumulate.

How SPJ guides are created

Usually, the task of creating SPJ guides has been accomplished by small groups of colleagues working together. Typically these working groups contain a mixture of clinicians and researchers. It has been helpful to borrow from the Hare PCL-R the idea of using a limited number of items, around 20, in the design of the various schemes. It is sometimes tempting to use considerably more. Yet there has to be a realistic limit. Professionals tend to be hard pressed in terms of the amount of time they have available. Similarly, it might be thought that a three-point scale (i.e. 0, 1, or 2, or L, M or H) might be restricting; yet, again, allowing very fine-grain scaling may bog the assessment process down without accomplishing much.

Once a scheme has been developed in draft form it tends to be circulated among a broader group of colleagues for opinion and perhaps preliminary testing. Originators of SPJ schemes make no claim that their guides will offer unfailingly accurate projections of future violence. They do argue, however, that the schemes will help *stimulate discussion among colleagues*, and, it is to be hoped, with patients themselves. It is expected that these often challenging conversations will lead to enhanced treatability without sacrificing safety in the hospital, or in the community.

The general characteristics of SPJ schemes

In Table 11.1 we depict, in the form of a mnemonic device, the main qualities of most SPJ schemes. We then comment on each of these characteristics in turn.

Table 11.1: SPJ Principles
Scientific integrity
Precision in definition
Judgment enhancing capability
Past/present/future time frame
Relevant risk factors
Individualised intervention planning
Narrative clinical underpinnings
Clinical utility
Interprofessional collaboration
Patient involving
Literature based
Evaluation in situ
Safety planning for victims

1. Scientific integrity

Of all the various SPJ risk assessment schemes in existence the HCR-20 V3 is the most general in its application. Since it now has a long history and has gone through three iterations, it is reasonable to expect that it would have a good-sized body of scientific evidence in its support (see HCR-20 V3 manual Chapter 2, pp17–34). Doubtless, it would have disappeared from view had it not been shown unequivocally to possess reliability and validity. This much said, at the level of the particular mental health unit or service, it is important to stress that, ideally, all members of a team will be involved in research in some fashion. Not all research has to involve a thousand patients randomly assigned to conditions according to a multi-factorial statistical design. Not all investigations have to be conducted by personnel solely dedicated to the development and conduct of scientific studies.

Important research work can, and often should, be done collaboratively with the individual client. Single-subject, repeated-measures designs can yield information with high practical value.

2. Precision in the definition of items and risk factors

A large part of the work in creating SPJ devices involves arduous but good-natured wrangling among clinicians, researchers and administrators. These conversations must be informed by both clinical experience and information culled from research studies. They must also take into account the content of psychiatric classificatory systems (e.g. DSM-5; ICD-10, as they themselves are altered and re-focused). Since different types of violence come into existence with the passage of time and with shifts in social, political and economic circumstances, revisions to the content of items *must* be made periodically.

3. Judgment enhancing capability

At the outset of this book it was pointed out clearly that various legally constituted bodies have to make practical decisions in respect to persons deemed to have committed offences while mentally disordered (see Chapter 2, by Richard Schneider). Although the actual decisions rest with the courts and tribunals, mental health professionals are required to offer opinion in these matters. So any SPJ, or other such decision-enhancing guide, must be able to help practitioners as they advise these bodies as to the options that lie before them. And the guides must help clinicians as they offer opinions about the likely outcomes of the alternative conditions. It is necessary that mental health professionals, as they write reports and testify, be able to state the frameworks within which their opinions were formed.

4. Past/present/future time-frame

Sometimes people commit serious violent offences 'out of the blue'. After an unblemished life, she or he exhibits extreme violence. Yet even in these atypical circumstances (as, for example, of a murder carried out while the perpetrator was sleep-walking), there will have to be a thorough exploration of the individual's history. This analysis may well – possibly with the help of persons who can collaborate in providing historical information – turn up chains of events which will show that the attack was not as 'one off' as might have been thought. This kind of historical digging, often completed by social work professionals, is essential when it comes time to formulate plans for the future (see Chapter 22 by Joanne Eaves-Thalken). This aspect of the HCR-20 V3 organisational framework fits with ordinary, time-honoured clinical practices. As Douglas *et al* (2013) put it: 'In the case of violence risk assessment, it is necessary to assess people's past and present functioning, as well as their goals and plans for the future...' (p4).

5. Relevant risk factors

As noted by Hart and Douglas (Chapter 9) the HCR-20 framework has, from the beginning, recognised that not all items are going to be equally relevant to each and every person under assessment. As well, the originators presumed that the driving factors at one time may not be the same as those at work at a different time. That is why, at the end of the assessment, one of the main judgments made by evaluators is left to the assessing clinicians (i.e. as to overall risk being Low, Moderate, or High – see bottom of Table 11.2 on p106). In V3, assessors are invited to discern and record which items are relevant and which are not. This simplifies and clarifies the task considerably (i.e. it increases focus on the factors that are at play in the particular case under assessment). As well, it increases the chances that evaluators will be able to figure out how key factors *have interacted* or *will interact* with one another.

6. Individualised intervention planning

The HCR-20 V3 framework is intended to help clinicians, and patients themselves, monitor progress over time and over changed conditions. It takes some trouble to ascertain dependable 'baseline' scoring of the items within the scheme. The 'capture' of such information is generally valuable for the purpose of conducting assessments in the clinical, legal and correctional arenas. But that information can also, importantly, be put to further use to index change over time. When carefully and consistently achieved, repeated measurement can point up the extent to which change is or is not occurring. This idea of continuous monitoring using an already existing SPJ framework is well described by Viljoen *et al* (2014, p105). Psychologists have long been acquainted with ABA experimental designs for use with individual persons. A stands for baseline, B stands for intervention. By comparing B scores with A scores, it becomes possible to 'see' and document change. The actual effectiveness of the intervention can often be verified by returning to baseline and continuing measurement (though obviously this may be unnecessary or even ill-advised). It should be noted that what constitutes treatment or intervention will be determined by the particular issues of concern. Effectiveness of medications can be gauged in this way (though seldom are, in actual practice). Smoking cessation programmes can be developed along these lines. Violent incidents, however defined, can be the target. The important point is that the SPJ scheme can frequently provide the basic framework and definitions to make such individualised research possible.

7. Narrative clinical underpinnings

Once relevant items have been isolated via a V3 analysis, they must, to be useful, become integrated into a 'formulation'. This requires '...evaluations to integrate separate risk factors into a conceptually meaningful framework that explains a person's violence' (Douglas *et al*, 2013, p53). These authors go on: 'Ideally, we need to *tell a story* about an individual that integrates the main pieces of information available to us'. (p54, emphasis added). Their idea is that: 'It is necessary to derive *an individual theory of risk*, to help us make sense of risk, and therefore how best to intervene and manage such risk' (p54, emphasis added). The notions of 'reframing', 'promoting alternative thinking strategies', 'story editing' and related concepts are well expounded by Wilson (2011).

8. Clinical utility

The HCR-20 V3 devotes a section (Chapter 2, pp18–19) to 'Clinical and Practical Utility'. The authors note '...it was also of utmost importance for us to produce a revision that agencies and systems could integrate into their practices and would meet their risk-relevant obligations and duties...' (p18). The originators also '...sought to ensure there was a reasonable level of flexibility and adaptability of HCR-20 V3' (p19). This notion of flexibility, as a necessary feature of a contemporary SPJ device, was echoed in the START: AV. Viljoen *et al* (2014) say the scheme '...offers some flexibility and draws from professionals' expertise'. They note that the scheme, like V3, invites assessors '...to add Case-Specific Items and Case-Specific Adverse Outcomes that are unique to an individual and to make structured professional judgments of Low, Moderate or High risk (rather than rely on numerical algorithms)' (p2).

9. Interprofessional collaboration

The V3 Guide makes to clear that professionals need knowledge of violence, expertise in individual risk assessment, and complete familiarity with the various forms of mental disorder (Chapter 3, p38). The authors also endorse the idea that there can be an advantage in using *teams* of professionals. They note that psychiatrists or psychiatric nurses can be very helpful in improving understanding of mental illness, that psychologists can often add information about personality disorder, and that social workers or probation officers can illuminate future plans (Chapter 3, p38). Authors of the START: AV call upon the involvement of teachers and others. They note, too, that the '...families ideally should be included as active collaborators alongside the professional team' (Chapter 3, p11).

10. Patient involving

When the HCR-20 V1 was first developed (in 1995), the originators had not fully seen the advantage of drawing some clients as completely as possible into the assessment and treatment processes. Yet there can be a marked advantage in having clinicians and clients 'on the same page' of using a common language. It can help ensure that nothing highly individual or particular is missed (i.e. through, if need to be, adding a 'Case-Specific/Other Consideration Item'). It can, as has already been noted, help clients monitor their own progress. This kind of attention can be especially important during times of transition from one care team to another. It helps to have a framework within which crucial information can be transferred.

11. Literature based

In our view it is necessary for users of SPJ devices to keep abreast of the scientific and professional literatures. These are consolidated from time to time and appear on websites. One of the most comprehensive reviews of SPJ literature ever completed was undertaken by Viljoen et al (2015). It is extremely important that the literatures be re-examined periodically. It is ethically necessary to ensure that, so far as is humanly possible, decisions are based on the strongest available evidence. And ideally this literature should not be confined to item-by-item descriptions but, as well, these portrayals should indicate how particular mental and personality characteristics interact with one another.

12. Evaluation-in-situ

It is not ideal simply to adopt a particular SPJ scheme and follow it slavishly without test for months or years. It may well be that, overall, the HCR-20 V3 or other such device yields some statistical correspondence between prediction and outcome. Heartening though this may be, it remains the case that, properly, the device should be tested – for reliability and validity – in the particular situation in which it is being employed. Validity needs to be checked (during inpatient stays, during time spent in the community). Although very likely the positive results from previously published reports will find some applicability, it remains the case that onsite descriptive and follow-up studies need to be launched (e.g. see Chapter 27 by Anne Crocker and Chapter 12 by Webster & Chatterjee).

13. Safety planning for victims

It is important that the victim and other persons involved be urged and encouraged to react quickly and definitely to conditions which are changing rapidly. As the V3 authors say, 'The ability of these people to respond effectively depends, critically, on the extent to which they have accurate and complete information concerning the risks posed to victims. This means that good victim liaison is the cornerstone of victim safety planning' (p61). Persons often need advice about how to handle phone calls and how to look after themselves more generally. Viljoen et al (2015) urge that it is crucial to warn the school, the police or other persons or agencies. If the person has plans to injure or kill an identifiable victim or victims it is vital to notify the individuals and the authorities concerned. Suicidal patients need close monitoring (p91).

The content of HCR-20 V3 (2013)

Douglas *et al* (2013) state that SPJ is a *guided* clinical approach to decision-making. They say '...decision-making is assisted by guidelines that have been developed to reflect the "state of the discipline" with respect to scientific knowledge and professional practice' (p8). The authors note that such guidelines are common in medical practice (but are less widely used in psychiatric, psychological or correctional assessments). As noted above (Point 2), SPJ approaches hinge critically on defining terms. 'Violence', for example, is said to be '...actual, attempted or threatened infliction of bodily harm on another person' (2013, p2). Each individual item in the V3 and related guides must be defined. It is not thought that these definitions should extend into the indefinite future; rather, they are expected to serve for a time – perhaps a few years. Readers can gain a general impression of the content of V3 by examining Table 11.2. Here are listed the 'set' items of the scheme. Colleagues *must* consult the manual to obtain definitions of the items and sub-items (Chapter 4, pp67–102)

Table 11.2: HCR-20 V3 risk factors	
Historical Scale (Framed as 'Problems with...')	
H1	Violence
H2	Other Antisocial Behavior
H3	Relationships
H4	Employment
H5	Substance Use
H6	Major Mental Disorder
H7	Personality Disorder
H8	Traumatic Experiences
H9	Violent Attitudes
H10	Treatment or Supervision Response
OC-H	Other Considerations
Clinical Scale (Framed as 'Recent problems with...')	
C1	Insight
C2	Violent Ideation or Intent
C3	Symptoms of Major Mental Disorder

C4	Instability
C5	Treatment or Supervision Response
OC-C	Other Considerations
Risk Management Scale (Framed as 'Future problems with…')	
R1	Professional Services and Plans
R2	Living Situation
R3	Personal Support
R4	Treatment or Supervision Response
R5	Stress or Coping
OC-R	Other Considerations
Low ☐ Moderate ☐ High ☐	

The creative expansion of SPJ thinking

In Figure 11.1 (p108) we present a schematic based on a transportation network with milestones, destinations, zones, points and crossings. Such transportation systems are always evolving to deal safely with the multitudes of people with different plans for the day ahead. Our diagram helps show the current state of SPJ development in the field of violence risk assessment and management. This proliferation has all occurred over the past two and a half decades. As noted in Chapter 9, and above in this chapter, the earliest guide to be developed was the SARA. It is for this reason that we depict offending against intimates as Zone 1 (lower left). Zone 2 is given over to the basic HCR-20 V3. It is like a ring road, or the circle line within the London 'tube' system. Within Zone 2 we indicate how it is that the focus of the basic V3 can sometimes be altered to advantage. The use of 'Alignments', or supplements, can allow assessors to apply greater degrees of precision than might otherwise have been the case. In any transportation system there has to be central control to affect necessary minute-to-minute adaptations.

An alternative analogy would be to think of 'Alignments' as 'corrective eye lenses', which may improve focus. From time to time, colleagues in the SPJ risk assessment field have suggested ways in which the basic HCR-20 scheme can be modified or supplemented. A good example concerns the Hare PCL-R. In V2, item H7 was Hare PCL-R; in V3 this item was dropped. In its stead, item H7 is now termed 'History of Problems with Personality Disorder' (see Table 11.2). The V3 authors do however recommend that the Hare PCL-R still be administered in cases where it is important to assess and diagnose psychopathic personality disorder (pp79–80). It, or a similar measure, would be expected to add 'depth' in this domain. Below the Hare

PCL-R we list the HCR-CG, short for HCR-20 Companion Guide (Douglas *et al*, 2001). This edited volume encourages users, where appropriate, to shift the basic V2 toward an intervention-oriented approach.

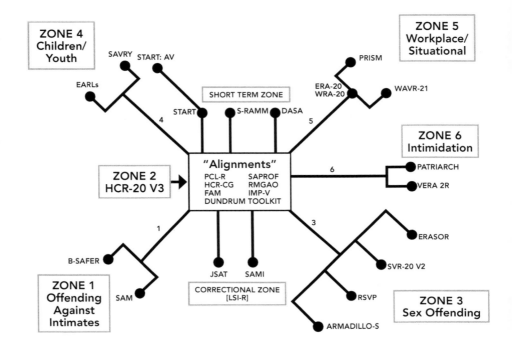

Figure 11.1: A transportation schematic illustrating directions pursued by colleagues involved in the creation of SPJ schemes,1995–present

The Female Additional Manual (FAM) (de Vogel *et al*, 2011) offers assessors suggestions as to how the HCR-20 can be adjusted as needed to take full account of gender. SAPROF offers guidelines for assessing protective factors for violence (de Vogel *et al*, 2012). In Chapter 18, Boer makes the point that is not appropriate to 'force' the use of schemes like the HCR-20 V3 on markedly distinct cultural groups. His *Risk Management Guide for Aboriginal Offenders* (RMGAO) (Boer *et al*, 2003) has gained no practical traction, so far as we are aware. Yet we have no hesitation in drawing this work to the attention of our present readers. The general approach is sound, and it may yet provide a platform that will enable other clinicians and researchers to spare effort as they strive to develop evaluation schemes for members of different cultures. Another way of adding depth to a particular V3 item can be found in the area of 'Impulsivity' as Item C4 was called in V2. This item is now termed 'Stability' in V3 – but still encompasses the

'Impulsivity' construct. The IMP-V is authored by Weizmann-Henelius *et al* (2019). The DUNDRUM Toolkit (Kennedy *et al*, 2010) suggests ways the HCR-20 V3 or other such SPJ devices should be embedded within an administrative or clinical framework (i.e. to assist with admission, transfer and discharge decisions).

As already noted, in Figure 11.1, Zone 2 is depicted as a kind of hub. It is reasonable to think of the HCR-20 V3 as being both at the core and as being the 'jumping off point' for other lines. This is so because experienced SPJ assessors will know that it is very common to find that, at the conclusion of an HCR-20 V3 analysis, some more specific exploration is called for (e.g. into spousal assault, or the seeming presence of intimidating or highly threatening behaviour).

Turning again to Figure 11.1, we have already mentioned that Zone 1 is devoted to 'Offending Against Intimates'. The third version of the Spousal Assault Risk Assessment Guide (Version 3) has recently been published (SARA-V3) (Kropp & Hart, 2015). Related to this is the version developed specifically for use by police officers, the B-SAFER (Kropp *et al*, 2005) and, as well, the Stalking Assessment Manual (SAM) (Kropp *et al*, 2008)

The 'Sex Offending Zone' is represented at the lower-right of Figure 11.1. The most recent version of the Sexual Violence Risk-20 has just been issued (SVR-20) (Boer *et al*, 2017). An SPJ guide for the Estimate of Risk of Adolescent Sexual Offense Recidivism has been in existence for several years (ERASOR) (Worling & Curwen, 2001). The Risk for Sexual Violence Protocol (RSVP) (Hart *et al*, 2009) is notable for the attention it devotes to formulation of sexual offending risks. Many of these ideas were later incorporated into the more broadly focused HCR-20 V3.

Schemes related to children and youth are depicted in the upper left quadrant of Figure 11.1. The Early Assessment Risk Lists for Boys (EARL-20B) (Augimeri *et al*, 2001) and Girls (EARL-21G) (Levene *et al*, 2001) were designed for children aged six to 11. These devices are discussed in more detail by Leena Augimeri in Chapter 25 of this book. A device for assessing risks in adolescents is called the Structured Assessment of Violence Risk in Youth (SAVRY) (Borum *et al*, 2006). A departure in this scheme was the inclusion of a half-dozen 'protective factors'. The notion of balancing risk or vulnerability factors with 'strengths' was brought even more strongly into play with the development of the Short-Term Assessment of Risk and Treatability (START) (Webster *et al*, 2009). In that systematisation, equal attention is devoted to strengths and vulnerabilities. This characteristic is explained in detail by Mary-Lou Martin in Chapter 13 of this volume. She notes that, out of the basic START, Jodi Viljoen *et al* expounded a scheme designed specifically for adolescents, the Short-Term Assessment of Risk and Treatability: Adolescent Version (START: AV) (Viljoen *et al*, 2015).

In the upper right quadrant of Figure 11.1 is depicted a zone having to do with workplace and situational risks. The Employee Risk Asessment-20 provides a guide for assessing individual perpetrators of violence in the workplace (ERA) (Bloom *et al*, 2002). In the Workplace Risk Assessment-20 the attention shifts away from the employee himself or herself onto the circumstances related to the work environment (WRA-20) (Bloom *et al*, 2000). As with the RMGAO, already mentioned, we are not aware that either the ERA-20 or the WRA-20 have found any practical application. But, as previously suggested, it can be a mistake to think that 'lack of uptake' should be the sole criterion of usefulness. It turns out that the WRA-20 had influence in the development of a highly practical SPJ scheme to assess risks in institutions like prisons and hospitals. We refer here specifically to the Promoting Risk Intervention by Situational Management (PRISM) (Johnstone & Cooke, 2008). The idea in this formulation is to take account of the fact that risks of violence not only inhere within the individual, but that they can be and are brought into play by features of the physical plant and the staffing and management policies in effect within the organisation. The WRA-20 likely also had some influence in the development of the Workplace Assessment of Violence Risk-21 (WAVR-21) (Meloy & White, 2016). Importantly, the WAVR-21 includes risks to be found on university campuses.

Zone 6 in Figure 11.1 is reserved for group-based violence, intimidation, and terrorism (see Chapter 19 by Steve Hart). The Violent Extremist Risk Assessment (VERA-2R) (Pressman *et al*, 2016) is an important contribution in this line. Also included in this branch is the Assessment of Risk for Honour Based Violence (PATRIARCH) (Kropp *et al*, 2013).

The Correctional Zone, centre bottom of Figure 11.1, lists the Jail Screening Assessment Tool (JSAT) (Nicholls *et al*, 2005). This SPJ guide is intended to assist mental health and correctional professionals as they evaluate inmates for mental and personality disorders, for suicide risk, and for becoming victims of violence. The Suicide Assessment Manual for Inmates (SAMI) (Zapf, 2006) is specifically designed to help isolate risks of suicide in custodial settings. Readers of V3 will note that the authors of that basic scheme credit strongly the influence of Andrews *et al* (2010). These colleagues, coming at risk assessment from a strictly correctional point of view, draw attention to the fact that the level of Supervision Inventory of 1982 influenced the subsequent development of the HCR-20 (see V3 footnote 3, p11). But the V3 authors also note that the LSI-R is directed to *general* criminality, not to violence as such. The literature surrounding the LSI-R is reviewed in detail by Andrews (2012).

In between Zones 4 and 5 in Figure 11.1 are two branches. One is for the Suicide Risk Assessment and Management Manual (S-RAMM) (Bouch & Marshall, 2005). It is patterned on the HCR-20 format (i.e. items scored 0, 1, or 2). The other, the Dynamic Appraisal of Situational Aggression: Inpatient Version (Ogloff & Daffern, 2006), borrows from the C Scale of V3 (and the Brøset Violence Checklist (BVC) (Almvik & Woods, 2003). The DASA is based on a mere seven items and is used for the prediction of violence over the very short term (e.g. 24 hours).

Developing SPJ schemes

Above, we mentioned that it is possible for small groups of clinicians, researchers and policy makers, using the HCR-20 general framework (or something like it), to evolve new schemes to fit particular requirements (e.g. as did Douglas Boer and colleagues, Chapter 18[18]). But readers should not be beguiled into thinking this is a simple undertaking. More is required than 'skimming' the main components from already-existing devices and companion guides. A review of Chapter 2 in V3 (pp17–34) shows what the authors went through as they re-formulated the scheme. They had to re-think the purpose of the decision-enhancing guide and revisit its ethical and legal acceptability. Crucially, they had to do new research to ensure its scientific soundness. This research, because the device had come into play in several countries around the world, had to be conducted on an international basis. Colleagues in different locations had to be willing to 'try out' draft versions with new rating schemes. There had to be periodic meetings among the principal researchers. Differences had to be hashed out. Colleagues then had to undertake further trial applications in their various settings. In the end, with all the information in and agreed, the entire manual had to be rewritten. Chapter 2 of the V3 manual ends with a plea for colleagues to publish individual case studies based on HCR-20 assessments (and follow-ups). Since that time such articles have begun to appear (e.g. Guy *et al*, 2012; Hickman *et al*, 2018; Logan, 2014; Storey *et al*, 2017). There is no reason, of course, that consenting patients, or former patients, cannot be invited to assist in this vital task (i.e. Starr, 2002).

---

18 A good example might be with respect to the elderly (see Almik *et al*, 2006). An SPJ device is in fact being forwarded for application in this area. Jennifer Storey is currently leading the development of an SPJ device called the 'Elder Abuse Risk Level Index' (EARLI). Two contributors to this volume are co-authors (Stephen Hart and Randy Kropp). It is similar to the SARA and the SAM and was developed in the same fashion. It contains 29 items in four domains – Nature of abuse, Perpetrator risk factors, Victim vulnerability factors, and Community and institutional responsivity factors.

References and further reading

Almvik R, Rasmussen K & Woods P (2006) Challenging behaviour in the elderly – monitoring violent incidents. *International Journal of Geriatric Psychiatry* **21** 368–374.

AlmvikR & Woods P (2003) The Brøset Violence Checklist. *Journal of Psychiatric and Mental Health Nursing* **10** 231–238.

Andrews DA (2012) The risk-need responsivity (RNR) model of correctional assessment and treatment. In: JA Dvoskin, JL Skeem, RW Novaco & KS Douglas (Eds) Using Social Science to Reduce Violent Offending (pp127–156). New York: Oxford University Press.

Andrews DA, Bonta J & Wormith SJ (2010) The Level of Service (LS) assessment of adults of older adolescents. In: RK Otto & KS Douglass (Eds) *Handbook of Violence Risk Assessment* (pp199–225). New York: Routledge.

Augimeri LK, Koegl CJ, Webster CD & Levene K (2001) *Early assessment risk list for boys: EARL-20B, Version 2*. Toronto, Canada: Earlscourt Child and Family Centre (Child Development Institute).

Bloom H, Eisen RS Pollock N & Webster CD (2000) *WRA-20, Workplace Risk Assessment: A Guide for Evlauating Violence Potential, Version 1*. Toronto, Canada: Workplace.calm, Inc.

Bloom H, Webster CD & Eisen RS (2002) ERA-20, *Employee Risk Assessment: A guide for evaluating potential workplace violence perpetrators*. Toronto, Canada: Workplace.calm, Inc.

Boer D, Couture J, Geddes C & Ritchie A (2003) *Yokwtol. Risk Management Guide for Aboriginal Offenders: Structured Guidelines for the Assessment of Risk Manageability for Aboriginal Violent Offenders (Research Version)*. Harrison, Canada: Aboriginal Initiatives Branch, Pacific Region, Correctional Service of Canada.

Boer DP, Hart SD, Kropp PR & Webster CD (2017) *Manual for Version 2 of the Sexual Violence Risk-20*. Vancouver, Canada: Protect International Risk and Safety Services.

Borum R, Bartel P & Forth A (2006) *Manual for the Structured Assessment of Violence Risk in Youth (SAVRY)*. Odessa, US: Psychological Assessment Resources.

Bouch J & Marshall JJ (2003) *S-RAMM: Suicide Risk Assessment and Management Manual (Research Edition)*. Glamorgan, Wales: The Cognitive Centre Foundation.

de Vogel V, de Ruiter C, Bouman Y & de Vries Robbé M (2012) *SAPROF: Guidelines for the Assessment of Protective Factors for Violence Risk, 2nd ed*. Utecht, The Netherlands: De Forensiche Zorgspecialisten.

de Vogel V, de Vries Robbé M, van Kalmthout W & Place C (2011) *Female Additional Manual (FAM). Additional guidelines to the HCR-20 for assessing risk for violence in women*. Utrecht, The Netherlands: Van der Hoeven Stichting.

Department of Health (2007) *Best Practices in Managing Risk: Principles and evidence for best practice in the assessment and management of risk to self and others in mental health services.* London, UK: Department of Health.

Douglas KS, Hart SD, Webster CD & Belfrage H (2013) *HCR-20 V3 Assessing Risk for Violence – User Guide*. Burnaby, Canada: Mental Health, Law and Policy Institute, Simon Fraser University.

Douglas KS, Webster CD, Hart SD, Eaves D & Ogloff JRP (Eds) (2001) *HCR-20 Violence Risk Management Companion Guide*. Burnaby, Canada: Mental Health, Law and Policy Institute, Simon Fraser University and Tampa, Florida: Louis de le Parte Florida Mental Health Institute, University of South Florida.

Guy LS, Packer IK & Warnken W (2012) Assessing risk of violence using structured professional judgment guidelines. *Journal of Forensic Psychology Practice* **12** 270–283.

Hare RD (2003) *The Psychopathy Checklist-Revised, 2nd edition*. Toronto, Canada: Multi-Health Systems.

Hart SD, Kropp PR, Laws DR, Klaver J, Logan C & Watt KA (2003) *The Risk for Sexual Violence Protocol (RSVP): Structured professional guidelines for assessing risk of sexual violence*. Burnaby, Canada: Mental Health, Law, and Policy Institute, Simon Fraser University.

Heilbrun K Yashuhara K & Shah S (2010) Violence risk assessment tools. In: RK Otto & KS Douglas (Eds) in *Handbook of Violence Risk Assessment*. Routledge/Taylor & Francis, Oxford.

Hickman G, Thrift S & Taylor C (2018) Case study illustrations of a psychological treatment pathway in a secure intellectual disability service. *Journal of Intellectual Disabilities and Offending Behaviour* **9** 102–114.

Johnstone L & Cooke DJ (2008) *PRISM: Promoting Risk Intervention by Situational Management: Structured professional guidelines for assessing situational risk factors for violence in institutions, 1st edition*. Burnaby, Canada: Mental Health, Law, and Policy Institute, Simon Fraser University.

Kennedy HG, O'Neill C, Flynn G & Gill P (2010) *The Dundrum Toolkit: Dangerousness, Understanding, Recovery, & Urgency Manual (The Dundrum Quartet)*. Dublin, Ireland: Dundrum Hospital.

Kropp PR & Hart SD (2015) *SARA-V3: User Guide for the Third Edition of the Spousal Assault Risk Assessment Guide*. Vancouver, Canada: ProActive ReSolutions.

Kropp PR, Belfrage H & Hart SD (2013) *Assessment of Risk for Honour Based Violence: User Manual (PATRIARCH)*. Vancouver, Canada: ProActive ReSolutions.

Kropp PR, Hart SD & Belfrage H (2005) *The Brief Spousal Assault Form for the Evaluation of Risk (B-SAFER): User Manual*. Vancouver, Canada: ProActive ReSolutions.

Kropp PR, Hart SD & Lyon D (2008) *Guidelines for Stalking Assessment and Management (SAM)*. Vancouver, Canada: ProActive ReSolutions.

Levene KS, Augimeri LK, Pepler DJ, Walsh MM, Koegl CJ & Webster CD (2001) *Early assessment risk list for girls: EARL-21G, Version 1, Consultation Edition*. Toronto, Canada: Earlscourt Child and Family Centre (Child Development Institute).

Logan C (2014) The HCR-20 Version 3: A case study in risk formulation. *International Journal of Forensic Mental Health* **13** 172–180.

Meloy R & White S (2016) *Workplace Assessment of Violence Risk-21, 3rd edition*. San Diego, US: Specialised Training.

Nicholls TL, Roesch R, Olley MC, Ogloff JRP & J Hemphill (2005) *Jail Screening Assessement Tool (JSAT): Guidelines for Mental Health Screening in Jails*. Burnaby, Canada: Mental Health, Law, and Policy Institute, Simon Fraser University.

Ogloff J & Dafern M (2006) *Dynamic Appraisal of Situational Aggression: Inpatient Version (DASA: IV)*. Australia: Forensicare/Monarch University, VIC.

Pressman DE, Rinne T, Duits N & Flocton J (2016) *Violent Extremism Risk Assessment, Version 2 (VERA-2R)*. The Netherlands: Institute of Forensic Psychiatry and Psychology.

Starr R (2002) A successful reintegration into the community: one NGRI acquittee's story. *Federal Probation* **66** 59–63.

Storey JE, Hart SD & Lim YL (2017) Serial stalking of mental professionals: case presentations, analysis, and formulation using the Guidelines for Stalking Assessment and Management (SAM). *Journal of Threat Assessment and Management* **4** 122–143.

Viljoen JL, Nicholls TL, Cruise KR, Desmarais SL & Webster CD (2015) *Short-Term Assessment of Risk and Treatability: Adolescent Version (START:AV)*. Vancouver, Canada: BC Mental Health and Substance Use Services.

Viljoen JL, Nicholls TL, Cruise KR, Desmarais SL & Webster CD (with contributions by Beneteau, JL, Petersen K, Barone C & Fusco-Morin S) (2014) *Short-Term Assessment of Risk and Treatability: Adolescent Version, Knowledge Guide.* Vancouver, Canada: BC Mental Health and Substance Use Services.

Webster CD, Martin M-L, Brink J, Nicholls TL & Desmarais SL (2009) *Manual for the Short-Term Assessment of Risk and Treatability (START), Version 1.1.* Coquitlam, Canada: British Columbia Mental Health & Addiction Services.

Weizmann-Henelius G, Putkonen H, Rissanen T, Eronen M & Webster CD (2019) Exploring a new structured professional judgment measure (impulsivity measure related to violence) after an average follow-up of 10 years: a study of Finnish offenders. *Criminal Behaviour and Mental Health* DOI: 10.1002/cbm.2107.

Wilson TD (2011) *Redirect: The surprising new science of psychological change.* New York: Little Brown & Company.

Worling JR & Curwen T (2001) *Estimate of Risk of Adolescent Sexual Offense Recidivism (ERASOR), Version 2.* Toronto: SAFE-T Program, Thistletown Regional Centre.

Zapf PA (2006) *Suicide Assessment Manual for Inmates.* Burnaby, Canada: Mental Health, Law and Policy Institute, Simon Fraser University.

Chapter 12: Implementing SPJ schemes – getting from manual to day-to-day clinical practice

By Chris Webster and Sumeeta Chatterjee

Cast of characters:

Him (David): An elderly forensic mental health researcher.

Her (Millie): A young but experienced forensic psychiatrist.

Kevin: Millie's husband.

Butch: Child of Millie and Kevin. Boy aged 10. Nick-name derived from *The Butcher Boy* by Patrick McCabe (1992).

Scout: Other child of Millie and Kevin. Girl aged 8. Nickname derived from Atticus's daughter in *To Kill a Mockingbird* by Harper Lee (1960).

Interlocutor: Any person with a suitably commanding voice.

A pedagogical play in four acts

Act I: Corridor

A conversation in a corridor following a formal board hearing. Millie has been testifying. David had been sitting as a member of a five-person board.

Him: I noted, Millie, from the hearing, that you're still using the 1997 Version (V2) of the HCR-20. The new Guide came out in 2013. Have you thought of shifting to these new guidelines?

Her: What I like about the original is its relative straightforwardness and simplicity. I do find it helpful to me, especially comparing numeric totals from year-to-year, to track broadly the progress of my individual patients over time.

Him: Well, you can use Form 1 included in the V3. This isn't a big departure from what you're already doing – beyond asking you and colleagues to rate the *relevance* of each item to the particular patient. And, in actual fact you have to take relevance into account anyway. To come up with a formulation you have to figure out which risk and strength variables are at play and what needs to be done to put forward a workable treatment plan. All the V3 authors are offering is a set of guidelines which may help improve practice. I take your point about the handiness that numbers can have in tracking the week-by-week progress of patients. But, do remember it's a simple matter to convert the V3 Low (L), Moderate (M), High (H) ratings to 0, 1, 2, scores.

Her: Look, I have to go now but I'm beginning to see we do indeed have work ahead of us. You're asking me re-think my resistance to V3, and challenge my views on what I perceived to be advantages of the V2. I will, I promise, now make it a priority to proceed with V3, and use it in my risk discussions with patients and staff. I have yet to analyse the full impetus behind my change in attitude, but fundamentally I agree that the use of numbers can be misleading or unhelpful, especially if this instrument is being widely used and interpreted not just by clinicians for daily management guidance, but by judges and board members who are charged with making important decisions about the liberties of others.

[Pauses]

I take your point. The V3 authors are offering guidelines. And, yes indeed, what I use must be current. I do need to get up-to-speed on the V3. *[Peers deep into her cell phone.]* So let me see, I have an hour next Thursday at 2pm. I think that after all I've done for you in the past, I deserve your full attention. Anyway, could you come to my office then? And maybe bring me a Starbucks tall, no fat, decaf latté, with soy?

Interlocutor: David wonders what she is talking about. He is trying to remember what, if anything, she has ever done for him. But as a result of years working as a humble mental health researcher, his face 'leaks' none of this – deeply repressed – feeling.

Him: Sure.

ACT II: Millie's office

On the appointed day, David arrives bearing the tall decaf latté with soy.

Her: I see you have both HCR-20 versions with you. What's the diff?

Him: First off, there are some changes in the way the items are framed, and there are some changes in item content. We don't have time to go into detail on the content of individual items. As with V2, the V3 authors recommend that users keep the manual open at the right item and refresh their memories as they go along. By the way, no one says you have to slug your way through the items exactly in the order in which they're laid out in the guide. So long as you ensure all items are taken into account, that's fine.

Her: But can we go through the items together today, even if superficially?

Him: Sure, you go through V2, I'll follow with V3.

Her: Item H1, 'Previous Violence'.

Him: Item H1, 'History of Problems with Violence'.

Her: Why complicate with the 'Problems with' thing?

Him: Just to make sure that the ratings for all items go in the same direction – that wasn't so in V2.

Her: OK, I get it – every one of the items starts with 'Problems with'. Otherwise you can't be sure you are rating in a consistent direction. Item 2, 'Young Age at First Violent Incident'.

Him: Item H2, 'History of Problems with Other Antisocial Behavior'.

Her: Wow! That sounds a pretty radical departure.

Him: Yes and no. The definition was indeed broadened from 'Violent Attitudes' to 'Other Antisocial Behavior'. But, as described in the manual, the item still includes emphasis on the *stage* of life at which this anti-sociality begins to occur.

Her: OK, I get the idea. Item H3, 'Relationship Instability'.

Him: Item H3, 'History of Problems with Relationships'. Notice in V2, which until recently you were still working from, this item 'applies *only* to romantic, intimate, non-platonic partnerships'. And notice also that the 'old' definition excluded relationships with family. V3 has *broadened the definition*. It now says that evaluators should consider intimate *and* non-intimate relationships.

Her: These are pretty big changes. Who dreamt these up?

Him: *[With just a touch of menace and puffing himself up to his age-related, ever-diminishing height]* No one dreamt them up. The changes, as with all the items, came about as a result of examining and taking advantage of the scientific evidence, and, importantly, consultations undertaken with clinicians on an international basis.

Her: Moving on – Item H4, 'Employment Problems'.

Him: Item H4, 'History of Problems with Employment'.

Her: SNAP!

Him: What are you talking about? Oh, I see, you mean the item titles are much the same. Sure, that's so, but you will – as you go over this later – see that the description of item content is clearer and fuller now.

Her: Item H5, 'Substance Use Problems'.

Him: Item 5, 'History of Problems with Substance Use'. Again, the guide uses consistent language, but please remember to look over the detailed text.

Her: Item H6, 'Major Mental Illness'.

Him: Item H6, 'History of Problems with Major Mental Disorder'.

Her: I see. From pages 76, 77, and 78 we now have to make sure to consult the manual for the details about different kinds of mental disorders. The guide refers now to General Indicators, Psychotic Disorders, Major Mood Disorders, and 'Other' Mental Disorders. I get the idea.

Him: V2 made no real attempt to deal with different *types* of mental disorder. And of course the DSM-5 did not exist when V^2 was published in 1997.

Her: Item 7 in V2 was Psychopathy. This item I've always liked a lot. You can send the patient off to Psychology and they'll come up with a score out of 40. This can be very helpful. And everyone knows that Psychopathy tends to be a prime predictor of future violence. In fact, I think you said it was the *very best* of the 12 predictors which make up the original 1993 VRAG, right? I feel on secure ground with this. The V3 is unchanged presumably?

Him: Well, no. It's now called 'History of Problems with Personality Disorder'.

Her: You've got the pages mixed up. Personality Disorder is H9 in V2.

Him: This *is* a change of real consequence. In V2, there were in essence two items covering much the same territory – H7 and H9. Research and clinical consultations by the V3 authors convinced them that the items needed to be conflated.

Her: OK, I get it. So Hare's PCL-R has gone completely?

Him: Not necessarily. The authors still recommend its use if the evaluator is interested specifically in the assessment and diagnosis of Psychopathy. There is a note in V3 on pages 79 and 80.

Her: Yeah, I'm with you. But it still seems a bit strange to leave out your most powerful predictor of violence.

Him: Couple of things to say on this. First, I don't have to tell you that 'Psychopathy' is not a DSM-5 diagnosis. It is an amalgam of Antisocial Personality Disorder, Borderline Personality Disorder, Histrionic Personality Disorder, and Narcissistic Personality Disorder. These are the 'Cluster B' ones described in pages 659–672. But the new DSM also allows for other kinds – Paranoid, Schizoid, Avoidant, Dependent, Obsessive-Compulsive. It also permits the assessor to take into account Personality Change due to Another Medical Condition as well as Other Specified and Unspecified Personality Disorders.

[Pauses]

Another thing, too, is that the HCR-20 scheme is *not* about 'prediction'. It's not in any way an actuarial device. It is a guide to assist clinicians *prevent* violence risks by developing a comprehensive risk formulation, and identifying relevant targets for treatment and management planning. Moving on…

Her: I know all that. But the fact is that when I see Personality Disorder in my forensic work I see mostly Cluster B persons.

Him: True, but surely from time to time you assess persons who are Dependent and so on that are relevant to your risk formulation. One of the purposes of an SPJ scheme is to get colleagues to cast their conceptual net as wide as possible. This can help evaluators as they wrestle with diagnostically complex individuals, in order to gain clarity that aids in their formulation and treatment.

[Pauses]

Can I add one more thing? You say you're inclined to refer patients to psychology to be assessed for Hare Psychopathy. I know you've taken a workshop with Bob in the recent past. I might venture that, having established rapport with the client, it may pay to do the Hare PCL-R assessment yourself. By the time you have reviewed the records and done the interviews it's very little extra work. The Hare PCL-R is, after all, *not* a psychological test. This has the joyous effect of releasing the psychologists to conduct specific and detailed psychological testing with the client that is beyond your ken (or in fact, mine).

Another thing is this. It's true that the vast amount of statistical research points to a link between Hare-Psychopathy and violence at later follow-up. It is a predictor of some consequence. But that applies to *published research studies*. What the V3 authors found as they undertook the revisions was that, in actual day-to-day practice with V2, assessors very frequently *omitted* the item altogether (which they were allowed to do). Also, V2 stated: 'The authors specifically warn against use of this item unless formally-obtained PCL-R or PCL:SV scores are available' (p41). So colleagues were 'within their rights' to skip the item if the scores were not at hand. So although Hare PCL-R Psychopathy might have been the single-item best predictor in theory, its inclusion as an item in the V2 scheme could, and probably did, work against improving overall prediction accuracy in practice.

Her: *[Looks at iPhone and gulps back the last of her soy non-fat latté.]* We're almost out of time.

Him: OK.

Her: I've already read Item H8 pretty thoroughly. I see that Kevin Douglas, Steve Hart and their V3 pals have generalised away from an emphasis solely on traumatic experiences in childhood. Given the fact that many of our patients come to us having suffered trauma from very many sources over the course of their lifetimes, I see the need for this revision in thinking.

Him: OK. And you'll know too that Item 9 has now been cast as 'History of Problems with Violent Attitudes'.

Her: Yes, I know that. I appreciate that we can't be maximally helpful clinically until we've got a handle on basic attitudes and motivations. Cognitive Behavior Therapy and such approaches can only be applied well if we have first undertaken a scan of those fundamental attitudes.

Him: Finally – for today anyway – H10 was 'Prior Supervision Failure'. The essence, as you know, has been retained. But the new item is broadened to 'History of Problems with Treatment or Supervision Response'.

Her: *[Looking at her watch.]* Well, our hour is up. It's been good to talk. I realise I need to go through these Historical Items very thoroughly by myself and need to ask my team members to do the same. Likely, we'll arrange a small workshop to help with this. I do have a better sense of what the originators have been trying to do. Could we have another meeting in about a month? I undertake to read the C Items and the R Items in advance. I'll even go a step further and, with my team, start using the V3 Historical Items with my team on all of our new clients. So why don't we meet here in a month? Wait! *[consults phone.]* I have a better idea. Why don't you come to our place on Friday the 15th? You can have dinner with us... You haven't seen my lesser-half in a while. And the kids often talk about you – mostly in an attempt to mimic your weird accent.

Him: That sounds great! Maybe that day you could slide off from work here a bit early and we could finish this off – without glass in hand. I could come around 4 o'clock, perhaps?

Her: Great, I'll do that! I'll tell you what though. Why don't you stay on after dinner and put the kids to bed? You have a have a new book on 'Edward the Bear' right? Bring a copy. They'll love it. If Edward fails, you can use my V3 manual. And it'll get them to sleep very fast. And I promise that Kevin and I'll be home before, say, 2 o'clock – not like last time when it was 4.30, if I remember correctly.

Him: *[Weakly]* Fine...........

ACT III: Outside Millie and Kevin's home
On the appointed day he rings doorbell.

Her: Oh hi, David, do come on in.

Interlocutor: There is silence in the house, which had not been anticipated.

Her: I've sent Kevin out with the kids – so we have an hour to work on V3. Let's go to my home-office.

[They sit.]

Him: We had managed to get through all the Historical Items, as I recall.

Her: That's so. And, good to my word, my team and I have rated eight new admissions with the V3 Historical Items over the past month. It was fine. We're going to test for inter-rater reliability among five team members using the next six persons admitted. Once we have those data across the items, can you or one of your students figure out the correlations for us?

Him: Sure.

Her: As well as all this, Suzanne, our social worker, took it upon herself to go over the Historical Items with two of our patients on the inpatient unit. In one instance the individual agreed with the team's ratings almost exactly. But in the second there were some seemingly serious discrepancies between our scores and hers. In her view, the file information we are working with is in serious error in respect to Item 5, 'Problems with Substance Abuse' and Item 6, 'Problems with Mental Disorder'. Suzanne is taking this very seriously and is seeking additional information from hospitals which have offered treatment and care in the past. We've got to get this straightened out, and will do so.

Him: Sounds sensible to me. If nothing else, in the instance you are referring to, it's an opportunity for both Suzanne and the patient to get agreed on the 'facts'. So let's get on with our review of the HCR-20 V3 and C and R Items.

Her: Actually, this need not take long. I've gone over these very thoroughly as have the members of my team. We can read you know. We always have the item definitions before us as we proceed with assessment.

Let's get on with C1, 'Problems with Insight'. We really like the way the V3 now splits the items into three dimensions – Mental Disorder, Violence Risk and Need for Treatment. My team saw real advantages of using the Rating Sheets in Appendix B in which users can break out type of deficiency in insight. Indeed in Appendix C of the new version, clinicians can elaborate these matters. So there's a real advance, or so we think.

Him: You're being very generous to the authors.

Her: Don't be smart. C2, 'Recent Problems with Violent Ideation' gave us no trouble. Again, the new description is better fleshed out than in its predecessor. Going on, C3, 'Recent Problems with Symptoms of Major Mental Disorder' represents a real advance both in terms of the description given in the manual and on the forms. As in Item H6, it's helpful to be able to differentiate symptoms of Psychotic Disorders, Major Mood Disorders and other Disorders. It's also good that the notes under these descriptions connect with the DSM-5.

Him: OK, we're getting there.

Her: We understand what the authors did in Item C4, which was 'Impulsivity' in V2, it has now become 'Recent Problems with Instability'. I find it interesting that the authors have reintroduced from Version 1 (V1) the notion of 'Stability' in favour of 'Impulsivity'. It's just that they have broadened the definition. Again, it's useful and clinically relevant to think instability in terms of Affective, Behavioural, and Cognitive functions. I seem to remember that in Psychology 101, the instructor, who wore the most dreadful ties, went on a lot about William James' notion that psychology had to do with thinking, feeling and willing. It appears to me that the authors of V3 have been leaning on some quite old ideas.

Him: It's interesting that one of our Finnish colleagues, Dr Ghitta Weissman, has, with others, recently put forward an entire SPJ scheme to pin down the concept of impulsivity (in press). Impulsivity remains a key construct under stability. Her advice may be helpful in elucidating the various components within the Impulsivity construct.

Her: Thanks for the scholarly dissertation. We see C5, 'Recent Problems with Treatment or Supervision Response' has been broadened to include both response to treatment and to supervision. This makes sense. It is in line with Item H10.

Him: I'm so glad you agree.

Her: My colleagues and I have also noted that the content of R1 has also been broadened somewhat. The V2 emphasis on 'Plans' remains but it makes sense to include specific reference to 'Professional Services'. We find in clinical practice that a plan in and of itself may be well-conceived, but it is liable to run aground if there are insufficient or inadequate resources within the hospital or within the community. The item, as now construed, helps make the assessor wonder: is this plan actually feasible?

Him: Sure.

Her: R2 in V3, 'Future Problems with Living Situation', is more or less what it used to be in V2 except now that living situation is now the overall theme. It was always hard in V2 to distinguish R2 ('Exposure to Destabilizers') and R5 ('Stress'). The detailed wording in V3 now makes it clear that the new R2 is environmentally/situationally/*externally* centred, whereas R5 focuses on *internal* psychological actualities.

Him: Yes, I agree with that, Doctor.

Her: R3, 'Future Problems with Personal Support', seems little changed. And we can see that the future-oriented R4, 'Future Problems with Treatment or Supervision Response', is like H10 which links to the past, and C5 which relies on reporting from the present.

Him: That's right.

Her: And finally, to R5, 'Future Problems with Stress or Coping'. My team and I now really understand that this item hinges upon how the individual *experiences* situations as being stressful.

[The front door slams. Moments later, Butch and Scout burst into the home-office. They're trailed by weary-looking Kevin.]

Her: That's it, job done, wrapped up, over and done with. Yeehaw!

Him: Well, not really, we need one more session.

Her: What for?

Him: To deal with Risk Formulation, Risk Scenarios and Management Strategies.

Her: Ok, I'd agree to anything right now. Shoot me an e-mail as to when we can next meet and let me know whether it's best here at home or at the office.

[Pauses]

I've laid out their pajamas. Kevin and the kids ate on their way home. I hope they've not been allowed too much sugar, eh, Kevin? Good night, kids. We're off, see you later David. Toodaloo!

Interlocutor: The 'later' turns out to be 4:30 in the morning.

ACT IV: Millie's office

Three weeks later.

Her: Sorry we couldn't arrange to meet at home.

Interlocutor: David thinks – never at home again!

Her: I have looked over pages 50–65 of the V3 manual.

Him: That's good. What did you get out of that reading, may I ask?

Her: I made a list: Four Things. Aren't I good? Here they are.
            [Looks at sheet of paper.]

            First, the importance of rating items not just for presence but for *relevance* is clear. It helps us bring into focus the items that are critical in the particular case, when it comes to trying to figure out the antecedents of violence, and how to prevent similar, or indeed any, kind of violence in the future. Any useful risk management plan must address pertinent risk factors that are person and context-specific.

Him: OK. Agree. The idea is to *'See'* the relevant factors and then more clearly than before, think about how they do interact, or might interact under particular circumstances.

Her: Second, we get to 'risk formulation'. What I take from this is that the V3 originators are actually leaning on tried-and-true principles derived from the literature on psychotherapy. We, as clinicians, are looking here for the 'roots' with a down-the-road eye toward figuring which interventions might be best under the circumstances. I found this idea very compelling and useful. At university I studied, before medicine, a good deal of English, American, Russian, German and other literatures. I nearly fell off my chair when I read at the top of page 54 of V3: '…we need to tell a story about an individual that integrates the many pieces of information available to us'. The guide tells us on the same page to develop 'an individual theory of risk'.

            [Pauses]

            I was also intrigued to see that the V3 authors have 'reached out', as people say these days, to some very standard, and well-established principles in psychiatry – the 'Four P' model of 'Predisposing', 'Precipitating', 'Perpetuating' and 'Protective Factors'. All this was drummed into my head as a junior resident.

Him: It's true that the HCR-20 authors seem to have no trepidation when it comes to incorporating established ideas or, for that matter, moving notions from business or other domains way outside the mental health field.

Her: My *third* point has to do with the creation of 'risk scenarios'. These are formulations oriented toward the future, or as the manual says 'possible futures'. This idea, as you just said, arose from the business context. It's important, if I have it right, to be able to *imagine* not only the present state of affairs but also possible future ones. To be successful in this kind of assessment, it appears to be necessary to *project* reasonable scenarios on behalf of, or with, the patient. The manual says, if I remember, that it may often be possible and necessary to create to three to five such scenarios.

Him: That's so.

Her: For my *fourth* point I note that the V3 draws on the Don Andrews Risk-Need-Responsivity (RNR) principle from general criminology. I learned about that in a Crim course years ago. The instructor at the time hammered home the idea that it is best to apply the strongest efforts and programmes towards high-risk persons. She also pointed out that if you want to help persons reduce criminal behaviours, it is best to direct resources towards there criminogenic needs. I also grasped from Crim the idea of *responsivity* – the idea that members of staff need to help persons select and participate in programmes that are well-suited to their actual requirements. There has to be a 'fit'. Putting the wrong person in the wrong programme can do much more harm than good.

Him: I'm glad to know they're still teaching the right stuff in university undergraduate courses.

[Pauses]

Well, we got over that very well. Would it be OK if I were to sit in on one of your V3 team meetings sometime soon?

Her: For sure, just so long as you don't try to take over – like the last time you came along. I'm in charge, not you.

Him: I don't doubt it...

Chapter 13:
From false starts to the real START – the practical integration of patients' strengths in clinical assessment and research work

By Mary-Lou Martin

> *'…even when people present with obvious vulnerabilities they also have strengths. Their strengths are in their passions, in their skills, in their interests, in their relationships and in their environments. If mental health practitioners look for strengths they will find them.'*
> (Deegan, 2012, pviii)

Recently, in the field of forensic mental health there has been a growing interest in clients' strengths and protective factors as they may be associated with positive outcomes. This represents a distinct shift from clinicians and researchers being interested only in vulnerabilities and risks. Strengths need to be integrated from the very beginning into strategies and approaches for conducting assessments because the results of such evaluations usually lay the groundwork for the later planning of interventions. Clients and clinicians, working together, can figure out how best to bring into play residual positive qualities and personal assets (see also Chapter 20). A recovery approach demands that strengths be identified and brought fully into account. It is now clear from recent research that non-violence can be predicted from knowledge of patients' strengths (Webster *et al*, 2009, Table 9, p101).

Clinical work with forensic and some correctional clients is influenced by practice models. Traditionally, forensic psychiatric assessments have followed a standard medical model and problem-based perspective. The focus has been on discerning pathology, identifying symptoms of mental illness, isolating behavioral problems and estimating risks of violence of various kinds. A deficit or problem-focused approach limits the information collected and emphasises the negative aspects of the client. A number of reliable and valid guides exist for the assessment of risks. Many risk assessment schemes and risk management plans centre solely on deficits and social adjustment problems.

Strengths may help to reduce or manage risks. But all too often strengths are underused in forensic mental health care. Integration of strengths into risk assessment and management helps ensure that clients receive treatment that is properly rounded and balanced. Most forensic clinicians have not been trained in assessing strengths or using strength-based approaches. A focus on strengths can promote clients' willingness to consider new ways of coping. A focus on strengths also means taking into account the strengths of the clients' family and their community. Discussing strengths as part of routine forensic care can help support clients and their families to build on existing strengths and capacities so that unanticipated challenges can be overcome. A focus on strengths may also help shift the focus from risk to prevention (see Chapter 9).

The evolution of START

As distinct from the HCR-20 V3 (Douglas *et al*, 2014), the START focuses, as its title implies, on the *short-term*. There is a reason for this. Peter Scott pointed it out (see Chapter 1). He said quite specifically, *'Our disappointment* [about our inability to make accurate predictions of violence] *may be alleviated if we accept that short-term assessment (which permits the scanning of the subject's present environment and associates, and his reactions to these) is likely to be much more reliable than long-term assessment, which, especially in the present setting of a mobile and changing society is likely to be totally beyond our reach.'* (1977, p25)

In recent years, several reliable and valid structured assessment guides have emerged that specifically focus on a positive approach that assesses strengths and protective factors. Among these are:

■ Short–Term Assessment of Risk and Treatability (START) (Webster *et al*, 2009).

■ Short-Term Assessment of Risk and Treatability Adolescent Version (START:AV) (Viljoen *et al*, 2014).

■ Structured Assessment of Protective Factors (SAPROF) (De Vogel *et al*, 2009; de Vries Robbé, 2014).

■ Structured Assessment of Violence Risk in Youth (SAVRY) (Borum *et al*, 2006).

The START is an example of an SPJ guide that assesses strengths, vulnerabilities and risks. It has now existed for some 15 years (Webster *et al*, 2004). At the time of the START's development, the HCR-20 V2 (Webster *et al*, 1997) was the most-available and most-used general-purpose SPJ risk assessment scheme.

It took the START's interdisciplinary development group several years to evolve the scheme. Initially it was called the Short-Term Assessment of Risk (STAR), but it soon became clear that the fledgling device needed to be propelled toward the notions of prevention and treatability. The first step was to identify and test out 'STAR Items', which eventually became 'Short-Term Assessment of Risk and Treatability (START) Items'. The next challenge was to define the 'Items' in both directions with 'Strengths' in one direction and 'Risks' in the other. This required an extensive literature review, consultation with an array of forensic mental-health clinicians, and considerable discussion within the development group.

Part of the challenge emerged from the fact that, initially, in STAR, the development group had based the scaling around a 5-point set-up (-2, -1, for Vulnerabilities; +2, +1 for Strengths), with a common '0'. Yet this rating scheme did not pass the 'hard test'. Forays into actual practice left colleagues thinking it was not 'quite right'. The group eventually realised that it was the common '0' that was working against the device. If in fact the 'Items' on one side of the coin were not precise opposites of those on the other side, it made no sense to be using the same zero. The only way out of this quandary was to introduce a zero on the 'Risk' (later called 'Vulnerabilities') scale and a zero on the 'Strengths' scale. When the group tested this out clinically it was found that progress was being made. The group realised that it was necessary to elucidate more clearly 'Vulnerabilities' on one side and 'Strengths' on the other. Once that was done, it was then important to think about how assessors would have to deal with the fact that it is possible to locate risk and vulnerability *within the very same item*. All individual items had to be viewed from both angles. A dictionary of antonyms was only of slight help. The originators had to slug out the two-sided definitions based on their clinical and research experience. They then had to reflect as to how the set of defined 'Items' on both the 'Vulnerabilities' and 'Strengths' sides might interact among one another. This is where the ideas about scenario planning and risk formulation fit in (see Chapter 9 by Hart and Douglas). In START, seminars the trainers always point out and demonstrate that, with respect to a particular 'Item', it is often the case that a client can demonstrate some quantum of 'Strength' (i.e. +1, +2) and *at the same time*, some discernable 'Vulnerability' (i.e. -1, -2).

From the outset of this project, the development group was interested in breaking new ground in using an SPJ approach to assess strengths, vulnerabilities and risks. It was a crucial departure from tradition and the thinking of the time. Specifically, the development group set out to develop a device that could be used in practice or research that would remind people to consider a range of possible outcomes. The 'Specific Risk Estimates' include historical and present risks for violence, self-harm, suicide, unauthorised leave, substance abuse, self-neglect, and being victimised. The START coding form is flexible and allows colleagues to write in additional, seemingly idiosyncratic risks that could arise in a specific client case. The development team also determined it was important to assess clients for the ability to establish and maintain therapeutic relationships and peer support relationships. In addition, a prediction 'Risk Specificity' formulation statement is expected from the clinicians so that it can be addressed in treatment plans involving clients to the fullest extent possible.

The START has been translated into eight languages (Danish, Dutch, Finnish, French, German, Japanese, Norwegian and Swedish) and is being used in 11 countries around the world. Over 70 articles and chapters have been published about the START[19].

Experience with STAR and START over two decades

The main thing that has caught the attention of the authors of START is the number of publications which have emanated from the scheme since its inception. Space precludes a review of these various papers. A few, though, are referred to at the end of this chapter. Our most recent review is contained in an article by Nicholls *et al* (in press). There are many lessons that have been learned from the START over the years. Generally, the START fits well with practice standards, recognition of clients' strengths, assisting with clinical decision-making and it asks clinicians to specify any negative outcomes. Research demonstrates that the START predicts future violence on the risk side about as well as most current risk assessment schemes, and that future violence can be predicted about as well from the absence of strengths. The START scheme supports and enables treatment planning and risk management. The process entails reminding clinician assessors at every stage of the necessity of entertaining risks and vulnerabilities *at the same time*. This can be of much value when the START is used by an interdisciplinary team.

Failure in client care and support are especially likely to occur during phases of client transition. In our and others' experience, the completion

---

19 Information about the START summary sheet, START training workshops and publications about the START can be found at: http://www.bcmhsus.ca/health-professionals/clinical-resources/start (accessed February 2019)

of START with the involvement of both clients and clinicians can do much to 'bridge the gap' between one set of circumstances and another. Under ideal circumstances, the 'out-going' team and the client meets with the 'new taking-over team' to promote continuity and transition of care, and together they go over the client's experience, START details, the formulation and the management plan.

Strengths are often overlooked by clinicians. Many clients are challenged to identify their own strengths. It is important to hear evidence of strengths when listening to clients' stories. Often clients are so oriented to unveiling their deficits and limitations that they are challenged to identify and disclose their strengths and capacities. Clinicians can support clients to identify their strengths by asking questions such as: what are you doing well? What's currently working in your life? How are you coping during this difficult time? Tell me what you are good at? What are your strengths? What have you been successful at? What strengths would other people identify about you?

The role of the clinician includes supporting clients to identify and explore their strengths and past successes. It is important for both clinicians and clients to focus on the positive. Clinicians need to be supported in their practice as they learn to focus on plans to maintain and increase strengths and decrease risks.

Understanding the client's strengths can inform plans of treatment by helping with targeted intervention and supporting clients' resiliency under conditions of stress. When patients hear strengths identified in their meetings with clinicians and see strengths described in reports, it can enhance the engagement and the therapeutic relationship between clients and clinicians. This can also help clients to feel empowered, motivated and increasingly willing to be involved in collaborative relationships with their clinicians.

Strengths and risks are complex and multi-dimensional. Little is known about how risks and strengths operate in combination in relation to positive and negative outcomes. More research is needed to determine the extent to which strengths reduce or ameliorate risks and how risks and strengths are associated in multiple ways with eventual outcomes of various kinds.

References

Borum R, Bartel P & Gorth A (2006) *Manual for the Structured Assessment for Vioene Risk in Youth (SAVRY)*. Odessa, FL: Psychological Assessment Resources.

De Vries Robbe M (2014) *Protective Factors, Validation of the Structured Assessment of Protective Factors for Violence Risk in Forensic Psychiatry*. Utrecht: Van der Hoeven Kliniek.

DeVogel V, De ruiter C, Bouman Y & De Vries Robbe M (2009) *SAPROF: Guidelines for the assessment of protective factors for violence risk*. Utrecht: Forum Educatief.

Deegan P (2012) Foreword. In: CA Rapp & RJ Goscha (Eds) *The Strengths Model: A Recovery-Oriented Approach to Mental Health Services.* New York: Oxford University Press.

Douglas KS, Hart SD, Webster CD, Belfrage H, Guy LS & Wilson CM (2014) Historical-Clinical-Risk Management-20, Version 3 (HCR-20V3): Development and overview, *International Journal of Forensic Mental Health* **13** 2 93-108.

Nicholls TL, Desmarais S, Martin ML, Brink J & Webster CD (In press) Short Term Assessment of Risk and Treatability (START). In: RD Morgan (Ed.) *The SAGE Encyclopedia of Criminal Psychology.* Thousand Oaks, CA: Sage Publishing.

Scott PD (1977) Assessing dangerousness in criminals. *British Journal of Psychiatry* **131** 127–142.

Shepherd SM, Strand S, Viljoen JL & Daffern M (2018) Evaluating the utility of 'strength' items when assessing the risk of young offenders. *The Journal of Forensic Psychiatry & Psychology* **29** (4) 597–616.

Viljoen JL, Nicholls TL, Cruise KR, Desmarais SL & Webster CD (2014) *Short-Term Assessment of Risk and Treatability: Adolescent Version (START: AV): User Guide.* Burnaby, BC: Mental Health, Law and Policy Institute.

Webster CD, Douglas K, Eaves D & Hart S (1997) *HCR-20: Assessing Risk for Violence, Version 2.* Burnaby, BC: Simon Fraser University.

Webster CD, Martin ML, Brink J, Nicholls TL & Middleton C (2004) *Short-term assessment of risk and treatability (START).* Hamilton, ON: St Joseph's Healthcare Hamilton.

Webster CD, Martin ML, Brink J, Nicholls TL & Desmarais S (2009) *Manual for the Short-Term Assessment of Risk and Treatability (START) (Version 1.1).* Port Coquitlam, BC: Forensic Psychiatric Services Commission and St. Joseph's Healthcare Hamilton.

Section 4
Specific applications of SPJ

Chapter 14:
Principles for violence risk assessment with perpetrators of intimate partner violence

By Randall Kropp

Intimate partner violence (IPV) is one of the most common forms of interpersonal violence and may lead to acute and chronic consequences for the victim, such as psychological trauma, serious physical injury, and even death. IPV – sometimes also referred to as domestic violence, spousal assault, wife assault or spousal violence – can be broadly defined as the *actual, attempted or threatened physical harm of a current or former intimate partner*. The definition is intended to include violence in any intimate relationship (i.e. sexual, romantic), regardless of the gender or legal status of the people involved.

IPV, like many acts of family violence, is typically different from violent crime perpetrated against strangers. The perpetrator and victim in IPV are more likely to be strongly emotionally attached, and such strong emotions may lead to severe reactive violence. Both may also be physically close, thus allowing opportunity of access for repeated and sometimes frequent violence.

Serious acts of IPV are more likely to be perpetrated by males toward females, though as mentioned above, IPV may occur in any intimate relationship. IPV is prevalent across most countries of the world. All nations and jurisdictions face challenges in the prevention of IPV, as effective risk management often requires co-ordinated communications and actions between different professional agencies working within local laws. Risk assessment and effective risk management is vital however when helping policing, correctional and health agencies to match interventions and services with the level of risk and need presented in each individual case, and to delineate any protective measures to support the (potential) victim.

As noted by Stephen Hart and Kevin Douglas (Chapter 9), the primary goal of violence risk assessment is to *prevent* violence; that is, to manage and minimise any risks posed by the individual. In other words, IPV risk assessment should inform *risk management* by generating ideas regarding the monitoring, supervision and treatment of offenders, and safety planning for victims. Procedures which only focus on the narrow question of predicting the likelihood or probability of offence do little to inform us about prevention and management.

Structured Professional Judgment

Those conducting risk assessments should employ the Structured Professional Judgment (SPJ) to IPV risk assessment. Such guidelines should reflect the 'state of the discipline' with respect to the scientific literature and professional knowledge.

Indeed, many professionals across health, justice and policing agencies have valued the development of the SPJ professional guideline approach in the field of IPV. Kropp *et al* first developed the Spousal Assault Risk Assessment Guide (SARA) in 1994, which was soon updated to a second edition the following year. These guides were adopted and evaluated by institutional and community organisations across many countries, states and provinces.

The authors also developed a similar but more concise guideline for use by law enforcement agencies. This shorter, simpler guide, known as the Brief Spousal Assault Form for the Evaluation of Risk, or B-SAFER (Kropp *et al*, 2005) was also noteworthy for another reason. Risk assessment schemes in the field of IPV (e.g. actuarial tools – Danger Assessment (DA) (Campbell, 1995) and the Ontario Domestic Assault Risk Assessment (ODARA) (Hilton *et al*, 2004)) often require an exclusive rigorous examination of perpetrator risk factors. The B-SAFER did this, but also required the evaluator to consider the psychosocial adjustment and background of the (potential) victim i.e. victim vulnerability factors.

Version 3 of the SARA, released in 2015, is an important evolution of the guideline, fully in keeping with the refinement of related guidelines developed roughly around the same era (notably the HCR-20 Version 2 and SVR-20). All of these guidelines now incorporate steps related to the formulation of violence perpetration and management plans. This includes the coding of relevance for each risk factor, a feature that is described elsewhere in this text. The factors considered in the SARA-V3 are divided into three domains.

■ First, the nature of IPV includes eight factors related to the pattern of any IPV behaviour (i.e. intimidation; threats; physical harm; sexual harm; severe IPV; chronic IPV; escalating IPV; and IPV-related supervision violations).

- Second, perpetrator risk factors are 10 factors reflecting the background and psychosocial adjustment of the evaluee (i.e. intimate relationships; non-intimate relationships; employment/finances; trauma/victimisation; general antisocial conduct; major mental disorder; personality disorder; substance use; violent/suicidal ideation; and distorted thinking about IPV).

- Finally, the SARA-V3 includes victim vulnerability factors supported by literature review that are '...barriers to victims' ability, opportunity, or motivation to engage in self-protective behaviour' (SARA-V3, p9). These six items are barriers to security; barriers to independence; interpersonal resources; community resources; attitudes or behaviour; and mental health.

Application

SPJ schemes such as the SARA Version 3 should not be seen as simple checklists. Risk assessment is complex and should be conducted by individuals who are experienced working with offenders or victims. It is recommended that evaluators understand that: (a) risk assessment is complex; it is not simply a matter of checking boxes and summing up scores; (b) the dynamics of intimate partner violence are unique and must be understood to properly evaluate the reliability of information available.

Those conducting risk assessments should consider multiple sources of information and multiple methods. Possible sources of information include the (alleged) perpetrator, the victim(s), other collateral informants, correctional file information, criminal records, mental health reports, etc.

Although it is extremely important to incorporate victim information into a risk assessment, the evaluator should always be aware that a number of victim barriers exist that might compromise the reliability of information provided. Further, while there is much literature to suggest that victims can be accurate predictors of future violence, there is also evidence that victims can underestimate risk for violence, especially violence of a serious or lethal nature.

Risk assessments should produce a risk management or case management plan that includes recommendations for monitoring, supervision, treatment and safety planning. Whenever possible, risk management plans should be implemented by multiple professionals from multiple agencies (e.g. police, corrections, health, victim services and child protection, etc.).

The SARA V3 is intended for use with common or typical forms of IPV. This does not make it suitable for use as a general purpose risk assessment guide. Risk in the context of IPV is often rapidly changeable and may present in multiple guises at different times. We as professionals should not see guidelines as exhaustive or fixed, and be quick to recognise that evaluees may represent with other forms of risk (including harm to self), which will need the complementary use of other SPJ guidelines.

References and further reading

Campbell JC (1995) Prediction of Homicide of and by Battered Women. In: JC Campbell (Ed) *Assessing Dangerousness: Violence by sexual offenders, batterers, and child abusers.* Thousand Oaks, CA: Sage.

Hilton NZ, Harris GT, Rice ME, Lang C & Cormier CA (2004) A brief actuarial assessment for the prediction of wife assault recidivism: The ODARA. *Psychological Assessment* **16** 267–275.

Kropp PR & Cook AN (2014) Intimate Partner Violence, Homicide, and Stalking. In: R Meloy & J Hoffman (Eds) *The International Handbook of Threat Assessment.* Oxford University Press.

Kropp PR & Hart SD (2015) *User Manual for Version 3 of the Spousal Assault Risk Assessment Guide (SARA-V3).* Vancouver, BC: Protect International, Inc.

Kropp PR, Hart SD & Belfrage H (2005) *The Brief Spousal Assault Form for the Evaluation of Risk (B-SAFER) (2nd Edition).* Vancouver, British Columbia: Proactive-Resolutions, Inc.

Storey JE, Kropp PR, Hart SD, Belfrage H & Strand S (2014) Assessment and management of risk for intimate partner violence by police officers using the Brief Spousal Assault Form for the Evaluation of Risk. *Criminal Justice and Behavior* **41** (2) 256–271.

Belfrage H, Strand S, Storey JE, Gibas A, Kropp PR & Hart SD (2012) Assessment and management of intimate partner violence by police officers using the Spousal Assault Risk Assessment Guide. *Law and Human Behavior* **36** (1) 60–67.

Chapter 15:
SPJ and the elucidation of sexual violence risk

By Caroline Logan

Introduction

The structured professional judgment (SPJ) approach to risk assessment, formulation and management is the recommended approach to understanding the risks presented by individuals, dyads, or groups in order to prevent or limit harmful outcomes (Hart *et al*, 2016). The harmful outcomes to be prevented or limited are by their nature poorly understood and forecast only with uncertainty, but, in response to the threat of their occurrence, we are compelled to act. In doing so, the SPJ approach guides us from a position of uncertainty to one of greater certainty using the empirical and professional literature on the nature of the threat posed as, in effect, a map of the terrain.

Guidance based on the SPJ approach – such as the *Historical, Clinical,* and *Risk Management-20 Violence Risk Guide 3rd Edition* (the HCR-20 V3) (Douglas *et al*, 2013) – begins by directing the attention of evaluators to a minimum number of variables or risk factors that the literature tells us are important to consider in an assessment of the general violence potential of an individual. The HCR-20 describes those risk factors in detail so that the evaluator knows what to look for and the potential relevance of what they observe. The evaluator may add additional risk factors to their assessment, but the 20 described in the HCR-20 guidance must always be considered. The HCR-20 guidance then supports the evaluator to prepare a formulation of the risks posed by the individual, that is, a statement of their understanding of that person's harm potential based on what they have abducted about the person's past violent conduct (Chapter 9). And on the basis of that understanding, scenarios for the occurrence of harmful behaviour in the future are outlined, providing a platform for both the refinement of the formulation and the preparation of bespoke risk management strategies. These strategies must address the range of direct interventions, supervision options, observations or monitoring objectives to enable the earliest detection of a change in risk, and victim safety plans.

The outcome of early efforts to risk manage an individual whose harm potential has been appraised using the HCR-20 guidance then feeds back into the original evaluation of the relevance of risk factors in the individual case and then formulation and risk scenarios derived from that collective assessment. Thus the evaluation of risk is a dynamic process of assessment, understanding and action, back to assessment again, over and over, with timescales dependent on the nature of the risks posed, their imminence, the context in which risks are being assessed, and the needs and wishes of the key stakeholders in the process.

Sexual violence risk

As Kropp noted in the previous chapter, evaluators who understand both the application of the assessment approach and the nature of the threat to be prevented or minimised should carry out risk assessments. Therefore, to understand and manage risk of sexually harmful behaviour, which is the focus of this chapter, an evaluator must have expertise in both the SPJ approach as outlined above *and* harmful sexual behaviour. Expertise in one area does not guarantee good practice in the other.

With respect to sexually harmful conduct, practitioners who hope to understand the risks posed by their clients, must have at least a basic understanding of:

1. The nature of harmful sexual behaviour and the myriad ways in which it can be enacted in men and women, and in young people as compared to working age adults and older adults.
2. The aetiology and development of sexual violence.
3. The range of needs that may be met by this form of conduct.
4. The impact of the various efforts at risk management, from direct interventions via long-term individual or group therapy (e.g. sexual offender treatment programmes) through to imprisonment, long-term supervision and specific schemes to restrict access to potential victims (e.g. Laws & O'Donohue, 2008; Phenix & Hoberman, 2016; Ward & Stewart, 2003; Ward *et al*, 2006).

Such a knowledge base will facilitate the evaluator's appreciation of how and why the client used sexual violence to meet their needs on the occasions on which they consciously chose to do so.

Risk management in the long term – leading to the prevention or limitation of any kind of sexually violent act – is based on an understanding of how risk and protective factors interplay, or indeed fail to do so. Understanding what has protected the individual from harming others more often or more seriously will be as important to managing risk in the future as understanding what has actively steered that person towards sexual violence, encouraged and nurtured it as an outcome – and failed to divert it – in the past. SPJ guidance specific to sexual violence will assist the evaluator by directing his or her attention to key factors known in the literature to be important in any consideration of sexual violence risk. Such guidance will then assist the evaluator in melding their knowledge of sexual violence in general with their understanding of risk in the individual case, the product of which will be their risk formulation, which is in turn the foundation to bespoke risk management planning. It is in the formulation that the evaluator's understanding of the individual's risk is crystallised and it is this that forms the basis for communication with others towards managed risk (Sturmey & McMurran, 2011).

SPJ guidance on assessing and managing risk of sexual violence

What options are available to evaluators who want to use the SPJ approach to apply their expertise on sexually harmful behaviour to the question of the risks posed by their specific client? There are two options available.

First, there is the Sexual Violence Risk-20 version 2 (SVR-20 V2) (Boer *et al*, 2017). This guidance is intended for use by evaluators who possess at least a basic level of knowledge about sexually harmful behaviour and the SPJ approach. It is intended for application to clients who have a known history of actual, attempted or threatened sexually harmful behaviour. The guidance encourages evaluators to gather an adequate range of information related to 20 risk factors for sexually harmful behaviour (e.g. sexual deviation, sexual health problems that disturb an individual's sexual drive or ability to experience sexual satisfaction, psychopathic personality disorder, relationship problems, employment problems, extreme minimisation or denial of sexual offending, negative attitudes towards interventions and supervision). Other factors may be taken into consideration depending on the nature of the individual case.

Evaluators are guided to determine the presence of each of the risk factors identified in their client, noting recent change. The assessment is concluded with a summary risk rating (focusing on level of effort or intervention required to manage risk based on the information known), a rating of the risk of serious physical harm, a rating of the requirement for immediate action and the nature of the action recommended, any other risks indicated, and a statement about both the date of next review and the specific issues to be considered at that time. The SVR-20 V2 guidance does not support risk formulation and scenario-planning activity. In this sense, the evaluation supported by the SVR-20 V2 is comparatively superficial.

The second option for SPJ guidance on sexual violence is the *Risk for Sexual Violence Protocol* (RSVP) (Hart *et al*, 2003). The RSVP is comparable to the

SVR-20 V2 in the sense that both require the assessment of a broad range and depth of clinical information in relation to, in this case, 22 risk factors for sexual violence. However, two features differentiate the RSVP from the SVR-20 V2. First, similar to the HCR-20 V3, the RSVP goes beyond the evaluation of the mere presence of risk factors in the individual case to a study of their relevance to that person's future potential for sexually harmful behaviour. Thus, relevance ratings are required of all 22 risk factors in the RSVP, where a risk factor may be deemed relevant if it has a bearing – causal, correlational, temporal – on the occurrence of sexual harm.

Second, also akin to the HCR-20 V3, the RSVP evaluation requires a sophisticated formulation and scenario planning process prior to comprehensive risk management, exploring options around treatment, supervision, monitoring and victim-safety planning. Consequently, the RSVP is intended for use by experts in both sexually violent behaviour and its risk assessment and long-term management, and in particular the communication of harm potential in the form of a statement of understanding, namely the formulation. Therefore, the RSVP is comparable to the HCR-20 V3 in terms of the depth of the assessment its use supports, and an evolved form of the SVR-20 V2 in terms of the specific focus on sexually harmful behaviour, its understanding, and its bespoke management.

Risk formulation

Formulation is critical to the application of the most developed SPJ guidance. But what exactly do we mean when we talk about risk formulation? Formulation is the process of creating one or more linked hypotheses about the underlying mechanism of a complex clinical problem (or problems), such as sexually harmful behaviour, in order to prepare action to facilitate positive change. Essentially, the formulation process allows evaluators the opportunity to *organise* often quite disparate information about the client in order to expose the key elements of the case. Ideally, a formulation is a narrative – also brief and succinct – that represents the shared or *mutual understanding* between the practitioner and client (and/ or key others) which is then used as a basis for generating hypotheses that are psychologically *informed connections* between events and outcomes or inferences about motives or the function of problem behaviour. The hypotheses derived in this way are then the basis for *communication* between the practitioner who is its author and the client as well as key others, and are used as a springboard for ameliorative *action* that is intended to mitigate the distress experienced and the problems caused.

Key to the formulation process is scenario planning, which is the forecasting of at least two possible ways in which harmful behaviour may manifest in the future, given what is understood about the nature and drivers of similar harmful behaviour in the past (Douglas *et al*, 2013). Evaluators are required to describe the nature of each possible scenario, how severe its many consequences could be for the victim or victims, how soon the scenario may happen given what is known about existing risk management plans, how often might the sexually harmful behaviour occur and whether the problem is acute or chronic, and finally, the likelihood that that scenario will occur compared to the others forecast. Those scenarios then form the basis for detailed risk management plans, intended to assist in their prevention or considerable limitation.

Therefore, in the application of SPJ guidance at the highest level – as in the RSVP or the HCR-20 V3 – formulation-based risk management is at the core. But how might we know a good risk formulation from a poor one – or even a formulation from a case summary or case description? In the UK, the Offender Personality Disorder Pathway provides psychologically informed care and risk management to in excess of 30,000 men and women in prison and probation services across England and Wales thought to be at risk because of severe personality problems. Formulation has been placed at the heart of this work – the development of good practice in formulation and the means of examining the impact of formulation on risk management is therefore paramount to the demonstration of the effectiveness of the approach taken.

This work is ongoing but preliminary findings are promising (Ramsden *et al*, 2014; Shaw *et al*, 2017). To evaluate formulations and their impact, a set of quality standards have been developed, which will allow practitioners to know both whether what they have written is a formulation rather than anything else and to give them a basis for determining its value. Based on the quality standards described in Hart *et al* (2011), these simplified standards are being applied across a wide range of settings and formulations, with a particular focus on risk formulations (see Logan, 2017; NOMS & NHSE, 2015):

1. A formulation should state clearly *what* it is seeking to explain (i.e. the risk, such as sexual violence) and *why* (i.e. the purpose to which the formulation will be put).

2. A formulation should include an indication of the range, depth and quality of the *evidence* upon which is it based, and make clear whether it is a formulation expressed with confidence or whether it is a preliminary formulation.

3. A formulation should account for the *developmental history* of the risk that is its focus and any patterns in its presentation over time.

4. A formulation should provide a *psychological explanation* for the risk. Thus the formulation should:

   a. *organise* information relevant to its purpose

   b. provide a balanced view about areas of vulnerability and areas of strength, including protective factors

   c. *connect* pieces of information about the risk presented in order to create an explanation for it

   d. propose hypotheses about the *activation* and *maintenance* of important risk-relevant behaviours

   e. be developed from an *active collaboration* between its main author and at least one other relevant person

   f. be clearly and coherently *anchored* in relevant psychological theory.

5. A formulation creates *hypotheses* about action to *facilitate change* and therefore guides interventions and their prioritisation. That is it should:

   a. provide a basis for *decisions* about risk management

   b. make explicit reference to *difficulties* that may be encountered and how they could be *overcome*

   c. it should comment on how the client could be both *motivated* and *enabled* to engage with the actions and interventions proposed.

6. A formulation should be *easily understood and relevant* to those for whom it is intended (e.g. other practitioners, legal bodies such as the courts, the client him or herself, his or her carers). That is a formulation should:

   a. be expressed in language that is *accessible* to all those for whom it is intended and avoids unnecessary use of jargon

   b. be *brief* enough to be read easily by the individuals for whom it is intended

   c. be *meaningful* and *add* to what is already known about the client

   d. *avoid* the use of judgmental language

   e. provide a coherent explanation of the risk – that is, *the explanation should make sense*.

Concluding comments

■ SPJ is an approach to risk assessment and management whose objective is to prevent or significantly limit the harm potential presented by the individual under scrutiny.

■ The SPJ approach prioritises the gathering of information relevant to the reason for the risk assessment, the examination of the client in terms of a minimum number of risk factors that the empirical and professional literatures in the field say are important to the particular harmful behaviour the evaluator is seeking to prevent, and on the basis of that examination, careful risk management planning.

■ There exist a variety of sets of SPJ guidance that offer route maps through the risks presented by individual clients. Guidance may be differentiated by the depth or granularity of the evaluations offered (e.g. the RSVP offers a more comprehensive or granular evaluation than the SVR-20 V2) and by their focus (e.g. sexual violence using the RSVP, general violence using the HCR-20 V3). More granular evaluations are recommended for use by more experienced practitioners. In addition, more granular evaluations are characterised by a greater focus on the relevance of risk factors to risk in the individual case, and to the important but sophisticated process of formulation and scenario planning.

References and further reading

Boer DP, Hart SD, Kropp PR & Webster C (2017) *Manual for Version 2 of the Sexual Violence Risk-20: Structured professional judgment guidelines for assessing and managing risk of sexual violence*. Vancouver, Canada: Protect International Risk and Safety Services Inc.

Douglas KS, Hart SD, Webster CD, Belfrage H, Guy LS & Wilson CW (2014) *Historical-Clinical-Risk Management-20, version 3* (HCR-20 V3): Development and overview. *International Journal of Forensic Mental Health* **13** 93–108. DOI: 10.1080/14999013.2014.906519.

Hart SD, Douglas KS & Guy LS (2016) The structured professional judgment approach to violence risk assessment: Origins, nature, and advances. In: L Craig & M Rettenberger (Vol Eds) and D Boer (Series Ed) *The Wiley Handbook on the Theories, Assessment, Treatment of Sexual Offending: Volume II. Assessment* (pp643–666). Oxford, UK: Wiley.

Hart SD, Sturmey P, Logan C & McMurran MM (2011) Forensic case formulation. *International Journal of Forensic Mental Health* **10** 118–126.

Hart SD, Kropp PK, Laws DR, Klaver J, Logan C & Watt KA (2003) *The Risk for Sexual Violence Protocol: Structured professional guidelines for assessing risk of sexual violence*. Mental Health, Law and Policy Institute. Vancouver, Canada: Simon Fraser University.

Laws DR & O'Donohue W (2008) *Sexual Deviance: Theory, assessment and treatment* (2nd ed.). New York: Guilford Press.

Logan C (2017) Formulation for forensic practitioners. In: R Roesch and A Cook (Eds) *Handbook of Forensic Mental Health Services* (pp153–178). New York: Routledge.

National Offender Management Service & NHS England (2015) *Working with Personality Disordered Offenders: A practitioner's guide* [online]. Available at: https://www.gov.uk/government/uploads/system/uploads/attachment_data/file/468891/NOMS-Working_with_offenders_with_personality_disorder.pdf (accessed December 2018).

Phenix A & Hoberman H (2016) (Eds) *Sexual Offenders: Predisposing antecedents, assessments and management*. New York: Springer.

Ramsden J, Lowton M & Joyes E (2014) The impact of case formulation focussed consultation on criminal justice staff and their attitudes to work with personality disorder. *Mental Health Review Journal* **19** 124–130. DOI: 10.1108/MHRJ-12-2013-0039.

Shaw J, Higgins C & Quartey C (2017) The impact of collaborative case formulation with high risk offenders with personality disorder. *Journal of Forensic Psychiatry and Psychology* **28** 777–789.

Sturmey P & McMurran M (Eds) (2011) *Forensic Case Formulation*. Chichester: Wiley-Blackwell.

Ward T, Polaschek DLL & Beech AR (2006) *Theories of Sexual Offending*. Chichester: Wiley.

Ward T & Stewart CA (2003) Good lives and the rehabilitation of sexual offenders. In: T Ward, DR Laws & S Hudson (Eds) *Sexual Deviance: Issues and controversies*. Thousand Oaks, CA: Sage.

Chapter 16:
Intellectual disability and violence – minding the gaps

By Beate Eusterschulte

'What we know is a drop, what we don't know is an ocean.'
Sir Isaac Newton

Individuals with intellectual disability who present to mental health services in forensic psychiatric or correctional settings often require assessment and treatment for a variety of complex, often overlapping needs and associated risks. Yet our understanding of the optimal approaches toward assessment and treatment remain limited when compared to other mental health conditions (see Chapter 3). This chapter considers the gaps in our knowledge and suggests pragmatic approaches towards employing effective risk management strategies.

The knowledge gap

In the broadest terms, epidemiological research in the field of intellectual disability is very limited compared to that for other psychiatric disorders. The reasons for this are diverse in nature. According to data of the World Health Organization, intellectual disability is likely to occur in 1-3% of the general population. The considerable differences in population prevalence figures are sometimes due to the application of different diagnostic criteria across studies.

People with intellectual disabilities are more vulnerable to the development of psychological disorders, so that they require higher levels of medical attention and care. The forms of these psychological disorders frequently differ from those presented in classic psychiatric diagnostic criteria. A well-accepted standardised set of diagnostic criteria as the prerequisite for targeted treatment has not yet been established.

The health care gap

The UN Convention on the Rights of Persons with Disabilities (CRPD) (2006) was intended to promote equality of opportunity for persons with intellectual disability, prevent discrimination and advance inclusion. The principle of equality of opportunity to access and receive medical/psychiatric care is also an important aspect of the Convention. However, there is often a shortage of corresponding clinics and experts who can provide this medical care. Country-specific differences can be observed (Crocker *et al*, 2017, pp3–61).

The recording of somatic illnesses is particularly important. The physical health of persons with intellectual disabilities is generally poorer compared to that of the general population (Emerson *et al*, 2012). Overall life expectancy is typically shorter and individuals are constitutionally more prone to neurological disorders and medical conditions that must be taken into account with regard to therapy planning and treatment with medication.

Links with violence risk: the research gap

While there is extensive research on the correlation between schizophrenia and violence, for example, there is only a limited number of studies on the correlation between intellectual disability and violence. In Europe, research results come mostly from the UK, and occasionally from other European countries.

The proportion of persons with an intellectual disability is much higher in forensic psychiatric units, but also in the general penitentiary system (Casey & Keilitz, 1990; Hall, 1999; Hodgins, 1992) compared to the total population. But here as well, the prevalence figures referenced in the literature vary between 0.5% and 45% depending on the population studied (prison, forensic hospital, police station, outpatient setting), the selected criteria for the diagnosis of intellectual disability (e.g. including borderline intellectual functioning with an IQ < 85, only intellectual disability in the narrower sense with an IQ < 70), and the diagnostic method used (overview in Lindsay, 2002). A proportion of approximately 10% would represent a relatively good approximation for forensic hospitals in Germany.

The obvious conclusion that people with intellectual disability commit crimes more frequently due to their disability does not suffice: in addition to an indisputably higher risk of aggressive behavior (e.g. Hodgins, 1992). Some studies suggest a higher success rate in solving cases owing to the accused having less successful strategies for concealing the offense. Individuals facing criminal proceedings may also have greater 'vulnerability vis-à-vis the judicial system' through having less knowledge of their own rights, being prone to suggestibility during hearings, and having poorer representation before the court (see Casey & Keilitz, 1990). It is also unclear whether intellectual disability itself leads to higher rates of delinquency.

Another problem when researching any link with violence is the relatively high comorbidity of other mental health conditions – sometimes as high a total prevalence as 40.9% (Cooper *et al*, 2007). In the group of forensic psychiatric patients with intellectual disability, the comorbidity rate is once again significantly higher. In a meta-analysis, Hobson and Rose (2008) found varying rates of prevalence of psychological disorders of up to 74.5% depending on the methodology and sample used. The most frequently diagnosed mental disorders were schizophrenia and psychotic disorders, with rates up to 44%. In a separate analysis of 80 intellectually disabled offenders who were imprisoned between 2000 and 2019 in the German state of Hesse (84% with mild intellectual disability, 16% with moderate intellectual disability), comorbid mental disorders were diagnosed in accordance with ICD-10 in 89% of all cases. The most frequent disorders were substance use disorders (46%), personality disorders (36%), schizophrenia (28%) and paraphilic disorders (6%).

In view of the possible existence of comorbid disorders, there must be a particular focus on the diagnostic clarification of anti-social personality traits (entries in the German Federal Central Register, antisocial/dissocial personality disorder, disorder of social behavior, PCL:SV score, previous hospitalisations in child and adolescent psychiatric clinics), substance use disorders, paraphilic and schizophrenic disorders.

It should be noted that psychopathological forms of mental disorders in intellectually disabled persons do not always necessarily meet the classic ICD-10 or DSM IV/5 criteria, and that intellectually disabled patients are often limited in their ability to describe these symptoms in specific terms. This results in an overall tendency towards under-diagnosis with the risk that the crucial factors in delinquency are not identified under the circumstances.

In particular, the diagnosis of personality disorders is of fundamental importance with regard to the precise classification of behavioral abnormalities, the development of treatment strategies and the risk of recidivism. However, there are very few systematic studies on the occurrence of personality disorders in intellectually disabled persons. In a literature review, Alexander and Cooray (2003) came to the conclusion that the range of variation in the published prevalence rates between 1% and 92% could hardly be explained by genuine differences in the samples. They suggest that more attention must be paid to delayed personality development (i.e. a valid diagnosis can only be stated from age 21 years); any differences in the classification systems; the blurring between behaviors associated with disability and characteristics of personality disorders; the specific manifestations of mental disorders in the individual case; and any shortcomings in the methods of data acquisition.

However, there is no doubt that particularly persons with mild intellectual disability can develop personality disorders (Voss, 2014). With regard to prevalence and significance in the forensic context, Lindsay *et al* (2006) found personality disorders in just under 40% of the patients across three treatment settings (community, medium-security and high-security), whereby an antisocial personality was diagnosed most frequently (22%). In a second study, the authors examined the connection between personality disorder and various measures of the risk of recidivism, which was well documented for other patient groups, and stated that in particular there was a significant correlation with the prediction of 'generally' violent behavior.

Due to limited cognitive, social and daily living skills, a systematic analysis of the environment at the time an offense is committed is also of considerable importance. Due to insufficient consideration of these limitations, persons with intellectual disabilities often experience excessive pressure, for example, through exploitation by peers that can lead to criminal actions. These factors need to be included in any analysis of delinquency.

The classification of harm gap

The blurring of classification systems that make research in this area more difficult are found not only in the assessment of intellectual disability itself and of comorbid disorders (diagnostic gap); this blurring is also found in the differing understanding of violence (harm definition gap). While on the one hand aggressive behavior is frequently defined as 'challenging behavior' and thus part of communicative behavior (Murphy & Clare, 2012), the same behavior in other contexts may be defined as violent behavior under the circumstances.

This can mean that figures for the frequency of violent behavior in intellectually disabled persons vary considerably. The real problem thus arises that issues of criminal responsibility, risk assessment and management of violent behavior are not discussed in numerous cases.

The accuracy of risk prediction gap

Studies showed that offenders with intellectual disability do not differ from the overall group of mentally ill offenders in many respects. Here as well, the offenders are young, male and have a previous history of violence. This leads to the consideration that the classic risk assessment instruments also have acceptable predictive validity for this group. The scope of research that examines the applicability of the risk assessment instruments to the specific subgroup of persons with intellectual disability is still limited.

■ With regard to the structured risk measurement of repeated (violent) offenses, structured schemes applicable to generic forensic population have demonstrated some predictive capacity (e.g. HCR-20, VRAG, PCL: SV). For an overview, see the systematic review by Hounsome *et al* (2018)).

■ Several authors have proposed modified assessment criteria for the individual risk factors to better adapt them to this specific group of patients, e.g. Pouls & Jeandarme (2014) for PCL-R and PCL-SV; Boer *et al* (2010a; 2010b) for HCR-20 and SVR-20; Boer *et al* (1997) for SVR-20. However, upon review, these have not substantially improved the predictive quality of the instruments up to now.

■ Boer *et al* (2007) use a specifically expanded approach with the Assessment of Risk and Manageability for Individuals with Developmental, Intellectual, or Learning Limitations who Offend (ARMIDILLO). This instrument is available in a version for sex offenders (http://armidilo. net/). In a comparative study (Blacker *et al*, 2011) with multiple predictive methods, the instrument was the most reliable in predicting the risk of relevant recidivism in sex offenders with intellectual disability.

■ The majority of studies in this area refer to groups of offenders with mild to moderate intellectual disability; the applicability to the total group of offenders with intellectual disability including specific subgroups, such as women or persons with severe intellectual disability, has not been documented up to now.

■ There have not been any studies on protective factors so far.

■ Beyond recidivism with violent offenses, the assessment of the intramural (i.e. inside the hospital, during hospital order treatment) risk of violence is becoming increasingly important: the data with regard to SPJ instruments is not only very limited, but also very heterogeneous. Predictive validity for offenders with intellectual disabilities was shown in individual studies, e.g. HCR-20 (O´Shea *et al*, 2015) or VRAG (Pouls & Jeandarme, 2018).

Criminogenic needs – no gap?

Offenders with intellectual disability differ very little from other patient groups in their criminogenic needs.

Relevant identified factors may include reduced introspection; emotional deficits and lack of ability to see things from different perspectives; lack of social skills; a dysfunctional environment of inadequate social support associated with a pronounced dissocial lifestyle; the lack of ability to plan or to anticipate consequences of behavior; reduced impulse control; low frustration tolerance; immature sexuality; dissocial personality traits up to and including features of psychopathic personality disorder; lack of integration of social norms and values; an unrealistic, uncritical perception of self and their possibilities; and low self-esteem.

These characteristics, combined with wishes that are partially experienced as urgent (through a reduced ability to delay gratification) but which are nonetheless frequently frustrated, such as desires for sexual activity, social assertion or material possessions, can lead to delinquent behaviors.

The goals of therapy therefore include:

- acquisition of social and action competence
- promotion of emotion perception and expression
- adoption of social norms and values
- teaching problem-solving skills
- promotion of self-esteem and independence with acceptance of responsibility for one's own actions
- improvement of impulse and anger control
- development of a realistic self-perception and outlook on life subject to the acknowledgment of one's own dangerousness
- development of a meaningful use of leisure time
- sometimes detachment and dissociation from the family in order to be able to lead a life free from crime within a protective facility.

In particular, due to frequently complex problems and limited cognitive and social skills, treatment should be provided on specialised wards with specific treatment programmes in order to adequately address the criminogenic needs. However, a survey by Kestel (2010) showed, for example, that in Germany only a few of the forensic psychiatric clinics maintained corresponding departments (for details, see Weber, 2012).

The treatment of offenders with intellectual disabilities should be expected to be based on the established forensic rehabilitation models, the risk-need-responsivity (RNR) principle, the Good Lives model (GLM) and the recidivism prevention model (Müller *et al*, 2017).

Conclusion

In view of the numerous evidence gaps stated above, the following points should be taken into account in research and practice in the future:

- Intellectual disability and comorbid disorders require consistent, standardised diagnostic instruments and procedures. The Diagnostic Manual-Intellectual Disability (Fletcher *et al*, (2017) could be a promising guide.

- Certain diagnostic subgroups may show different risks of recidivism. Evidence in this regard should be included in structured risk assessment instruments. This applies particularly to the risk of intramural violence as well.

- As for mainstream offenders, there is a need for the further development of structured assessment instruments with protective factors for offenders with intellectual disability (e.g. SAPROF: De Vogel *et al*, 2012).

- Evidence for other biopsychosocial factors that support effective risk assessment and effective risk management would be desirable.

- Given the increasing importance of fundamental rights and freedoms in forensic psychiatry, research on the cumulative effects of the gaps discussed above on length of stay in forensic-psychiatric services is vital.

References

Alexander R & Cooray S (2003) Diagnosis of personality disorders in learning disability. *British Journal of Psychiatry* **182** (suppl. 44) 28–31.

Blacker J, Beech AR, Wilcox DT & Boer DP (2011) The assessment of dynamic risk and recidivism in a sample of special needs sexual offenders. *Psychology, Crime and Law* **17** 75–92.

Boer DP, Frize M, Pappas R, Morrissey C & Lindsay WR (2010a) Suggested Adaptions to the HCR-20 for Offenders with Intellectual Disabilities. In: LA Craig, WR Lindsay & KD Browne (Eds) *Assessment and Treatment of Sexual Offenders with Intellectual Disabilities.* New York: Wiley (pp177–192).

Boer DP, Frize M, Pappas R, Morrissey C & Lindsay WR (2010b) Suggested Adaptions to the SVR-20 for Offenders with Intellectual Disabilities. In LA Craig, WR Lindsay & KD Browne (Eds) *Assessment and Treatment of Sexual Offenders with Intellectual Disabilities.* New York: Wiley (pp193–209).

Boer DP, Hart SD, Kropp PR & Webster CD (1997) Manual for the Sexual Violence Risk – 20. Professional Guidelines for Assessing Risk of Sexual Violence. Burnaby, BC, Canada, Simon Fraser University, Mental Health, Law, and Policy Institute.

Boer DP, McVilly KR & Lambrick F (2007) Contextualising Risk in the Assessment of Intellectually Disabled Individuals. *Sexual Offender Treatment* **2** (2).

Casey P & Keilitz I (1990) Estimating the prevalence of learning disabled and mentally retarded juvenile offenders. In PE Leone (Ed) *Understanding Troubled and Troubling Youth.* Newbury Park: Sage.

Cooper SA, Smiley E, Morrison J, Williamson A & Allan L (2007) Mentally ill – Health in adults with intellectual disabilities: Prevalence and associated factors. *British Journal of Psychiatry* **190** 27–35.

Crocker AG, Livingston JD & Leclair MC (2017) Forensic mental health systems internationally. In: R Roesch & A Cook (Eds.) *International Perspectives on Forensic Mental Health. Handbook of forensic mental health services.* New York, NY, US: Routledge/Taylor & Francis Group (pp3-76).

De Vogel V, de Ruiter C, Bouman Y & de Vries Robbé M (2012) *SAPROF. Guidelines for the assessment of protective factors for violence risk (2nd Ed.).* Utrecht: De Forensische Zorgspecialisten.

Eady N, Courtenay K & Strydom A (2015) Pharmacological management of behavioral and psychiatric symptoms in older adults with intellectual disability. *Drugs Aging* **32** 95–102.

Emerson E, Baines S, Allerton L & Welch V (2012) *Health inequalities and people with learning disabilities in the UK: 2012*. Department of Health.

Fletscher R, Barnhill LJ & Cooper SA (2017) *Diagnostic Manual-Intellectual Disability (DM-ID) 2. A Textbook of Diagnosis of Mental Disorders in Persons with Intellectual Disability*. New York: NADD.

Hall I (1999) *Young people with a learning disability in Secure Health and Social Services Care: A descriptive Study*. MPhil Thesis. University of London, St George's Hospital Medical School.

Hobson B & Rose JL (2008) The mental health of people with intellectual disabilities who offend. *The Open Criminology Journal* **1** 12–18.

Hodgins S (1992) Mental disorder, intellectual deficiency and crime: evidence from a birth cohort. *Archives of General Psychiatry* **49** 476–483.

Hounsome J, Whittington R, Brown A, Greenhill B & McGuire J (2018) The structured assessment of violence risk in adults with intellectual disability: a systematic review. *Journal of Applied Research in Intellectual Disabilities* **31** e1-e17.

Kestel O (2010) *Delinquentes Verhalten bei Menschen mit geistiger Behinderung und deren Situation im Massregelvollzug aus interdisziplinärer Sicht – Explorative Untersuchung eines Praxisfeldes*. Erfurt: Universitätsverlag.

Lindsay WR (2002) Integration of recent reviews on offenders with intellectual disabilities. *Journal of Applied Research in Intellectual Disabilities* **15** 11–199.

Lindsay WR, Hogue T, Taylor JL, Mooney P, Steptoe L, Johnston S, O'Brien G & Smith AHW (2006) Two studies on the prevalence and validity of personality disorder in three forensic intellectual disability samples. *Journal of Forensic Psychiatry and Psychology* **17** 485–506.

Müller JL, Saimeh N, Briken P, Eucker S, Hoffmann K, Koller M, Wolf T, Dudeck M, Hartl C, Jakovljevic AK, Klein V, Knecht G, Müller-Isberner R, Muysers J, Schiltz K, Seifert D, Simon A, Steinböck H, Stuckmann W, Weissbeck W, Wiesemann C & Zeidler R (2017) Standards für die Behandlung im Massregelvollzug nach §§ 63 und 64 StGB. Interdiszipinäre Task-Force der DGPPN. *Nervenarzt* **88** (1) 1–29.

Murphy GH & Clare ICH (2012) Working with offenders or alleged offenders with intellectual disabilities. In: E Emerson, C Hatton C, K Dickson, R Gone, J Broomley & A Caina. *Clinical Psychology and People with Intellectual Disabilities* (pp235–272). Chichester: Wiley.

O´Shea LE, Picchioni MM, McCarthy J, Mason FL, Dickens GL (2015) Predictive validity of the HCR-20 for inpatient aggression: the effect of intellectual disability on accuracy. *Journal of Intellectual Disability Research*. **59** (11) 1042–1054.

Pouls C & Jeandarme I (2014) Psychopathy in offenders with intellectual disabilities: A comparison of the PCL-R and PCL:SV. *International Journal of Forensic Mental Health* **13** 3 207-216, DOI: HYPERLINK "https://doi.org/10.1080/14999013.2014.922138" 10.1080/14999013.2014.922138.

Pouls C & Jeandarme I (2018) Predicting institutional aggression in offenders with intellectual disabilities using the Violence Risk Appraisal Guide. *Journal of Applied Research in Intellectual Disabilities* **31** 265–271.

UN (2006) *Convention on the Rights of Persons with Disabilities (CRPD)* [online]. Available at: https://www.un.org/development/desa/disabilities/convention-on-the-rights-of-persons-with-disabilities.html (accessed December 2018).

Voss T (2014) Persönlichkeitsstörung und Intelligenzminderung. *Forensische Psychiatrie, Psychologie und Kriminologie* **8** 169–174.

Weber E (2012) *Perspektiven für Menschen mit geistiger Behinderung im Massregelvollzug*. Düren: Eigenverlag DHG.

Chapter 17:
Risk assessment and risk management – in what ways must gender enter the fray?

By Tonia Nicholls

Principle

The extent to which risk assessment measures are optimised for use with girls and women is far from settled. Simply because the same variables are predictive of offending and violence in both males and females does not preclude the need for ongoing examination into the value of gender-specific (i.e. variables that are uniquely relevant to female offending) or gender-informed (e.g. attending to gender with respect to determining relevance/ importance) risk assessments. Perhaps even more importantly, risk factors that are seemingly gender-neutral (i.e. predictive of offending in both female and male populations) may possess variable relevance with respect to risk management and treatment. In short, predictive accuracy is not equivalent to conducting a patient needs assessment, constructing interdisciplinary care plans, and implementing risk reduction strategies.

Female offending

The distinction between male and female involvement in crime and violence is not trivial. Epidemiological research, self-reports and administrative data confirm time and again that violence and crime are predominantly the domain of males and that women and girls consistently represent a small minority of individuals in correctional and forensic settings. Based on administrative and government resources, de Vogel and Nicholls (2016) estimated that women and girls comprise just 6%–10% of these populations, respectively. However, experts remind us that the dark figure of crime may be greater for females than for males (e.g. because females tend to offend against people known to them) and that there are pockets of antisocial and criminal behaviour that reflect comparable rates of offending by males and females (e.g. abuse of children and intimate partners) (for a review, see Nicholls *et al*, 2015). Finally, females are more likely than their male counterparts to be in custody for non-violent, often trivial offences.

Moreover, the number of women incarcerated in many developed nations is at an all-time high. For the past several decades, burgeoning numbers of girls and women have been entering prisons. Interestingly, this often is in direct contrast with decreasing numbers of males. Consider, for instance, that the Canadian Correctional Investigator reported an increase of almost 30% in the number of women federally sentenced women in Canada (i.e. two-years, plus a day) in the past ten years; this is in stark contrast to a reduction of 4% among federally incarcerated men within that same time period (Zinger, 2018).

Further concerning is that these increases in the rates of incarceration among women and girls are disproportionately within minority populations, with the number of black and indigenous women growing, in some cases while the number of Caucasian women being incarcerated is dropping.

Specifically, the expanding proportion of inmates who are women is particularly evident among women of colour across the US and those of Aboriginal/Indigenous heritage in places like Canada (Zinger, 2018) and Australia (Walmsley, 2016). Walmsley (2016) reported that the rate of incarcerated women in Australia has doubled in the past decade but that is accounted for almost entirely by Aboriginal women (95%). The differential growth in the female incarcerated population has made the female offender population a priority for researchers, clinicians and decision-makers alike for several decades and there is little evidence the tide is turning (e.g. Walmsley, 2016; Zinger, 2018). Service providers are therefore increasingly suggesting resiliency and crime prevention should be addressed upstream by social services/community providers to prevent women coming into contact with the criminal justice system at all (e.g. UK, 2018). Similarly, experts recommend that diversion and community sentences should be strongly considered when appropriate, and that all aspects of our work with women who come into conflict with the law need to be gender-informed (e.g. see UK, 2018).

Similar but different

Although there remains debate in the literature, proponents of 'feminist/gender-informed' and 'gender-neutral' perspectives largely agree that gender matters. There is widespread agreement that gendered approaches to understanding the emotional experience of crime, informed by the predominant two-factor model (pleasure-displeasure and degree of arousal) provide useful insights into understanding the extent to which the motivations for criminal behaviour, and thus the most efficacious interventions, might differ by gender (eg. a community versus custody). Theory (e.g. the responsivity principle of the RNR model; bio-psycho-social model) and qualitative and quantitative research findings alike suggest that although the same variables are relevant to both male and female offending, females experience some shared risk factors to a greater degree than males (e.g. history of childhood abuse, victimisation as an adult, difficulty with child rearing, self-worth, autonomy, intimate relationships and low socio-economic status) (UK, 2018).

Research in forensic and correctional samples demonstrates that women share many characteristics with their male counterparts but have unique profiles (for reviews, see de Vogel & Nicholls, 2016; de Vogel *et al*, 2019; Nicholls *et al*, 2015). Compared to men, women may be particularly negatively affected by the disempowering environment of psychiatric and correctional institutions. For instance, due to higher rates of victimisation and associated trauma and resulting mental health and behavioural needs, such as self-harm and suicide, female offenders may find the experience of being an inmate or an inpatient to be particularly stressful (e.g. Covington & Bloom, 1999). Finally, compared to male offenders, women offenders are more often the primary care providers of dependent children and are differentially harmed by the stigma of being identified as an offender (UK, 2018). It stands to reason that community sentences versus custody is preferable for low risk/ non-violent women as a means of reducing the disruption to the individual and to families. Similarly, reintegration efforts with women inmates need to be particularly attentive to empowering women to enter the workforce through education and employment support (UK, 2018).

Women and girls who come into contact with the law, regardless of whether they enter the system via forensic or correctional gates, present with profiles that are overlapping but distinct from males representative of the same populations. Female offenders generally are less entrenched in criminal lifestyles, meaning they often have less extensive criminal histories and less diverse forms of offending in their histories; this translates into important differences in treatment needs. Female offenders are less likely to hold pro-criminal attitudes and they typically have lower rates of prior offending and recidivism than their male counterparts, particularly when it comes to violent and sexual offences (e.g. UK, 2018). The National Trajectory Project, examining persons found Not Criminally Responsible on Account of Mental Disorder (NCRMD) in Canada demonstrated that although women spent less time in custody and/or under the supervision of the Review Board, and had similar index offences, they were significantly less likely to have extensive criminal histories and were significantly less likely to reoffend.

Particularly compelling is evidence that the life course persistent pathway (i.e. lengthy, persistent criminal careers) is virtually non-existent in female samples, comprising as little as 1% of a sample of female offenders. Similarly, although it is widely recognised that childhood adversity and violence is also relevant to male offending (e.g. HCR-20-item H8 – traumatic experiences; RNR –family/ marital relationships; VRAG –lived with biological parents), female offending is thought to be propelled more often by a history that is marred by trauma, dysfunctional relationships, economic hardship, difficulties with substance use and problem solving (e.g. UK, 2018; though, see Andrews *et al*, 2012). Evidence that girls and women make their way into offending via somewhat unique pathways suggests that the pathway to desistance and successful community reintegration may also need to be gender-specific. Consistent with this perspective, a recent rapid evidence assessment concluded that women's offending is related to antisocial personality, antisocial peers and substance abuse, but found that gender-responsive interventions yielded superior outcomes to gender-neutral approaches (Stewart & Gobeil, 2015).

Assessment

Lateral and downward extensions of risk assessment measures to women and girls reflect the assumption that violence risk assessment schemes should function equally well within female and male populations. That the theoretical and quantitative foundation of these measures had been derived almost exclusively from work with males had been largely ignored until the past decade. As Cooke and Logan (2018) recently observed, it is as if women are treated as 'funny-shaped men' (p198). Although considerably more work remains (e.g. evaluating the psychometric properties of measures such as the FAM (de Vogel *et al*, 2019)) we now have a handful of meta analyses and extensive reviews that provide considerable evidence that most variables relevant to the assessment of violence in men also are relevant to an assessment of the risk of violence among females, though not necessarily equally.

A forensic assessment should begin with a thorough consideration of the available empirical evidence. For instance, meta analyses of the 'Big Eight' and examinations of the LS/CMI and YLS/CMI specifically suggest the interaction of gender and risk is minimal, or even favours the validity of assessments with female offenders. Similarly, research, including meta analyses, with the HCR-20 has demonstrated that the measure largely performs well with women, a fact widely acknowledged by the authors of one of the only measures developed explicitly for the assessment of violence in women (i.e. the FAM (see de Vogel *et al*, 2019)). Similarly, studies with the Short-Term Assessment of Risk and Treatability (START) have generally demonstrated strong psychometric properties with women. For instance a recent systematic review and meta analysis concluded that the START had stronger predictive validity for females (though note that they were unable to replicate these findings in a later study).

Despite the relevance of established risk assessment measures for assessing violence risk with women, commentators agree that there are risk factors that are of particular importance when assessing and treating female offenders. Landmark studies, such as the MacArthur study (Monahan *et al*, 2001), have revealed the substantial overlap in risk factors as well as variables that have a differential impact on women. For instance, substance abuse, intellectual disabilities and severe psychiatric disorders might have a more substantial effect on violence in women than in men. As we noted above, women are similar but different; there are variables that are more commonly of concern to women (e.g. childhood sexual abuse; sexual assaults across the lifespan), others that appear to have a differential effect on female populations (e.g. social support/relationships) and variables seemingly unique to females (e.g. pregnancy at a young age; prostitution) (de Vogel *et al*, 2019). Acknowledging considerable overlap in risk variables, de Vogel *et al* (2019) recently concluded that multiple reviews of existing violence risk assessment measures with women and girls have found that the predictive validity is modest and further development and research is required.

Research at the intersection of risk assessment and gender suggests that risk assessments need to be attentive to the well-established risk variables and should additionally address gender-specific risk factors relating to women (e.g. a history of non-suicidal self-injury), involvement in sex work, and pregnancy experienced at a young age. For instance, experts who have been highly attentive to gender-informed evaluations recommend using the well-established HCR-20 *and* the Female Additional Manual (de Vogel *et al*, 2019). Similarly, the Early Assessment Risk List-21 is comprised largely of variables relevant to both boys and girls between six and 12 years of age and contains two additional items considered of specific relevance to violence risk among girls (care-giver-daughter interaction and sexual development). Another manner in which assessors can be attentive to gender is to consider the relevance of the item, in addition to its presence. The *extent* to which variables are relevant is now increasingly being recognised in the field generally. Webster (personal communication, October 30, 18) noted that this is the whole point of coding for 'relevance' in the newest version of the HCR-20 V3: '…risk factors may not be equally relevant to all persons' (p51). Many established structured professional judgment measures (e.g. the HCR-20, SARA, START, START:AV) prompt assessors to consider the importance of individual variables. For example, the START/START:AV include 'key items' – strengths of the individual that are thought to be particularly important to facilitating recovery and/or buffering the individual from deteriorating mental health or escalating risk. Similarly, 'critical items' refer to red flags – vulnerabilities that are known to be especially pertinent to prior offences or similar critical events for that individual.

In sum, when it comes to violence risk assessments, 'Gender neutrality is the rule and gender specificity is the exception' (Andrews *et al*, 2012, p119). Assessors should adopt measures with defensible psychometric properties relevant to the population (e.g. considering the individual's age, gender, culture) and the nature of risk being assessed, keeping in mind the importance of considering the relevance of the variables to the individual and the extent to which any additional (gender-specific or otherwise) variables should be taken into consideration. Finally, depending on the nature of the measure(s) used, mental health professionals will want to give careful consideration to the meaning ascribed to risk bins/categories or cut-off scores, given concerns that over-intervening with low risk individuals may be particularly relevant to females (Andrews *et al*, 2012).

Treatment

Similar to the risk assessment field, gender neutrality is a common inference based on an extensive literature examining correctional treatment (Andrews *et al*, 2012); however, there is also evidence that gender-informed interventions yield superior violence/offending reduction among female offenders (Stewart & Gobeil, 2015). Despite ongoing debate in the field, there is widespread agreement that equivalent predictive accuracy does not equate to equivalent risks, needs and strengths. In other words, acknowledging that the same risk/protective factors are predictive of violence is not to deny gender inequities or the value of gender-specific treatment approaches. It is not evidence that the two genders have the same degree of those risks/strengths, that they have similar offending histories, life experiences or that the genders have comparable opportunities or experiences of discrimination, marginalisation and abuse.

Moreover, proponents of both gender-informed and gender-neutral perspectives acknowledge that a treatment developed for use with men will be unlikely to provide the same efficacy as interventions developed with the specific needs of women in mind. Rather, gender is well-recognised as an important consideration in how best to engage and motivate women (Andrews *et al*, 2012; Stewart & Gobeil, 2015; UK, 2018). Lifespan trajectories leading to offending and the characteristics of the offences perpetrated by women illuminate the importance of adopting a gender-lens when planning for prevention, management and treatment.

Gender-informed models of women's services largely reflect a consideration of the Pathways perspective and assert that the profound differences between men's and women's social (e.g. victimisation, trauma, substance abuse) and economic lives (e.g. homelessness, poverty) carve out the routes that bring women into the criminal justice system. Consistent with this perspective are criticisms of much of the risk management and treatment literature which some scholars have asserted tend to locate the problem of criminal involvement largely within the individual, providing insufficient emphasis on socio-structural inequalities that would be identified if we adopted a more macro-level perspective, particularly with respect to female offenders, and perhaps specifically among women of colour. There is also a body of work that suggests that women's motivations for offending may be unique, though the findings are often equivocal.

Following Martinson's (1976) seminal article asserting that 'Nothing Works', several watershed documents have been published attempting to ascertain 'What Works' with female offenders. Covington and Bloom (2006) provided a blueprint for gender-responsive services, calling for:

1. An acknowledgement that gender makes a difference.
2. An environment based on safety, respect and dignity.
3. Policies, practices and programmes that promote healthy connections and relationships.
4. Comprehensive, integrated and culturally relevant services for substance abuse, trauma and mental health.
5. Opportunities to improve socio-economic conditions.
6. A system of community supervision and re-entry with comprehensive, collaborative services.

Covington and Bloom (2006) further proposed that the theoretical foundations reflect theories of trauma. There can be little question that women and girls involved with the criminal justice system have trauma relevant risks and needs that typically are on par with, or are even in considerable excess of, their male counterparts (e.g. histories of physical and sexual abuse that have led to the destabilisation of personal and psychological health, victimisation as an adult, and difficulty with substances). Yet it is essential to note that the integration of variables of particular relevance to treating women offenders (e.g. trauma, parenting) needs to be with respect to how those variables are relevant to/may interfere with robust risk factors (e.g. antisocial attitudes, antisocial peers, substance abuse).

To demonstrate, research to date indicates that interventions that have a singular focus on trauma, to the neglect of these well-documented 'gender-neutral risk factors', are ineffective in reducing women's offending (Stewart & Gobeils, 2015). Similar findings have been reporting for in-custody parenting programmes (Stewart & Gobeils, 2015), whereas multi-target programmes employing cognitive behavioural and gender-responsive approaches that target relevant risk factors are effective in reducing recidivism. For instance, meta-analyses of substance abuse interventions employed with incarcerated women have revealed participants had significantly lower rates of recidivism than non-participants.

Contemporary theories of women's criminality can be used to lay the essential groundwork for the structural elements of programming. For instance, mental health and substance abuse services are integrated; a strengths-based model of treatment shifts the focus from all of the problems the woman has to contend with to the assets she has for developing healthy coping strategies; women-only groups must be seen as essential for primary treatment (substance abuse, trauma) and comprehensive services that must take culture into consideration. Treatment must also acknowledge that women cannot be treated in isolation from their social support systems. It would be difficult to argue that these are anything but fundamental principles of good practice, with males and females.

Polaschek (2012) asserted that the responsivity aspect of the RNR model requires further development, noting that 'why' gender and ethnicity are important is an unexplored aspect of the theory. She also goes on to propose that the implications of the central eight of the RNR model (i.e., history of antisocial behaviour, antisocial personality pattern, antisocial cognition, antisocial associates, family and/or marital, school and/or work, leisure and/or recreation, substance abuse (Andrews *et al*, 2006)) for treatment are not sufficiently established, noting that simply demonstrating that a variable is a correlate of future offending and of interventions that reduce risk does not equate to establishing a casual mechanism (Polaschek, 2012).

> '*A list of broad categories of treatment targets cannot and is not meant to substitute for an adequate understanding of (a) the central mechanisms driving current criminal propensity, and therefore (b) how different risk factors are related to each other, and further (c) how change processes work on these mechanisms for different offenders'* (Polaschek, 2012, p8–9).

Hannah-Moffat (2009) also discussed the limitations of the RNR's gender neutral approach stating that the level of risk differs between 'gendered, stratified and racialized groups' and that the failure to address these differences creates a 'conceptual problem' within the model's framework (p211).

Implications for research and future directions

We now have a reasonably robust literature that has evaluated diverse variables as to their relevance to violence and offending in female samples (e.g. MacArthur Study), and specific risk assessment measures (e.g. HCR-20, START). There is also a growing body of evidence to demonstrate 'what works' to reduce criminal offending within female populations (Stewart & Gobeils, 2015). Yet important knowledge-gaps remain, beginning with our guiding theories. For instance, Polaschek (2012) critiqued the utility of the RNR model to guide interventions generally and emphasised the importance of considering the pathways that lead to criminal behavior to establish more refined theories for women specifically. Further, there is little research that has examined certain subgroups (e.g. women who perpetrate sexual offences) or contexts (e.g. institutional violence within prisons or psychiatric hospitals). There also remains debate in the literature regarding the importance of gender-specific items or measures (e.g. the FAM (for a review, see de Vogel *et al*, 2019; also see Chapter 25)).

Although they appear to have considerable promise generally, and with women specifically, considerably more work is also required to truly understand the contribution of dynamic variables and how we can best operationalise strengths/protective factors (e.g. as *promotive* – i.e. demonstrating a negative correlation with risk, regardless of risk level vs. protective – i.e., demonstrating a buffering or moderating effect on risk similar to resilience, with a larger effect on high risk scenarios vs. low risk scenarios). In particular, the implications of implementing gender-informed perspectives into treatment planning and delivery for recovery and reducing risk and criminal offending/recidivism requires considerably more research.

Conclusions

Evidence-based practice requires the explicit use of the best available evidence available in the relevant literatures. Although there remains important gaps in knowledge with respect to violence risk assessment and risk management with women there will always be more work to be done, and that is no reason to not adopt the best available evidence at any given time. The importance of attending to gender has been firmly embedded as a requirement of professional and ethical guidelines with respect to the provision of general mental health services (e.g. APA, 2007) and forensic mental health services, specifically (APA, 2013). Further, the field's primary guiding theory, the Risk Need Responsivity model (Andrews & Bonta, 1994; 2007; Andrews *et al*, 2006) compels us to consider gender as a responsivity factor. The state of the literature and the evolution of patient-centred/individualised care and gender-informed care has resulted in a call for action among clinicians, policy-makers and researchers to inform a more gender-responsive approach to the assessment and management of violence among female offenders, with diverse international leaders recommending that effective management of violence among women requires a gender informed lens (de Vogel *et al*, 2019).

Mental health service providers should explore how gender and gender identity, as well as other relevant individual and cultural differences, may affect and be related to the basis for people's contact and involvement with the legal system

(APA, 2007; 2013) in their assessments, as well as in subsequently undertaking management and treatment decisions. Earlier chapters in this volume caution us to be wary of the 'perils of the biased "expert"' (see Chapter 2 p27,); Justice Schneider noted, however, all we can do is be wary as 'biases are inevitable' and this certainly seems to be relevant to gender. Research demonstrates that when clinicians attempt to integrate gender-informed perspectives the result is often gender-stereotyping. Therein lies the value of structured risk assessments and risk management plans. This is also a reminder that knowledge translation and continuing education should be a priority for actually implementing gender-informed approaches.

References

Andrews DA & Bonta J (1994) *The Psychology of Criminal Conduct.* Cincinnati, OH: Anderson.

Andrews DA, Bonta J & Wormith JS (2006). The Recent Past and Near Future of Risk and/ or Need Assessment. *Crime & Delinquency* **52**(1) 7-27. doi:10.1177/0011128705281756

Andrews DA, Guzzo L, Raynor P, Rowe RC, Rettinger LJ, Brews A & Wormith JS (2012) Are the major risk/need factors predictive of both female and male reoffending?: a test with the eight domains of the level of service/case management inventory. *International Journal of Offender Therapy and Comparative Criminology* **56** (1) 113–133 doi:10.1177/0306624X10395716.

APA (2007) *Guidelines for Psychological Practice with Girls and Women. A Joint Task Force of APA Divisions 17 and 35* [online]. Available at: http://www.apa.org/practice/guidelines/ girls-and-women.aspx (accessed January 2019).

APA (2013) *Guidelines Forensic Psychology* [online]. Available at: https://www.apa.org/pubs/ journals/features/forensic-psychology.pdf (accessed January 2019).

Cooke D & Logan C (2018) Capturing psychopathic personality: penetrating the mask of sanity through clinical interview. In: CJ Patrick (Ed) *Handbook of Psychopathy: Second Edition* (p189–210). Guilford Publications.

Covington SS & Bloom BE (2006) Gender-responsive treatment and services in correctional settings. *Women and Therapy* **29** (3/4) 9–33 doi: 10.1300/J015v29n03_02.

de Vogel V & Nicholls TL (2016) Gender matters: an introduction to the double special issue on women and girls. *International Journal of Forensic Mental Health* **15** (1) 1–25

de Vogel V, de Vries Robbé M, van Kalmthout W & Place C (2011) Female Additional Manual (FAM). *Additional guidelines to the HCR-20 for assessing risk for violence in women.* English version. Utrecht, The Netherlands: Van der Hoeven Kliniek.

de Vogel V, Wijkman M & de Vries Robbe M (2019) Violence risk assessment in women: The value of the Female Additional Manual. In: Ireland JL, Ireland CA & Birch P (Eds) *Violent and Sexual Offenders: Assessment, treatment and management* (2nd edition). New York: Routledge.

Hannah-Moffat K (2009) Gridlock or mutability: Reconsidering "gender" and risk assessment. *Criminology & Public Policy* **8**(1) 209.

Martinson R (1976) California research at the crossroads. *Crime and Delinquency* **22** 180–191.

Monahan J, Steadman HJ, Silver E, Appelbaum PS, Robbins PC, Mulvey EP, Roth LH, Grisso T & Banks S (2001). *Rethinking Risk Assessment: The MacArthur study of mental disorder and violence.* New York; Oxford; Oxford University Press.

Nicholls TL, Cruise KR, Greig D & Hinz H (2015) Female offenders. In: BL Cutler, PA Zapf (Eds) *APA Handbook of Forensic Psychology, Vol. 2: Criminal investigation, adjudication, and sentencing outcomes* (pp79–123). Washington, DC: American Psychological Association.

Polaschek DLL (2012) An appraisal of the risk-need-responsivity (RNR) model of offender rehabilitation and its application in correctional treatment: The RNR model of offender rehabilitation: An appraisal. *Legal and Criminological Psychology* **17** (1) 1–17 doi:10.1111/ j.2044-8333.2011.02038.x

Stewart L & Gobeil R (2015) Correctional interventions for women offenders: A rapid evidence assessment. *Journal of Criminological Research, Policy and Practice* **1** (3) pp116–130.

UK (2018) Female Offender Strategy [online]. Available at: https://www.gov.uk/government/ publications/female-offender-strategy.

Walmsley R (2016) *World Female Imprisonment List* (3rd ed). London: International Centre for Prison Studies.

Zinger I (2018) *Office of the Correctional Investigator Annual Report 2017-2018* [online]. Available at: http://www.oci-bec.gc.ca/cnt/rpt/annrpt/annrpt20172018-eng.aspx (accessed January 2019).

Chapter 18:
Ethical and practical concerns regarding the current status of risk assessment measures with Aboriginal offenders

By Douglas P Boer

Quite some time ago, it had become clear to me and several of my First Nations (Aboriginal) colleagues, that the Historical-Clinical-Risk-20 (HCR-20) (Webster *et al*, 1997), the premier structured professional judgment (SPJ) guide of the day, was not ideally suited for the assessment of Aboriginal offenders in Canada. A great deal of recent writing has indicated support for our early thoughts in this area: the cultural fairness of using actuarial or SPJ guides with Aboriginal offenders or groups different than those for which the instruments were designed is questionable at best for many reasons which have been elucidated by others at length (e.g. Shepherd & Lewis-Fernandez, 2016; Shepherd & Anthony, 2018) and proven to be particularly problematic in specific cases (e.g. Hart, 2016). There is no evidence that these kinds of devices, developed for mainstream application, are appropriate for Aboriginal offenders[20]. Indeed, there is no general evidence for the cross-cultural validity of actuarial or SPJ risk assessment measures across Aboriginal cultures within Canada (or likely elsewhere where mainstream assessment devices are simply cross-validated – and sometimes poorly – with Aboriginal offender groups).

Elders, particularly Arnold Ritchie and Joseph Couture, advised me some years ago that being labelled with a level of risk was seen as an insult by

---

20 Many professionals currently assess risks of sexual violence using 'actuarial' (statistically-based) devices developed in countries other than their own. This kind of practice can, though, be problematic when, as is likely to be the case, the characteristics of the individual in question differ from those included in the test-development sample. Also, misapplication is also possible not just between countries, but within a country. And finally, within both actuarial and SPJ contexts, there is a 'base-rate problem'. It may be that Aboriginal offenders have particular rates of offending and re-offending.

some Canadian Aboriginal offenders and not reflective of the traits or needs of the person being assessed. As a result, we set about constructing The Risk Management Guide for Aboriginal Offenders (RMGAO; Boer *et al*, 2003). The RMGAO was modelled on the HCR-20 to a certain degree – Risk issues, Management issues, and Guidance issues, but all of the items were derived in a unique manner – through a series of meetings with Elders.

The literature reviewed indicated that, with respect to the Aboriginal groups in British Columbia (which tend to be far from homogeneous in any event), there remains a lack of evidence regarding the identification of relevant risk (client and situational) and protective (and health promotive) factors. As a result, items (see Table 18.1) are rather distinct, but the RMGAO 'is designed to do what risk assessments are supposed to do: that is, provide guidance for the effective management of the offender both in the institution and the community' (Boer *et al*, 2003, p7).

While most of the items are self-explanatory, item 15 refers to 'relevance of Sections 81/84 [of the Canadian Corrections and Conditional Release Act, or CCRA, 1992[21]] to the offender'. These sections of the RMGAO manual, on pages 34–35, refer to the Gladue decision (*R v Gladue*, 1999). The Gladue decision resulted in important changes in how the Correctional Service of Canada (CSC) reported particular circumstances regarding Aboriginal offenders and culturally relevant risk management options available and appropriate to the offender in question (see Boer *et al*, 2003, pages 24–27, and Shepherd & Anthony (2018) for a broader discussion of these issues).

Table 18.1: RMGAO items

1. Traditional teachings, ceremonies and customs
2. Relationship of offender to heritage
3. Child abuse history
4. Historical/generational issues
5. Foster care history
6. Family and marital relationships
7. Alcohol and drug use
8. Impulsive behavior and violence
9. Attitudes regarding offending
10. Psychological or psychiatric issues
11. Self-harm risk

---

21 CCRA 1992, c20, s81; 1995, c42, s21(F) & (3) CCRA 1992, c20, s84; 2012, c1, s66.

| 12. Gains, insights and behavioral changes |
| 13. Support for the victim(s) |
| 14. Support for the offender |
| 15. Relevance of Sections 81/84 to offender |
| 16. Lifestyle stability |
| 17. Self-support skills |
| 18. Supervision attitudes and compliance |
| 19. Risk management plan |
| 20. Unique resiliency factors |

The idea of reaching a 'risk level' itself was eschewed by the RMGAO in favor of what we called a narrative describing the issue of 'risk manageability', which was defined as the 'degree to which an offender's dynamic risk factors (changeable factors) are under control or as the degree to which these factors have been ameliorated' (Boer *et al*, 2003, p9). In our view at that time, any other risk assessment measures (actuarial or SPJ) that might have proven predictive validity with Aboriginal offenders were worthy of consideration in an individual case, but any estimate risk value would only be helpful in guiding placements and treatment intensity as opposed to guiding release and reintegration assessment work.

The RMGAO tried to foster:

'...an optimistic, change-oriented view in which a person's risk is seen as something that can improve, be reduced, and become more manageable over time. All the items in the RMGAO were designed with positive change in mind. It [was] hoped that the offender [could be] seen in a more holistic manner by the RMGAO than by any actuarial instrument or structured clinical guideline instrument currently available. The RMGAO also [took] into account the resilience of the individual and promote[d] the view that an offender [could] recover, change, and attain the goals of finding his own path, as well becoming a responsible community member.' (Boer *et al*, 2003, p11).

Since the Ewert decision (*Ewert v. Canada*, 2015), many authors have noted that cultural sensitivity is not an option but an ethical (if not a legal) requirement. Shepherd and Anthony (2018) have recently noted that the Gladue decision and resulting reports provide a great deal of information that allows 'holistic narrative of the individual's circumstances and options' (p216).

Recently, Hart (2016) provided suggestions for working with 'diversity issues' and Tamatea and Boer (2017) provided suggestions to promote 'culturally responsive practice' in assessment. These suggestions are paraphrased and summarised in Table 18.2.

Table 18.2: Suggestions for culturally responsive practice regarding diversity issues

1. Make sure you try to get either a cultural mentor or advisor as well as a translator if you're interviewing or treating someone who is from a different cultural group.

2. Make sure you identify any potential cultural diversity issues that may bias your assessment, treatment or management work (don't wilfully use inappropriate measures).

3. If you have identified any potential cultural diversity issues that could bias your work, get educated about how such issues could bias your work and reduce its effectiveness.

4. Also, if you have identified any potential cultural issues that could bias your view, try to minimise the effect that such issues could have on your assessment, treatment or man agement work – make sure you include a statement qualifying your opinion in your reports (and whether you think bias could be an issue resulting in limitations to your appraisal).

5. Develop culturally appropriate assessment practices.

6. Increase awareness/decrease bias (we are not always aware of our biases but need to develop that awareness).

7. Address stereotypical beliefs via supervision.

8. Treat cultural issues as part of clinical engagements in general and assessing risk in particular.

9. Engage in educational cultural experiences.

10. Attempt to understand local social support structures.

11. Conduct case conferences with relevant cultural/social advisors.

12. Develop your skills to achieve credibility and trust with clients

13. Develop cultural competence. This takes practice, experience and time – get supervision from a mentor or cultural advisor.

14. Actively seek to discover that which is culturally salient – this information will emerge over time as rapport is established.

15. Build a body of knowledge of 'practice-based evidence' – that which works – new awarenesses; new knowledge and new skills.

In summary, many SPJ risk assessment instruments state that the goal of risk assessment is to guide risk management. The RMGAO posited that that the accurate assessment and description of the latter was more important than the former, and the completion of the former may indeed be a meaningless exercise if we can't assess the latter effectively. The RMGAO stressed the use of a narrative approach in the assessment process in order to develop trust and foster the involvement of the Aboriginal offender in co-operatively developing feasible strategies to attain his treatment needs and reintegration plans. There is no easy way of developing such instruments. As pointed out to me by the Elders (as I am not Aboriginal), the Aboriginal way of ratifying such an assessment protocol of such importance (at least in southern British Columbia at that time) was via the approval of an Elder Council, not via statistical proof of predictive validity. Think about the implications of that for validation research.

References

Boer DP, Couture J, Geddes C & Ritchie A (2003) *Yókw'tól: Risk management guide for Aboriginal Offenders (Research Version)*. Harrison Mills, B.C., Canada: Kwikwéxwelhp Healing Lodge (author).

Ewert v. Canada (2015) FC 1093

Hart SD (2016) Culture and violence risk assessment: The case of Ewert v. Canada. *Journal of Threat Assessment and Management* **3** 76–96. doi:10.1037/tam0000068.

R v Gladue (1999) 1 SCR 688.

Shepherd SM & Lewis-Fernandez R (2016) Forensic risk assessment and cultural diversity: Contemporary challenges and future directions. *Psychology, Public Policy, & Law* **22** (4) 427–438. doi:10.1037/law0000102.

Shepherd SM & Anthony T (2018) Popping the cultural bubble of violence risk assessment tools, *The Journal of Forensic Psychiatry & Psychology* **29** (2) 211–220. DOI: 10.1080/14789949.2017.1354055

Tamatea AJ & Boer DP (2017) Risk assessment and culture: Issues for Research and Practice. In: D Boer (Ed.) *The Wiley Handbook on the Theories, Assessment, and Treatment of Sexual Offending*. Volume II. L Craig & M Rettenberger (Eds.) Assessment (pp1181–1200). Chichester, England: John Wiley & Sons, Ltd.

Webster CD, Douglas KS, Eaves D & Hart SD (1997) *HCR-20: Assessing Risk for Violence, Version 2*. Burnaby, BC: Simon Fraser University.

Chapter 19:
Assessing risk for group-based violence

Stephen D Hart

'Collective fear stimulates herd instinct, and tends to produce ferocity toward those who are not regarded as members of the herd.'
Bertrand Russell (1872-1970)

Mental health professionals tend to conceptualise violence as something that is perpetrated by individuals and caused by intra-individual risk factors. This is understandable, given that the primary focus of mental health assessment and treatment tends to be people who have engaged in serious, repeated, cross-situational violence and who suffer from chronic impairments of psychological and social functioning. But the reality is that much violence – if not most of it – is perpetrated by people whose decisions and behavior are influenced by one or more social groups to which they belong, with which they are affiliated, or with which they identify, and it is often directed at people who do not belong to, are not affiliated with, or do not identify with the same groups. We may call this phenomenon 'collective violence' (e.g. Krug *et al*, 2002) or *group-based violence* (e.g., Hart, 2010; see also Cook *et al*, 2013).

The nature and dynamics of groups

With respect to group-based violence, a group is an identifiable collective of two or more people who interact based in part on shared attitudes, beliefs, norms, values or identity (Hart, 2010; Cook *et al*, 2013). Each group reflects some combination of kinship (shared ancestry, culture or nationality) and collaboration (shared activities or objectives). Examples include: local, national and transnational criminal organisations; cults and new religious movements; families, extended families and clans; and issue-oriented political or other social movements. Insofar as groups constitute part of the social context of violence, they are always relevant when understanding the violence risk of individuals, but sometimes they are crucial – it may be impossible to adequately assess and manage violence risk without understanding the influence of groups. A group may potentiate or mitigate a person's violence risk in ways that are not obvious from an exclusive focus on individual-level risk factors.

Groups can exert a powerful influence over individual decision-making and behavior related to violence through a number of different mechanisms (e.g. Arena & Arrigo, 2005; Borum, 2014; Pynchon & Borum, 1999). The first mechanism is the establishment, evolution and maintenance of intra-individual cognitive structures. The individuals who comprise a group each bring to it their own beliefs, attitudes, values and norms. But once they begin interacting and form a collective, individuals tend to develop consensual ways of thinking and acting, which in turn reinforces group consensus. These consensual beliefs, attitudes, values or norms may differ from – for example, be more polarised (extreme or rigid) than – those initially brought to the group by any individuals. Such consensus is critical for distributed cognition (sharing and extending individual cognitive resources to enhance group decisions and actions).

The second mechanism is modeling. Modeling is vicarious learning through observation of, or instruction by, others. It may or may not involve imitation (practise on the part of the learner). Modeling is particularly effective when the model is a close acquaintance of the learner (e.g. a family member or peer), is perceived by the learner as being high status, or reinforces the learner; thus, other group members make good models.

The third mechanism is the development of a group-based identity; a feeling that one belongs to the group and the incorporation of the group into one's sense of self. A strong group-based identity may exert an influence on thought, feeling and action that is greater than that of a person's individual sense of self. This is particularly true when people have a weak or disturbed sense of self, perceive they are powerless as individuals, or believe a group to which they belong is under threat. Under such conditions, individuals may 'lose' themselves in the group (i.e. fuse their individual sense of self with the group identity), thereby increasing their willingness to fight to protect the group or even sacrifice themselves for the group.

Major categories of group-based violence

Violence by criminal organisations

Criminal organisations can vary greatly in terms of their size, areas of operation, primary activities and structure – from street gangs, prison gangs, bandits and hooligans, to sophisticated networks involved in diverse illegal activities across geopolitical boundaries. Regardless, in all criminal organisations 'violence is a readily accepted and routinely available resource' according to Abadinsky (2016, p4). Indeed, he considers the 'willingness to use illegal violence' to be a core feature of criminal organisations (2016, p2). Some of the violence is between rival criminal organisations or within a criminal organisation, but some is committed in the context of other criminal activity (e.g. robbery, extortion, prostitution, human trafficking).

Violence by terrorist organisations

Terrorist organisations use violence that causes widespread fear to achieve social, political, religious or other ideological goals. These goals range from retribution for perceived wrongs committed by others, to coercing others to comply with the terrorist organisation's socio-political agenda, to observance of religious or spiritual edicts by the organisation's members. Although violence by terrorist organisations has been a fact of life around the world for more than a hundred years, it has become a major national security and public safety concern in the past three decades.

As most forensic mental health professionals have limited education, training and experience with respect to terrorism, it is worth emphasising three points here. First, not all terrorists operate as part of a group. Most have some degree of affiliation with and receive support from a group, but a few are 'lone actors' who develop or implement plans for a violent attack (virtually) on their own (e.g. Borum *et al*, 2012). Second, as discussed by Borum (2015), even when terrorists are members of the same group, they may play very different roles in violence: some are involved in direct action, whereas others are conspirators who play more distal roles such as operational support (directly helping actors), logistical support (indirectly helping actors), or organisational support (directly supporting terrorist organisations rather than specific actors). Third, although terrorists do not necessarily have the typical risk factors associated with general violence, neither are they immune from them. Indeed, those risk factors – including mental health problems such as major mental disorder, personality disorder or substance use – may make people vulnerable to becoming radicalised in their thinking or being recruited into a terrorist group (e.g. Borum, 2014; Corner & Gill, 2015).

Hate crime

Hate crime is violence motivated by prejudice against people who are perceived to have certain personal characteristics considered offensive by the perpetrators. The personal characteristics include such things as nationality, ethnicity, culture/language, religion/spirituality, gender, sexual identity or orientation, age or physical or mental disability. The violence ranges from intimidating communications to homicide or even mass homicide. It is intended to express animus toward and cause fear in not only the people who are directly victimised but, more generally, all people who possess the same personal characteristics.

From the brief description provided here, it is apparent that hate crime resembles terrorist violence. They are similar in terms of the basic underlying dynamic (i.e. the perpetrator's assertion of self-identity as fundamentally different from the victim), as well as the fact that perpetrators may act alone or as part of a group, may play different roles when they act as part of a group, and may have many of the risk factors commonly found in those who commit general violence. Indeed, research supports the view that hate crime and terrorism are more 'close cousins' than 'distant relatives' (Mills *et al*, 2017).

Honour-based violence

This form of violence is motivated by the desire to protect or restore the honour of a family, clan or community (e.g. Kropp *et al*, 2019). The honour is perceived by the perpetrators to have been threatened or harmed by violation of important religious or cultural norms. The concept of honour tends to reflect traditional masculine (patriarchal) views of gender and gender roles – how males and females should act, and how men should respond when females do not act properly.

It is sometimes assumed that honour-based violence is limited to the murder of females by males within Middle Eastern (and in particular Muslim) families, but both these assumptions are incorrect and may reflect a bias in media reports in Western countries (Gill, 2006). This statement is not at all intended to minimise the problem of honour killings, which is a global health concern, but rather to encourage recognition of the fact that honour-based violence itself is diverse in nature, including such acts as female genital mutilation, kidnapping or forcible confinement in the family home, forced marriage, forced abortion, forced or counseled suicide, physical or sexual assault and disfigurement, in addition to homicide. Also, the perpetrators and victims of honour-based violence are diverse with respect to culture, age, gender and acquaintanceship. Perpetrators may act on their own, but in most cases there are multiple people involved who play different roles in the violence.

Recommendations for practice

In light of the discussion above, we recommend the following with respect to the assessment of group-based violence.

Consider group involvement in all assessments of violence risk

Evaluators should always be open to or mindful of the possibility that acts of violence were group-based rather than individual in nature. When reviewing records or conducting interviews with collateral informants or the person of interest, look for evidence that the person's violent actions –

that is, their decisions and behaviour – were influenced by social groups to which they belonged, with which they were affiliated, or with which they identified. To avoid possible confirmatory bias, it is better to routinely look for evidence that violence was group-based than to assume it was not unless or until you encounter obvious or unmistakable evidence.

If it is unclear whether the violence was group-based, it may be helpful to analyse the assessment information gathered twice: first assuming that it was individual, and second assuming that it was group-based. Typically, if the violence was individual, then complicating the assessment to include factors related to group-based violence (see below) will not change the opinions about the person's violence risk.

Consider the presence and relevance or factors related to individual violence

It is always important to consider risk factors at the individual level, even when the person's violence is clearly group based. Members of the same group are not identical; some have different or more problems with personal adjustment than others, which may affect their willingness or capacity to play various roles with respect to group-based violence. Also, the fact that someone has a history of group-based violence does not mean that they cannot pose a risk for individual violence. Individual violence risk should be investigated using standard procedures (e.g. Douglas *et al*, 2013).

Consider the presence and relevance or factors related to group-based violence

When assessing risk for group-based violence, it is important to consider risk factors from beyond the individual level – for example, those that reflect how the person relates to the group in question, how the group itself is structured and operates, and how the group relates to rival groups or functions in the broader social context. The *Multi-Level Guidelines* (Cook *et al*, 2013) is a set of structured professional judgment guidelines that includes general factors from these various levels, which appear to be important across all kinds of groups. But there are also some tools designed for use with specific kinds of violence, such as terrorism (Lloyd & Dean, 2015; Meloy, 2018; Pressman & Flockton, 2012), hate crimes (Dunbar *et al*, 2016), and honour-based violence (Kropp *et al*, 2019).

Consult with professionals who have relevant expertise

It is impossible to be expert at everything. Forensic mental health professionals cannot have expertise in the nature, history, structure and operations of all the groups they may encounter in the course of their risk assessments. (Think of it: Albanian clans scattered throughout Scandinavia, Italian anarchist anti-globalisation protesters, radical animal rights or environmental groups operating around the world, Macanese triads, extremist Christian anti-abortion activists in the United States, UK football hooligans, indigenous Canadian prison gangs, neo-Nazis, sovereign citizens in Australia, Central American street gangs, transphobic thugs in Jamaica, nationalist motorcycle gangs in Russia, 'Ndràngheta based in Europe, charismatic cults from Korea, Sikh separatists in Pakistan...) Similarly, people who are experts in one or more of those groups are unlikely to have training in or experience with violence risk assessment of individuals. For this reason, group-based violence is best assessed by a multi-disciplinary team of professionals.

References and further reading

Abadinsky H (2016) *Organized crime (10th ed)*. Belmont, MA: Wadsworth.

Arena MP & Arrigo BA (2005) Social psychology, terrorism, and identity: a preliminary re-examination of theory, culture, self, and society. *Behavioral Sciences & the Law* **23** 485–506.

Borum R (2014) Psychological vulnerabilities and propensities for involvement in violent extremism. *Behavioral Sciences & the Law* **32** 286–305.

Borum R (2015) Assessing risk for terrorism involvement. *Journal of Threat Assessment and Management* **2** 63–87.

Borum R, Fein R & Vossekuil B (2012) A dimensional approach to analyzing lone offender terrorism. *Aggression and Violent Behavior* **17** 389–396.

Cook AN, Hart SD & Kropp PR (2013) *Multi-Level Guidelines for the assessment and management of group-based violence, Version 1*. Burnaby, Canada: Mental Health, Law, & Policy Institute, Simon Fraser University.

Corner E & Gill P (2015) A false dichotomy? Mental illness and lone-actor terrorism. *Law and Human Behavior* **39** 23–34.

Douglas KS, Hart SD, Webster CD & Belfrage H (2013) *HCR-20 V3: Assessing risk of violence – User guide*. Burnaby, Canada: Mental Health, Law, and Policy Institute, Simon Fraser University.

Dunbar E, Blanco A & Crèvecoeur-MacPhail DA (Eds) (2016) *The psychology of hate crimes as domestic terrorism: U.S. and global issues*. Santa Barbara, CA: Praeger.

Gill A (2006) Patriarchal violence in the name of 'honour'. *International Journal of Criminal Justice Sciences* **1** 1–12.

Hart SD (2010) Risk for terrorism: A multi-level, multi-disciplinary approach to threat assessment. In: M Scalora (Chair) *The Psychology of Terrorism and Extremist Violence*. Invited address, annual meeting of the American Psychology-Law Society (Div. 41 of the American Psychological Association), Vancouver, Canada.

Kropp PR, Belfrage H & Hart SD (2019) *Assessment of risk for honour based violence (PATRIARCH), Version 2: User manual*. Vancouver, Canada: Protect International Risk and Safety Services Inc.

Krug EG, Dahlberg LL, Mercy JA, Zwi AB & Lozano R (Eds) (2002) *World report on violence and health*. Geneva: World Health Organization.

Lloyd M & Dean C (2015) The development of structured guidelines for assessing risk in extremist offenders. *Journal of Threat Assessment and Management* **2** 40–52.

Meloy JR (2018) The operational development and empirical testing of the Terrorist Radicalization Assessment Protocol (TRAP-18). *Journal of Personality Assessment* **100** (5) 1–10.

Mills CE, Freilich JD & Chermak SM (2017) Extreme hatred: Revisiting the hate crime and terrorism relationship to determine whether they are "Close Cousins" or "Distant Relatives". *Crime & Delinquency* **63** 1191–1223.

Pressman DE & Flockton J (2012) Calibrating risk for violent political extremist and terrorists: The VERA 2 structured assessment. *British Journal of Forensic Practice* **14** 237–251.

Pynchon MR & Borum R (1999) Assessing threats of targeted group violence: Contributions from social psychology. *Behavioral Sciences & the Law* **17** 339–355.

Section 5
Treatment/
transition issues

Chapter 20:
Toward secure recovery in forensic care[22]

By Alexander IF Simpson

'Secure recovery' is the application of recovery-oriented principles to the practice of forensic mental health care. It is a set of ideas that helps to guide those who care for people with forensic mental health needs (FMHN) and who work in teams within systems of care. The aim is to help people progressively develop, in safety, 'a life worth living'. A major task is to help them understand the problems of illness and the role abuse and trauma may have had in their lives. Over recent years we have learned a great deal about the nature of the experiences and requirements of people with FMHN as they develop a life worth living. A good deal, too, has also been learned about how staff should apply the principles of good recovery-oriented forensic care.

The nature of recovery for forensic clients can be complex. But, by taking the ideas from recovery principles in general and using approaches to measure progress, clinicians and researchers are much more knowledgeable about this field than they were 10 years ago. Recovery-oriented schemes specific to forensic settings are still lacking, although Shinkfield and Ogloff (2014), in their review of forensic outcome measures, found six. This list of six included two recovery-centred schemes originating in general mental health – the Illness Management and Recovery Scales and the Mental Health Recovery Measure – and one designed specifically for forensic settings – the recovery subscale of the Dangerousness, Understanding, Recovery and Urgency Manual (DUNDRUM) (Davoren *et al*, 2015; considered later in this chapter). The dominant assessment paradigm, however, is still one of violence risk, and measured outcomes continue to be focused on adverse events such as violence, substance use and criminal recidivism (Chambers *et al*, 2009). Too little is known about the prevalence of strengths-based factors (see Chapter 12) and how success is achieved and experienced by forensic clients as they recover and move out of secure care (Livingston, 2018).

---

22 This chapter is based on work developed with Stephanie Penney and in two editorials we wrote together for *Criminal Behaviour and Mental Health* (Simpson, & Penney, 2011; 2018).

What do patients say about secure recovery?

There have now been a number of studies in which forensic clients have been asked about how they experience recovery in forensic care and what matters most to them as they are cared for. There are two literature reviews (Shepherd *et al*, 2016; Clarke *et al*, 2016). Clarke *et al* synthesised 11 qualitative studies on 'offender-patient' perceptions of personal recovery. They identified six overarching themes: connectedness, sense of self, coming to terms with the past, freedom, hope, health and intervention. The themes of connectedness and sense of self were noted to be especially important, with positive relationships with family and staff also seen as vital in aiding recovery. There was a recurring theme about the importance of the presence of nurturing relationships and the process of self-discovery. People get better when they are in supportive relationships with others. The sense of self refers to the development of an identity that is separate from the 'offender identity'. The loss of individuality experienced during hospitalisation is experienced as a barrier to recovery.

The Shepherd *et al* review (2016) of this literature came up with themes that overlapped with the Clark *et al* study. Their major themes for supporters of recovery were: hope and social networks, a personal sense of safety and security (provided by the physical environment and relationships with staff), and 'identity work' (making sense of past experiences, understanding the role of mental illness and constructing a sense of self). These themes overlap with key principles of recovery derived from non-forensic mental health areas. But they also highlight a particularly important area for forensic clients around safety and security and the need to come to terms with the past. This includes the offending that brought them into forensic care as well as past experiences.

In a study of 30 forensic inpatients, Nijdam-Jones *et al* (2015) found that in addition to factors that were perceived to help recovery (involvement in programmes, belief in rules and social norms, attachment to supportive individuals (family, friends and staff), commitment to work-related activities) they also found key variables that were barriers including the stigma and isolation associated with forensic hospitalisation. Such enforced removal from society disrupts key relationships and induces feelings of hopelessness which arise from uncertainty about the length of a hospital stay.

Livingston (2018) interviewed 18 forensic clients and 10 staff and asked them about what 'success' meant in terms of forensic recovery. Participants described multiple forms of success: the ability to lead a normal life, an independent life, a compliant life, a healthy life, a meaningful life, and a progressing life. Relevant markers of success (e.g. health, meaningfulness, normality) were thus much broader than outcomes related to an absence of violence or recidivism, or 'cure' of the mental disorder(s). While participants acknowledged the need for violence control and the protection of public safety, their view of success was much broader than risk management.

For these reasons, recovery for forensic clients encompasses features of general recovery, such as hope and optimism, re-establishing a positive identity and building a purposeful and productive life despite illness. However it also embraces offence-related recovery, which includes coming to terms with the offence and building a life in which reoffending has no part. This fits well with the 'conservative optimism' that forensic mental health staff describe in the process of helping forensic clients to reconcile a sense of personal guilt or responsibility with the rehabilitative and support needs that mental illness may create (Moore & Drennan, 2013).

There is a clear tension here between maintaining and developing circumstances that support recovery on the one hand, and the need of security and safety for the person and the public on the other. Institutions are experienced as both places with necessary security and safety, with programmes that can help and staff who can be supportive. But, at the same time, they also isolate the person from other enlivening and emboldening relationships. And, as already mentioned, maintaining hope is made more difficult when there is uncertainty over how long the detention will last. While this is so, it is well to take into account a remark by Drennan and Woolridge (2014), who noted that security requirements such as restrictions of movement or compulsory treatment also create an environment of safety and predictability. Properly used, this stable situation can help promote the first steps towards recovery. A person cannot begin to find a new path while still either perpetrating or being victimised by violence. The safeguards offered within secure hospital units may be a necessary new starting point. Similarly, coercive interventions such as the administration of medication against a patient's expressed desires may be necessary for the restoration of the person's ability to engage in treatment programmes and therapeutic opportunities.

What do staff think about secure recovery?

Forensic clients say staff relationships are central to their rehabilitation. How do staff feel about their clients' recovery? Earlier studies suggested that some staff perceived a fundamental incompatibility between recovery principles and secure care. These members of staff struggled to understand how they could encourage autonomy and self-determination on the one hand, while their client was under conditions of legal coercion on the other (Drennan et al, 2012). Fear of the hospital as an unsafe workplace also results in the use of unduly restrictive practices by staff to reduce risk (e.g. seclusion and restraint), rather than it feeling safe to engage with patients (Livingston *et al*, 2012).

Staff attitudes appear to be evolving, however. Chandley *et al* (2014) described that, in a high-security hospital setting, they had been able to address the perceived contradictions staff experienced in the course of applying a recovery-based approach. McKenna *et al* (2014) studied the themes that emerged from nursing staff's efforts to transform a secure model of care into a recovery paradigm. They found it was vital to have a clearly defined philosophy of care, with a manual to support it in order to guide staff through these tensions and contradictions. In their view, success in this process needed continuing education, reflective learning and leadership.

Niebieszczanski *et al* (2016) explored hope and recovery from interviews with 10 nurses in a medium-secure hospital service. The nurses felt that their ability to promote realistic hope within patients relies on their personal beliefs about hope and the importance of team atmosphere. The nurses also described the emotional effects on them as they performed their work, stressing how important it is to have good team support in order to manage the emotional demands of their work.

The therapeutic alliance between patient and staff is the key common ground between effective security and effective treatment (Bressington *et al*, 2011). It was deemed by these authors as one of the strongest factors associated with user satisfaction in forensic mental health services (see also Coffey, 2006). Poor engagement can result from high staff turnover or inconsistent staff processes.

Clients describe therapeutic connectedness as an essential element along with social support. Staff members must build 'hope-inspiring' relationships. For this there has to a reasonable degree of consistency in staffing to ensure that mental health personnel can adopt a straight-forward, personalised and strengths-based approach to risk assessment and care planning.

Can we make risk assessment and management recovery informed?

How do we perform the core processes of risk assessment and risk management *with* forensic clients rather than *on* them? Or, in other words, how do we perform risk assessment and management in a recovery-focused manner? Best-practices in risk assessment and management have in fact evolved with recovery principles and there are emerging examples of how we might do this.

There is a concept elsewhere in health systems and in the recovery movement called shared decision-making (SDM). This model has been advanced primarily in general psychiatry but its application to risk assessments in forensic mental health is of increasing interest (Barnao *et al*, 2016). Fluttert *et al* (2010) reported on results of a novel risk management method involving a collaboration between patients and nurses to identify early signs of aggression and generate preventive actions. This method was shown to reduce the number of seclusions as well as the severity of aggressive incidents in a maximum security hospital setting. Davoren *et al* (2015) developed a patient-rated version of their risk and recovery toolkit (DUNDRUM) to supplement the earlier staff-rated form. Staff and patient ratings were found to be significantly and positively correlated, although patients generally rated themselves as at lower risk and further along in their recovery than did staff. Importantly, though, agreement between staff and patients increased as patients progressed further along their rehabilitation pathways. Agreement was predictive of movement towards lower levels of security and eventual discharge.

Making risk assessment a collaborative enterprise should make it less opaque, and help to promote patient empowerment, engender trust and enhance therapeutic engagement (Barker, 2012). The commitment to understand and prevent repetition of harmful behaviours is a key recovery goal that can increase a patient's motivation to work on these areas. It can also contribute to an understanding that these maladaptive behaviours can be contrary to building a successful life. As noted within the Good Lives Model of offender rehabilitation (Ward & Maruna, 2007), individuals may have limited motivation to participate in risk management plans that emphasise avoidance goals and which are not linked to values and aspirations that are important to that individual (Barnao *et al*, 2015). A collaborative approach to risk assessment and management ensures that these formulations are both pertinent and understandable to forensic clients, thereby encouraging a deeper understanding of risk issues and how to help develop the mastery necessary to desist from harmful behaviour.

References

Barker R (2012) Recovery and risk: Accepting the complexity. In: G Drennan and D Aldred (Eds) *Secure Recovery* (pp23–40). New York: Routledge.

Barnao M, Ward T & Casey S (2015) Looking beyond the illness: Forensic service users' perceptions of rehabilitation. *Journal of Interpersonal Violence* **30** 1025–1045.

Barnao M, Ward T & Robertson P (2016) The good lives model: A new paradigm for forensic mental health. *Psychiatry, Psychology and Law* **23** 288–301.

Bressington D, Stewart B, Beer D & MacInnes D (2011) Levels of service user satisfaction in secure settings: A survey of the association between perceived social climate, perceived therapeutic relationship and satisfaction with forensic services. *International Journal of Nursing Studies* **48** 1349–1356.

Chambers JC, Yiend J, Barrett B, Burns T, Doll H & Fazel S (2009) Outcome measures used in forensic mental health research: A structured review. *Criminal Behaviour and Mental Health* **19** 9–27.

Chandley, M., Cromar-Hayes, M., Mercer, D., Clancy, B., Wilkie, I., & Thorpe, G. (2014). The development of recovery based nursing in a high-security hospital: nurturance and safe spaces in a dangerous world? *Mental Health and Social Inclusion*, **18**, 203-214.

Clarke C, Lumbard D, Sambrook S & Kerr K (2016) What does recovery mean to a forensic mental health patient? A systematic review and narrative synthesis of the qualitative literature. *The Journal of Forensic Psychiatry & Psychology* **27** 38–54.

Coffey M (2006) Researching service user views in forensic mental health: A literature review. *The Journal of Forensic Psychiatry & Psychology* **17** 73–107.

Coffey M (2012) A risk worth taking? Value differences and alternative risk constructions in accounts given by patients and their community workers following conditional discharge from forensic mental health services. *Health, Risk & Society* **14** 465–482.

Davoren M, Hennessy S, Conway C, Marrinan S, Gill P & Kennedy HG (2015) Recovery and concordance in a secure forensic psychiatry hospital – the self rated DUNDRUM-3 programme completion and DUNDRUM-4 recovery scales. *BMC Psychiatry* **15** 61.

Dorkins E & Adshead G (2011) Working with offenders: challenges to the recovery agenda. *Advances in Psychiatric Treatment* **17** 178–187.

Drennan G, Law K & Aldred D (2012). Recovery in the forensic organisation. In: G Drennan & D Aldred (Eds.) *Secure Recovery* (pp55–72). New York: Routledge.

Drennan G & Woolridge J (2014) *Making Recovery a Reality in Forensic Settings.* London: Centre for Mental Health and Mental Health Network, NHS Confederation.

Fluttert FA, Van Meijel B, Nijman H, Bjørkly S & Grypdonck M (2010) Preventing aggressive incidents and seclusions in forensic care by means of the 'Early Recognition Method'. *Journal of Clinical Nursing* **19** 1529–1537.

Livingston JD (2018) What does success look like in the forensic mental health system? Perspectives of service users and service providers. *International journal of offender therapy and comparative criminology* **62** (1) 208–228.

Livingston JD, Nijdam-Jones A & Brink J (2012) A tale of two cultures: examining patient-centered care in a forensic mental health hospital. *The Journal of Forensic Psychiatry & Psychology* **23** 345–360.

McKenna B, Furness T, Dhital D, Park M & Connally F (2014) The transformation from custodial to recovery-oriented care: A paradigm shift that needed to happen. *Journal of Forensic Nursing* **10** 226–233.

Moore E & Drennan G (2013) Complex forensic case formulation in recovery-oriented services: Some implications for routine practice. *Criminal Behaviour and Mental Health* **23** 230–240.

Niebieszczanski RJ, Dent H & McGowan A (2016) 'Your personality is the intervention': A grounded theory of mental health nurses beliefs about hope and experiences of fostering hope within a secure setting. *The Journal of Forensic Psychiatry & Psychology* **27** 419–442.

Nijdam-Jones A, Livingston JD, Verdun-Jones S & Brink J (2015) Using social bonding theory to examine 'recovery' in a forensic mental health hospital: A qualitative study. *Criminal Behaviour and Mental Health* **25** 157–168.

Shepherd A, Doyle M, Sanders C & Shaw J (2016) Personal recovery within forensic settings: Systematic review and meta-synthesis of qualitative methods studies. *Criminal Behaviour and Mental Health* **26** 59–75.

Shinkfield G & Ogloff J (2014) A review and analysis of routine outcome measures for forensic mental health services. *International Journal of Forensic Mental Health* **13** 252–271.

Simpson AI & Penney SR (2011) The recovery paradigm in forensic mental health services. *Criminal Behaviour and Mental Health* **21** 299–306.

Simpson AI & Penney SR (2018) Recovery and forensic care: Recent advances and future directions. *Criminal Behaviour and Mental Health* **28** (5) 383–389.

Ward T & Maruna S (2007) *Rehabilitation*. New York: Routledge.

Chapter 21:
Patient involvement and shared decision-making in risk assessment and management

By Quazi Haque

> *'Each patient carries his own doctor inside him. They come to us not knowing that truth. We are at our best when we give the doctor who resides with each patient a chance to go to work.'*
> (Albert Schweitzer, 1875-1965)

Perhaps the most striking advance in health care this century is the appreciation that the participation of the service user when managing their own health is not only morally right, but also the best professional approach. The evidence is clear: patient involvement in their own care generally leads to better health outcomes and scarce resources being allocated more efficiently (Berwick, 2003, pp18–20). Many mental health professionals who support the aspirations and hopes of their patients will argue that the greatest health and social rewards are achieved when this participatory tenet is applied to those labouring under severe mental health disability, disempowered through legal detention due to risk concerns, and unfamiliar with the idea of being asked to take shared responsibility for decision-making (Stringer *et al*, 2008).

Risk assessment is of course just one continuing process across a range of activities that occur within a mental healthcare setting designed to ensure individuals receive the optimal level of care. Services with patient co-production will do their level best to ensure that *all* of these activities include patient participation.

Key areas include:

■ Engaging people to keep healthy through lifestyle choices to better self-manage their weight, nutrition and the avoidance of smoking.

- Sharing decision-making for a better understanding of diagnosis, experience of ill-health, relapse triggers and treatment options.

- Supporting self-management through personalised care planning and educational programmes.

- Self-managing activities of daily living, such as budgeting, travel and gaining access to treatment.

- Involving families and carers. This is an important area with an emerging evidence-base and good practice resources (for example, see the Carer Support and Involvement in Secure Mental Health Services Toolkit, University of Central Lancashire, 2018).

- Choosing how, where and when treatment is delivered, balancing any legal constraints alongside the capacity and best interests of the individual.

- Participating in shaping the functioning of the services through patient involvement in audit and research.

Application of participatory tenets to the task of risk assessment

The evolution of SPJ guides (see Chapter 12) is emblematic of the move toward greater transparency and joint working with patients. For example, the single page score sheet common to SPJ guides developed in the 1990s (e.g. HCR-20 Version 2; Webster *et al*, 1997; SVR-20; Boer *et al*, 1997) is presently a markedly different document. In more recent guides (HCR V3; Douglas *et al*, 2013), this sheet is also available as a working document that can be completed *with* the patient at each stage. Information can be collected and collated around risk and protective factors, leading to a co-produced formulation. At its best the worksheet becomes a bridge toward a care plan belonging to the patient, one which is interlinked with that individual's needs and aspirations. Risk management thus becomes an enabling, positive and helpful experience for those receiving care. An experience that is more likely to lead to improved engagement with interventions and risk management interventions (Logan, 2003).

Van den Brink and colleagues (2015) introduced a self-appraisal risk assessment to 201 patients in a Dutch forensic out-patient setting. Content was based on key items derived from the Short Term Assessment of Risk and Treatability (START; Webster *et al*, 2004). The authors found poor concordance between clients and case managers when appraising key risk and protective factors. They concluded that, in most treatment plan evaluations, the client and case manager come to the evaluation with markedly different ideas about what the key risk and protective factors are and how the client is therefore progressing.

Horstead and Cree (2013) provide a helpful practical guide to implementing a collaborative multi-modal risk assessment programme based at their forensic psychiatric facility in England. The programme recognises from the outset the coercive and stigmatising elements of being in forensic care. They found that having one's risk(s) appraised fostered distrust and poor engagement. This needed to be addressed early and thoroughly. Risk assessment training, covering the nature and purpose of schemes such as the START (Webster *et al*, 2004) is thus delivered to new staff and patients *together*. This is then followed by an eight-week safety planning group through which patients are supported to complete SPJ schemes pertinent to their situation, usually the HCR-20 Version 2, START and SAPROF (de Vogel *et al*, 2009).

In recent years, two of the editors of this book (CDW and QH) have observed the growing emergence of structured programmes such as those already mentioned across different nations. All share common approaches that help foster patient participation and enable risk management programmes to achieve at least some success. The reader may find the acronym CONNECT helpful:

■ **C**ommunicate – Do not too readily state that someone is difficult to motivate or engage. This can lead to therapeutic nihilism. It takes perseverance, patience and politeness to build the groundwork for a collaborative relationship. Start a psychoeducational group about risk assessment.

■ **O**rganise – Make sure your written or electronic policies, risk worksheets, minutes and meetings allow space to directly include patient information and views. Ideally this information should be made easily accessible to frontline staff and patients working within the normal rules concerning confidentiality.

■ **N**ominate – Be clear to the patient which team member is responsible for which task in the assessment and intervention process. Also make sure that the patient is aware of his or her personal responsibilities within the team. Some clients may be safely encouraged to chair their own risk review meetings within such a framework.

■ **N**uance – Patients will process information based on their own life experiences. Subtle differences in the meaning of simple terms within risk assessment manuals can therefore exist between patients and professionals. This is striking and valuable when patients complete their risk assessments as described above. Safety plans can become strongly personalised and misunderstandings less acrimonious between the patient and the team.

- **Educate** – Set up collaborative risk training delivered by patients and staff to new patients and staff.

- **Co-produce** – Make sure that relevant risk factors and signature risk signs are transferred over to care and crisis plans in collaboration with the patient. Ensure intervention programmes actually include this information directly into group and individual-based harm reduction programmes.

- **Track** – Encourage clients regularly to monitor the relevance of each risk factor, alongside the emergence or diminution of personal strengths, and their overall formulation. Biofeedback is particularly crucial at times of transition. Individual outcome data should be made available to the clinician and the client. An old-fashioned personal diary remains a useful aid even during these times of technological acceleration.

About teams

Mental health treatments are often delivered by multi-disciplinary teams (MDTs) – a group of professionals of different disciplines using their skills to achieve a common set of goals. The reader may wonder when reading this chapter whether the composition of the 'multi-disciplinary team' is now so fluid, through patient and carer partnership arrangements, as to render the construct outdated. That notion, however, seems flawed when the truth is that little concerted effort has been directed to the important task of determining how to optimise decision making by clinical groups containing members with different skills, attitudes and sometimes values. Team members require support, education and opportunities for advancement to work effectively in the interests of service users. Members also require clarity of their role and the roles of others – blurring of roles can lead to conflict and also destructive opportunities for clients to split therapeutic boundaries.

There are, of course, many other important aspects to consider when teams are being composed (e.g. diversity, ethnic variety, gender balance, leadership). Effective leaders of teams will have a capacity to listen, reflect and galvanise members to that common purpose. An appreciation of the wider literature in this area can be fruitful, especially at times when teams require building or re-building. Lencioni, an influential American writer in this field (2002), believes that every effective team starts by building trust, which in turn allows constructive conflict, and results then in a shared commitment. This leads to high team 'performance'. Beyond the technical 'know-how', what are the features of an effective forensic MDT? Perhaps the following attributes are worth pursuing and evaluating:

1. Team members are interested and open in their discussion of issues.

2. Team members call out one another's unproductive behaviours and also raise difficult issues.

3. Team members know what their peers are working on and how they contribute to the collective good of the team and the patient.

4. Team members are curious and empathetic.

5. Team members quickly and genuinely apologise to one another when they do something inappropriate or possibly damaging to the team.

6. Team members willingly make sacrifices (such as budget/turf/head-count) in their departments or areas of expertise for the good of the team.

7. Team members openly admit their weaknesses and mistakes. They are slow to seek credit for their own contributions but quick to point out those of others.

8. Team meetings are compelling and purposeful.

9. Team members leave meetings confident that their peers are completely committed to the decisions agreed on during the meeting, even if there was initial disagreement.

10. Team members enjoy the benefits of good morale as team goals are achieved.

References and further reading

Berwick D (2003) *Improving the Safety of Patients in England*. William Lea.

Douglas KS, Hart SD, Webster CD & Belfrage H (2013) *HCR-20: Assessing risk for violence (3rd ed.)*. Vancouver, Canada: Mental Health Law and Policy Institute, Simon Fraser University.

Horstead A & Cree A (2013) Achieving transparency in forensic risk assessment: a multimodal approach. *Advances in Psychiatric Treatment* **19** (5) 351–357.

Lencioni P (2002) *The Five Dysfunctions of a Team: A leadership fable*. John Wiley & Sons.

Logan C (2003) Ethical issues in risk assessment practice and research. In G Adshead and C Brown (eds). *Ethical Issues in Forensic Research*. London: Jessica Kingsley.

Ray I & Simpson A (2019) Shared Risk Formulation in Forensic Psychiatry. *Journal of the American Academy of Psychiatry and the Law*. **47** (1) Pp1-7. DOI: 10.29158/JAAPL.003813-19.

Stringer B, van Meijel B, de Vree V & Van der Bijl J (2008) User involvement in mental health care: the role of nurses. A literature review. *Journal of Psychiatric and Mental Health Nursing* **15** (8) 678–683.

Van den Brink RHS, Troquete NAC, Beintema H, Mulder T, van Os TWDP, Schoevers RA & Wiersma (2015) Risk assessment by client and case manager for shared decision making in outpatient forensic psychiatry. *BMC Psychiatry* **15**:120. DOI 10.1186/s12888-015-0500-3.

Vogel V, de Ruiter C, Bouman Y, Vries Robbe & de Vries Robbé M (2009) SAPROF. *Guidelines for the assessment of protective factors for violence risk*. English Version. Utrecht, The Netherlands: Forum Educatief.

Webster CD, Douglas KS, Eaves D & Hart SD (1997) *Assessing Risk for Violence (Version 2)*. Burnaby, BC, Canada: Mental Health Law and Policy Institute, Simon Fraser University.

Webster CD, Martin ML, Brink J, Nicholls TL & Desmarais S (2004) *Short-term Assessment or Risk and Treatability (START)*. Hamilton, ON, Canada: St Joseph's Healthcare.

Chapter 22:
Calming turbulent seas – The role of social work and allied professions in practical risk assessment and risk management

By Joanne Eaves-Thalken

'The working life of a social worker is very much a mix of the "ideal" and the "practical", balancing the profession's high ideal with the reality of institutions and laws that can limit the capacity of an individual to deliver on such ideals.' (Hick, 2010, p85)

Steven Hick, in his classic text (2010), points out that social workers perform three main types of function: direct (providing services), indirect (forming policy and procedures), and macro-level (as in work with groups and communities) (p9). This chapter, consistent with the author's professional experience, centres on direct service to clients. Traditionally, social workers play a key role in the intake process. This involves a lot more than completing a checklist. As Hick puts it, 'The worker's function in this initial phase is a form of mediating an engagement between client and agency – a finding of common ground' (pp98–99). Hicks reminds us that 'Assessment is both a process and a product of understanding on which action is based... It involves gathering relevant information and developing an understanding' (p100).

As has been emphasised at some length by David Cooke in Chapter 4 of this book, there is an art to engaging with the client. David Cooke comes at the topic as a seasoned clinical psychologist, but the very same ideas apply to social work, nursing and the allied professions. Hick says: 'Assessment involves the art of asking questions. Purposeful and well-timed questions are the cornerstone of the assessment phase.' (p100)

Close up

Version 3 of the HCR-20 (Douglas *et al*, p41) stresses the importance of gathering information in assessments that is trustworthy and reliable, practically useful and relevant. Generally, this means interviews with the client, victims and collaterals (i.e. family members, friends, neighbors and professionals), reviews of criminal justice, health and educational records, and the study of formal reports arising from prior psychological testing. As the guide points out, it takes skill and experience to gather essential elements from a sea of information that potentially can be very large (p41). It is worth noting that the authors of V3 do not provide a protocol for conducting intake or other interviews. They rely on protocols established in social work and related disciplines. They say explicitly:

> '*An interview to complete HCR-20 V3 should not require evaluators to ask more questions than they otherwise would in a comprehensive, thorough, psychosocial interview intended to provide a full picture of an individual's history, risk factors, mental health status, past crime and violence, previous treatment and supervision experiences, current functioning, personality, and interpersonal relations*' (p41).

Social work is critical with regard to risk and risk management and the HCR-20 V3 continues to be an invaluable assessment guide for our profession. It provides a structured approach to gathering history and assessing risks of various kinds. As a psychiatric social worker in an acute in-patient setting, I and others on our multi-disciplinary team are constantly working together to prevent violence against others and self-harming behavior. It is a process that starts every day during our rounds when we share information about patients' histories, about their behavior on the unit, collateral data from their families, other hospitalisations, and forensic assessments.

We obtain much of this information directly from police and probation officers. We are on the phone a great deal. A large part of our work is gathering detailed and reliable information and sharing it, and assisting in making a plan that will protect the patient, the family and society. We spend many hours interviewing families and speaking to professionals involved in the client's care, often establishing whether there has been previous violence, detailing relationship and employment histories, substance use problems, mental illness and many other aspects of the person's history. This is crucial to risk management.

In the in-patient setting, we also work closely with patients to de-escalate emerging conflicts and eruptions. We use a multi-disciplinary approach of close communication. It is important to notice when patients need privacy or seclusion. We develop individualised therapeutic approaches that help to avoid escalation of violence. The patient's best interests and respect for confidentiality are at the centre. Social workers provide advocacy and strengths-based, client-centred support. They also assess, as carefully as they can, whether risk to self or others demands sharing of information and taking steps to protect others. The collateral information social workers gather is often used to inform review panels and the courts.

Acute and community social workers, psychiatric nurses and clinical counselors usually have team-based approaches to help provide crucial resources and supports to the patient, the lack of which are known to be risk factors. We are communicating constantly with one another. Webster *et al* (2001) state that mental health and correctional professionals should be 'attempting to create optimal, stable living arrangements' (p125). If a person at risk has basic income security, housing, mental health and substance use follow up, along with professional and family supports, she or he has a much enhanced possibility of avoiding problems. It helps greatly if the courts or review boards mandate forensic team involvement.

We have many patients who would be deemed high risk in terms of a standard V3 assessment. But most such persons have *not* been adjudicated by the courts. This, of course, does not mean that they do not require support and attention in order to prevent violence. With intensive discharge planning, we attempt to lower those risks as much as possible. This means collaborating with the substance-use nurses and counselors, psychiatrists, pharmacists, occupational therapists, vocational counselors, community mental health professionals, general practitioners and other service providers, and families. Social workers and their colleagues also work with the patient to develop their strengths and coping skills prior to discharge. This is a way of 'calming seas'.

Nonetheless, we often feel very limited in what we can do. There is, in most parts of the world, a severe lack of resources, particularly regarding income support and mental health housing. We need more tertiary mental health services, mental health housing, higher income support and more substance use services. Long waiting lists mean that patients are left vulnerable and at much greater risk of deteriorating mental health, with corresponding escalations in high-risk behaviors. No matter how thorough and evidence-based the assessment may have been, it fails if there are no matching resources. So part of our job necessarily involves advocating, at a macro-level, for improvements in the kinds of services we offer (see Hick, 2010, p9).

References and further reading

Corcoran J & Walsh JM (2014) *Mental Health in Social Work: A Casebook on Diagnosis and Strengths Based (DSM 5) (2nd Ed)*. London, England: Pearson.

Douglas KS, Hart SD, Webster CD & Belfrage H (2013) *HCR-20 V³: Assessing Risk for Violence: User Guide, Version 3*. Burnaby, Canada: Mental Health, Law, and Policy Institute, Simon Fraser University.

Hick S (2010) *Social Work in Canada: An introduction*. Toronto: Thompson Educational Publishing.

Webster CD, Eaves D & Halpin P (2001) Building stable environments. In KS Douglas, CD Webster, SD Hart, D Eaves & J Ogloff. *HCR-20 Violence Risk Management Companion Guide (pp125–133)*. Burnaby, Canada: Mental Health Law and Policy Institute, Simon Fraser University & Tampa, Florida: University of South Florida Dept of Mental Health Law and Policy.

Section 6
Research and implementation

Chapter 23: Implementation – Thinking, planning and integrating over the long term

By Rüdiger Müller-Isberner, with Petra Born, Sabine Eucker & Beate Eusterschulte

Introduction

Implementing new effective practices within a clinical service is an enormous challenge, however the existing knowledge about how to successfully implement new practices in organisations is not used. This might be one of the principal reasons why evidence-based practices are under-utilised in forensic mental health services. This chapter proposes that using knowledge about the implementation of change in organisations facilitates the implementation of evidence-based practices in forensic mental health services.

This chapter is divided into two parts. The first part reviews the literature on implementing change in organisations while the second briefly notes the key features necessary for successful implementation into an on-going clinical service. By using knowledge from studies of implementing change in organisations, the speed with which evidence-based practices are adopted in clinical services will increase (for a comprehensive recent overview, see Müller-Isberner *et al*, 2017)

The science of implementing change in organisations

This chapter focuses on performance implementation, which is defined as 'putting procedures and processes in place in such a way that the identified functional components of change are used with good effect for consumers'. Performance implementation produces actual benefits to consumers, organisations and systems, and requires careful and thoughtful efforts (Fixsen *et al*, 2005, p6). Performance implementation is distinguished from paper implementation or 'just do it', and from process implementation defined as 'train and hope'. Such a process is a planned, active and targeted approach to communicating knowledge about evidence-based interventions via determined channels to a target audience. It aims to convince a target group to adopt a new practice.

Models of implementation

Rogers's *Diffusion of Innovations-Model*, first published in 1962 and now in its 5th edition (2003), arose out of a study of how farmers in Iowa adopted best practice for growing corn. Recently, it has been widely used to structure investigations of health care innovations (Chambers, 2014, p14–15). Rogers (2003, Chapter 5) suggested that there are five stages of implementation: knowledge acquisition, persuasion, decision-making, implementation, and confirmation. He proposed that the rate of adoption of a new practice was explained by the characteristics of the practice: relative advantage, compatibility, complexity, trialability, and observability (Rogers, 2003, p15–16).

In detail:

1. *Relative advantage* is the degree to which the innovation is considered superior to existing practices.
2. *Compatibility* is the consistency of the new practice with existing values, experiences, and needs of the adopter.
3. *Complexity* describes the level of difficulty to understand and use the new practice.
4. *Trialability* is the possibility to experiment with the new practice on a limited basis.
5. *Observability* is the extent to which the results of the innovation are observable to others.

Adoption of a new practice is a process. Different concerns dominate different stages of the implementation. *'The adoption process in individuals is traditionally presented as having five stages: awareness, persuasion, decision, implementation, and confirmation'* (Greenhalgh *et al*, 2004, p600).

Researchers often use the RE-AIM Framework (Reach, Effectiveness, Adoption, Implementation, Maintenance) to organise the specific questions that arise when the process of implementing a specific intervention is studied within different settings. RE-AIM focuses on the pathway from the initial decision to implement a new practice to the degree to which the delivery of the intervention is maintained during the period after implementation (Chambers, 2014, p13–14).

Evidence-based practice

Given the state of evidence-based practice in forensic mental health services, the minimum standard for judging that a new practice is valid or effective is two rigorous studies showing similar results on meaningful key outcomes (Taxman & Belenko, 2013, p20). One of the difficulties in identifying effective practices in forensic services is the focus on recidivism as a key outcome variable. In order to document recidivism, lengthy follow-up periods are required.

Once the knowledge of an effective new practice has arrived in the 'real world', the next step is 'Who adopts when?' *Early adopters* are opinion leaders important in determining the rate of the adoption of a new practice. Once opinion leaders have adopted and tell others about the new practice, *'the number of adopters per unit of time takes off in an exponential curve'* (Rogers, 2003, p300). Interpersonal communication is the driving force *'creating a critical mass of adopters'* (Roger, 2003, p300).

Staff

Staff who are involved in the implementation process must be active participants. Their characteristics and behaviour fundamentally influence the success of an implementation process. Expert opinion leaders and peer opinion leaders influence the attitudes, opinions and actions of their colleagues. This influence can either be positive or negative. Expert opinion leaders exercise their influence through their rank, authority and status. Peer opinion leaders are effective through representativeness, integrity and credibility. The adoption of a new practice by individuals in an organisation is more likely if key individuals, often referred to as organisational champions, support the innovation within their social networks. Ideally, an organisation includes staff members with connections both inside and outside the organisation. Such individuals play an important role in identifying new practices that might be useful for their organisation (Greenhalgh *et al*, 2004).

If a new practice meets the needs of motivated and able adopters, the likelihood of successful implementation is increased. When the importance accorded to a new practice by individual staff members matches that of service leaders and service users, it is more likely to be implemented and maintained. The decision by a staff member within an organisation to adopt a particular practice can be individual, collective or authoritative. Making adoption by individuals obligatory may increase the chance of initial adoption but carries the risk of reducing the likelihood that the new practice will be successfully implemented and maintained (Greenhalgh *et al*, 2004).

Staff members at all levels require training in order to use a new practice. In general, effective training includes background information, theory and values of the new practice. Components of the new practice have to be introduced and demonstrated. The specific skills related to the new technology need to be exercised in a safe training environment. Feedback and opportunities for discussion are essential. Coaching and mentoring include observation, instruction, modelling, feedback and debriefing. However, while the skills needed to successfully undertake the new practice can be introduced and taught in training sessions, many of these skills are only fully developed during the supervised application of the new practice over lengthy periods of time by consultants or coaches. Training practitioners without providing follow-up support has been shown to be ineffective in implementing a new practice.

The context of implementation

The climate of an organisation can have a powerful effect on the success or failure of an implementation process. Conditions that make an organisation more or less innovative and those that indicate preparedness and capacity for implementation have been identified. Conditions that make an organisation more or less innovative, referred to as system antecedents, include characteristics of organisational structure, the capacity to absorb new knowledge, and a welcoming attitude towards change (Cook *et al*, 2012). A service that is able to systematically recognise, interpret and reframe new information is better able to absorb, integrate and correctly use a new practice. The link between new knowledge and existing knowledge is key. Openness and readiness for change includes the welcoming of new ideas. The characteristics of an organisation that is receptive to change include strong leadership with good management skills and a clear strategic vision, visionary staff in key positions, and a climate open to experimentation and data collection (Greenhalgh *et al*, 2004).

Systems-level networking is a core task of the leaders of the implementation process aimed at ensuring the availability of financial, organisational and human resources that are necessary for successful implementation. Internal networking must ensure that different parts of an organisation and different professions within the organisation share the same goal of implementing the new practice.

The outer setting is the economic, political and social context within which an organisation exists. The socio-political climate, incentives and mandates, inter-organisational norm-setting and networks, and environmental stability, are constructs of the outer setting (Cook *et al*, 2012). Changes in the outer setting can have a powerful influence on any implementation process (Greenhalgh *et al*, 2004).

A strong influence on an organisation's decision to adopt and implement a new practice is whether comparable organisations already use the new practice or are planning to implement it. An organisation that has extensive external networks is more predisposed to such influence. Organisations linked through common management structures and shared values and goals help disseminate information about effective new practices. Formal networks such as quality improvement initiatives may be effective in disseminating information about new, effective practices. External political mandates increase an organisation's motivation, but not its capacity, to adopt a new practice. Such mandates, however, may also be counterproductive as they block locally generated activities, ideas and priorities (Greenhalgh *et al*, 2004).

Implementation strategies

Implementation strategies are used to improve the adoption, implementation and sustainability of a new practice. Implementation strategies may be characterised as 'top down/bottom up', 'push/pull' and 'carrot/stick'. Implementation strategies comprise thoughtful and focused efforts to improve the uptake and sustainability of a new practice. Within forensic mental health services, implementation strategies must take account of the conditions imposed on each patient and their treatment by the courts. Often 'implementation packages' are available which, among other things, include techniques for training, intervention-specific tool kits, checklists, algorithms, formal practice protocols and guidelines (Proctor *et al*, 2014).

What do we know about education, the key part of implementation? One: that mailed guidelines, policies and/or information alone, or practitioner training alone, do not lead to the successful implementation of new practices. Neither mailing guidelines to clinicians nor the train-and-hope-approach (manuals plus two days of training plus follow-up consultations) lead to successful implementation. Two: longer-term, multilevel implementation strategies are more effective. Such implementation strategies include intensive involvement by programme developers on a continuing basis. Three: criteria for the selection and training of those who will use the new practice have been identified. And four: not enough is known about the functional components promoting and limiting implementation (Fixsen *et al*, 2005).

Implementation outcomes

Evaluating the implementation of a new practice includes the assessment of staff performance, adherence and compliance with the new practice, and the achievement of an advantageous outcome. Implementation outcomes must be distinguished and measured without confounding them with outcomes of patients who participated in the new practice. In order to determine the success of an implementation procedure a number of outcomes need to be measured: acceptability adoption, appropriateness, feasability, fidelity, cost and penetration (Proctor *et al*, 2014). The effectiveness of new practices is threatened by a **lack of sustainability, treatment integrity, drift** and **shift** (Chambers *et al*, 2013).

The science of implementation has not yet been used to improve patient outcomes in forensic mental health services. There are no empirical data on implementation outcomes, even for widely used risk assessment procedures such as the HCR-20.

Conclusion

The science of implementation provides considerable knowledge about how to implement a new practice within an organisation. When we began implementing new practices in our forensic mental health service, we were unaware of this literature and therefore did not use the available knowledge. We adopted several new evidence-based practices. Some failed. The principal reason for failed implementation attempts was the lack of knowledge about implementation. Both the task of implementing a new practice and the work required by staff were under-estimated. The management structures necessary for a complex implementation process were not sufficiently precise. And last but not least, it was only during the last decade that 'continuous improvement' as an on-going process was implemented in the hospital as part of the quality management structures (International Organisation for Standardization; ISO 9001). The discussion about these failed implementation projects resulted in the conclusion that the management of the implementation process largely determines success or failure.

The key points

Leadership

A clear and strong consensus that a new practice should be adopted and what its goals should be, or the additional value it will be bring, are necessary. This includes consideration of enablers and barriers to implementation, consequences for other procedures in the service, costs, and the importance of maintaining control over the implementation process. Barriers to implementation, such as the lack of qualified staff, lack of time, and general resistance of staff towards certain practices must be taken into account when planning the implementation.

Project group – not individuals

Successful implementation requires a long-term, multi-level strategy. This cannot be achieved by one or two staff members. A motivated work group and a project manager who is stubborn and obsessive are needed. Project group members should have some knowledge about the new practice and be able and willing to adapt the new practice to the characteristics of the organisation. Of course, groups have their own problems. Work group members leave and new members have to be integrated. The enthusiasm tends to decrease over time. Constant encouragement by senior staff is essential.

Control over the process

Due to the complexity of the organisation, the large number of interfaces, the different levels of skills of staff, the time frame, the complexity of the new procedures to be implemented, and the large number of staff to be convinced of the effectiveness of the new procedure, all studies show that implementation needs to be a highly structured project. The general framework of the implementation process, including the time-line, required funding and human resources, is carefully established in a first step, and continually revised as necessary during the implementation process by the steering group. The steering group ensures that they stay in control during the various stages of the implementation process. If, due to deficits in organisation or leadership, the connection to the top of the organisation loosens, an implementation process can easily take on a life of its own.

Staff: the critical human factor

Implementation of change will only be successful when employees are motivated and the change process is fueled by positive emotions. Positive emotions are promoted by focusing on the advantages of any new practice, for example saving time, optimising communication across professions, and better outcomes for patients. Not creating positive emotions and attitudes towards the new practice leads to resistance to change.

Control over the results

Regular meetings of staff with senior staff, structured documentation and continuous supervision ensure that a new practice is optimally adopted. Consequently the organisation has to provide leadership and the necessary structures for managing the change process.

Summary

The implementation of new evidence-based practices in a forensic mental health service is a change process. It requires time, planning and management. The complex institutional, legal and administrative rules, traditions and frameworks in which these services are embedded have to be considered. Senior staff must invest in establishing and using interfaces to the complex framework surrounding risk assessment, treatment and management. The whole process requires motivated, well-trained, well-prepared clinicians who have continuous support from competent superiors. Staff involved in the implementation process must be active participants rather than passive recipients. Implementation of new practices typically requires changes in the organisation and in individuals' practices. Commitment at every level of the organisation, dedicated leadership and the allocation of adequate resources is required in order to sustain a newly implemented practice that needs to be fitted into existing structures. Staff training should include demonstrations of the new practice, feedback when using the new practice, and ongoing supervision in order to ensure successful and sustainable change. Implementation science provides knowledge that is useful for adopting evidence based practices within forensic mental health services (for a detailed overview see, Müller-Isberner *et al*, 2017).

Take home message

Knowledge of how to implement change within a forensic mental health service is as important as knowing about evidence-based practice. Positive outcomes are achieved only when both the implementation process and the practice are effective.

References and further reading

Chambers DA (2014) Guiding Theory for Dissemination and Implementation Research: A reflection on models used in research and practice. In: RS Beidas & PC Kendall (Eds) *Dissemination and Implementation of Evidence-Based Practices in Child and Adolescent Mental Health* (pp9–21). Oxford: Oxford University Press.

Chambers DA, Glasgow R & Stange K (2013) The dynamic sustainability framework: addressing the paradox of sustainment amid ongoing change. *Implementation Science* **8** (117) https://doi.org/10.1186/1748-5908-8-117

Cook JM, O'Donnell C, Dinnen S, Coyne JC, Ruzek JI & Schnurr PP (2012) Measurement of a model of implementation for health care: toward a testable theory. *Implementation Science* **7** (59) https://doi.org/10.1186/1748-5908-7-59

Fixsen DL, Naoom SF, Blase KA, Friedman RM & Wallace F (2005) *Implementation Research: A synthesis of the literature* [online]. Tampa: Louis de la Parte Florida Mental Health Institute (FMHI Publication #231). Available at: http://ctndisseminationlibrary.org/ PDF/nirnmonograph.pdf (accessed January 2019).

Greenhalgh T, Robert G, Macfarlane F, Bate P & Kyriakidou O (2004) Diffusion of Innovations in Service Organisations: Systematic review and recommendations. *The Milbank Quarterly* **82** 581–629.

Müller-Isberner R, Born P, Eucker S & Eusterschulte B (2017) Implementation of Evidence –Based Practices in Forensic Mental Health Services. In: R Roesch & AN Cook (Eds) *Handbook of Forensic Mental Health Services* (pp443–469). New York: Taylor and Francis.

Proctor EK, Powell BJ & Feely MA (2014) Measurement in Dissemination Implementation Science. In: RS Beidas & PC Kendall (Eds) *Dissemination and Implementation of Evidence-Based Practices in Child and Adolescent Mental Health* (pp22–43). Oxford: Oxford University Press.

Rogers EM (2003) *Diffusion of Innovations* (5th ed). New York: Free Press.

Taxman FS & Belenko S (2013) *Implementing Evidence-based Practices in Community Corrections and Addiction Treatment.* New York: Springer.

Chapter 24: Risk in real time – Incorporating detailed chronologies into risk assessment and management

By Stephanie R Penney

'No episode is a priori condemned to remain an episode forever, for every event, no matter how trivial, conceals within itself the possibility of sooner or later becoming the cause of other events and thus changing into a story or an adventure. Episodes are like land mines. The majority of them never explode, but the most unremarkable of them may someday turn into a story that will prove fateful to you.'
(Milan Kundera, 1991)

Introduction

Over the past two decades, significant advances have been made in identifying robust and reliable risk factors for interpersonal violence. These advances have been translated into empirically validated instruments for assessing risk across diverse clinical populations and for different forms of violence (Douglas *et al*, 2013; Webster *et al*, 2009). Risk factors for violence that have received consistent empirical support include static or relatively stable historical variables (e.g. male gender, young age at first offense, history of substance use or relationship problems), as well as dynamic or theoretically modifiable indicators (e.g. active psychiatric symptoms, current substance use, insight, mood and affect, treatment or supervision compliance).

In this context, despite growing knowledge surrounding risk factors for future violence and offending (i.e. statistical predictors or correlates), considerably less attention has been paid to investigating proximal risk mechanisms (i.e. processes through which a risk factor increases the likelihood of an outcome such as violence). Consequently, surprisingly little is known about how empirically based risk factors actually translate into risk; that is, how these variables operate in real time to culminate in – or cause – an act of interpersonal violence. For example, despite the well-established finding that positive symptoms of psychosis are associated with a heightened likelihood of violence (Douglas *et al*, 2009; Fazel *et al*, 2009; Van Dorn *et al*, 2012), we know little about how or why these symptoms relate to violence: they may cause violence directly by focusing, destabilising, or disinhibiting behavior, but can also motivate violence indirectly by increasing stress, vulnerability to provocation, and exposure to tense or conflictive situations (Hiday, 1997). Other types of psychiatric symptoms (e.g. negative symptoms of psychosis, depression) may have a nonsignificant or inverse relationship with violence (Swanson *et al*, 2006; Witt *et al*, 2013; Douglas *et al*, 2009).

Prior methods of assessing risk for violence were similarly imprecise to the extent that they relied on the enumeration of risk factors as 'present' or 'absent' to arrive at a judgment of risk. Such methods did not routinely incorporate hypotheses about how or why certain risk factors contributed to a person's previous offending or violence, nor how they may influence a person's decision to act violently in the future. Fortunately, more recent clinical practice and research in the field has highlighted the importance of risk formulation alongside the rating of risk factors in arriving at a judgment about an individual's overall level of risk and the attendant risk management strategies.

Risk formulation, chronology and causality

As applied to the practice of risk assessment, 'formulation' refers to the integration of relevant risk factors into a meaningful explanatory model that accounts for an individual's violence. It is intended to facilitate hypotheses about the causes of an individual's problems and generate effective treatment plans. This type of exercise, by definition, necessitates careful attention to the chronology of violence: that is, the timeline of events leading up to each episode of violence in an individual's history, and the personal, social and contextual risk variables most proximally connected to them.

Ultimately, what informs judgments of risk for future harm most precisely and efficiently, as well as what is needed to reduce that risk, is an understanding of causation (Penney *et al*, 2013). An effective risk formulation should essentially generate a causal account of an individual's violence and thus optimally guide risk reduction treatment strategies.

Determining whether there is a temporal relationship between specific (antecedent) risk factors and (subsequent) violence is a prerequisite both for determining potential causality and for assessing whether interventions that reduce the risk factor would have any appreciable impact on the occurrence of violence (Douglas & Skeem, 2005; Kraemer *et al*, 1997). Furthermore, in addition to the temporal sequencing of risk factors and outcomes, recent literature points to the necessity of assessing changes in mutable ('dynamic') risk factors over time to conceptualise accurately an individual's risk status and focus treatment more effectively (Douglas *et al*, 2013). Even among ultra high-risk patients, violence risk ebbs and flows over time (Odgers *et al*, 2009), and the acuity and oscillation of relevant risk factors (e.g. psychiatric symptoms, hostility) are found to be better predictors of violence as compared to diagnostic status and other static risk indicators (Penney *et al*, 2016; Skeem *et al*, 2006). The study of how dynamic risk factors (a) precede violence, and (b) fluctuate in theoretically consistent ways with violent-related outcomes is thus necessary to establish causal processes. In the absence of longitudinal designs with repeated observations, however, these effects will go undetected.

Implications for research

Although many risk factors for violence are conceptualised as dynamic entities, they are assessed and measured as static indicators. With some notable exceptions (Odgers *et al*, 2009; Penney *et al*, 2016; Skeem *et al*, 2006; Wilson *et al*, 2013), few studies have adopted the types of repeated-measures, longitudinal designs which would permit an examination of change in dynamic risk indicators over time. The statistical methods most suited to examining change over time (e.g. dynamical systems models, structural cross-lagged longitudinal models) are also infrequently used. As a result, there is little research describing the trajectory of change among empirically based dynamic risk factors, the feasibility of trying to capture such change in clinical populations, and whether such change relates to relevant outcomes such as violence or offending. More commonly, studies have used either single time-point estimates of dynamic risk (e.g. Desmarais *et al*, 2012; McDermott *et al*, 2008), or have looked at change over time but without linking this change to prospectively measured outcomes (e.g. Belfrage & Douglas, 2002; Viljoen *et al*, 2012).

An important avenue for future research, therefore, is to incorporate time-sensitive methodologies and dynamic approaches to the measurement of risk factors and outcomes. More sophisticated measurement frameworks that incorporate theory-driven hypotheses regarding the anticipated nature of change (e.g. daily, weekly, yearly) for different classes of dynamic risk factors are needed. Longitudinal designs are also critically important not just to assess changes in risk factors over time, but to accurately measure the prevalence of violent outcomes accurately. For example, through our longitudinal follow-up of forensic patients being discharged into the community (Penney *et al*, 2018), we learned two important lessons. First, that dynamic risk indicators, measured as static entities, showed little predictive utility; rather, it was the change (increase, decrease) in these indicators that predicted adverse clinical outcomes. Second, that it is necessary to extend the scope of outcome measurement beyond violence perpetration. In our sample of forensic patients newly residing in the community, outcomes pertaining to hospital readmission, substance use and mental status decompensation proved far more common as compared to violence perpetration.

Implications for clinical practice

There is likely wide inter-individual variation in the translational process from risk factor to outcome, as well as how risk factors manifest just prior to an incident of violence. Further, we would expect significant intra-individual variation in the same risk factor over time. Indicators like active psychotic symptomatology may change on a daily basis, while others, like insight, may change only very slowly, over months or years.

For clinicians carrying out risk assessments, the task is not a simple one. We must consider the nature of change for specific risk factors (e.g. hourly, daily, monthly), and how this change relates to outcome. As noted, it is especially critical to consider the temporal quality of the relationship between risk factors and outcomes to ensure that a risk factor actually precedes, rather than simply co-occurs or follows violence, and to identify how and why specific factors result in violence. A detailed topography of the person's previous violence, as well as a chronological analysis of recent violence, is essential. In this way, an assessment can be produced that not only identifies relevant domains of risk, but outlines what these factors 'look like' when present for that person, and what they look like under conditions signaling increasing risk. Finally, to move closer to causal models of violence, we must seek to document that targeted interventions have the ability to influence risk factors, and that this ultimately reduces the likelihood of an adverse outcome.

Conclusory remarks

Ingrained in the science and practice of risk assessment is the concept of time. Much like assessments of criminal responsibility, where the ultimate legal question often hinges on the causal nexus between mental disorder and offending, violence risk assessments must attend to the temporal proximity between risk factors and outcomes, as well as how fluctuations in relevant risk factors relate to violence and other clinically relevant outcomes. In this way, effective explanatory models of behavior can be generated to optimally guide treatment efforts. From a research perspective, this means incorporating longitudinal and time-sensitive methodologies into our research designs. Future studies may consider increasing the frequency of data collection intervals over a longer period of time to better map the trajectory of change among dynamic risk indicators and more accurately connect changes in dynamic variables to violent incidents or other proxies of risk and recidivism. Finally, to move closer to causal models of violence perpetration and other outcomes, studies must also seek to document that targeted interventions have the ability to influence dynamic risk factors, and that this influence ultimately reduces the likelihood of an adverse outcome.

References

Belfrage H & Douglas KS (2002) Treatment effects on forensic psychiatric patients measured with the HCR-20 violence risk assessment scheme. *The International Journal of Forensic Mental Health* **1** 25–36.

Desmarais SL, Nicholls TL, Wilson CM & Brink J (2012) Using dynamic risk and protective factors to predict inpatient aggression: Reliability and validity of START assessments. *Psychological Assessment* **24** 685–700.

Douglas KS & Skeem JL (2005) Violence risk assessment: Getting specific about being dynamic. P*sychology, Public Policy, and Law* **11** 347–383.

Douglas KS, Guy LS & Hart SD (2009) Psychosis as a risk factor for violence to others: A meta-analysis. *Psychological Bulletin* **135** 679–706.

Douglas KS, Hart SD, Webster CD & Belfrage H (2013) *HCR-20V3: Professional guidelines for evaluating risk of violence.* Burnaby, Canada: Mental Health, Law, and Policy Institute, Simon Fraser University.

Fazel S, Gulati G, Linsell L, Geddes JR & Grann M (2009) Schizophrenia and violence: Systematic review and meta-analysis. PLoS medicine **6** (8) e1000120.

Hiday VA (1997) Understanding the connection between mental illness and violence. *International Journal of Law and Psychiatry* **20** 399–417.

Kraemer HC, Kazdin AE, Offord DR, Kessler RC, Jensen PS & Kupfer DJ (1997) Coming to terms with the terms of risk. *Archives of General Psychiatry* **54** 337–343.

Kundera M (1991) *Immortality.* New York: Grove Press.

McDermott BE, Edens JF, Quanbeck CD, Busse D & Scott CL (2008) Examining the role of static and dynamic risk factors in the prediction of inpatient violence: Variable- and person-focused analyses. *Law and Human Behavior,* **32**, 325–338.

Odgers CL, Mulvey EP, Skeem JL, Gardner W, Lidz CW & Schubert C (2009) Capturing the ebb and flow of psychiatric symptoms with dynamical systems models. *American Journal of Psychiatry* **166** 575–582.

Penney SR, Morgan A & Simpson AI (2013) Motivational influences in persons found not criminally responsible on account of mental disorder: A review of legislation and research. *Behavioral sciences & the law* **31** 494–505.

Penney SR, Marshall LA & Simpson AI (2016) The assessment of dynamic risk among forensic psychiatric patients transitioning to the community. *Law and Human Behavior* **40** 374–386.

Penney SR, Marshall L & Simpson AI (2018) A prospective study of pathways to hospital readmission in Canadian forensic psychiatric patients. *The Journal of Forensic Psychiatry & Psychology* **29** 368–386.

Skeem JL, Schubert C, Odgers C, Mulvey EP, Gardner W & Lidz C (2006) Psychiatric Symptoms and Community Violence Among High-risk Patients: A test of the relationship at the weekly level. *Journal of Consulting and Clinical Psychology* **74** 967–979.

Swanson JW, Swartz MS, Van Dorn RA, Elbogen EB, Wagner HR, Rosenheck RA, Stroup TS, McEvoy JP & Lieberman JA (2006) A national study of violent behavior in persons with schizophrenia. *Archives of General Psychiatry* **63** 490–499.

Van Dorn R, Volavka J & Johnson N (2012) Mental disorder and violence: Is there a relationship beyond substance use? *Social Psychiatry and Psychiatric Epidemiology* **47** 487–503.

Viljoen JL, Beneteau JL, Gulbransen E, Brodersen E, Desmarais SL, Nicholls TL & Cruise KR (2012) Assessment of multiple risk outcomes, strengths, and change with the START:AV: A short-term prospective study with adolescent offenders. *The International Journal of Forensic Mental Health* **11** 165–180.

Webster CD, Martin ML, Brink J, Nicholls TL & Desmarais SL (2009) *Manual for the Short-Term Assessment of Risk and Treatability (START)* (Version 1.1). Port Coquitlam, BC: Forensic Psychiatric Services Commission and St. Joseph's Healthcare.

Wilson CM, Desmarais SL, Nicholls TL, Hart SD & Brink J (2013) Predictive validity of dynamic factors: Assessing violence risk in forensic psychiatric inpatients. *Law and Human Behavior* **37** 377–388.

Witt K, van Dorn R & Fazel S (2013) Risk factors for violence in psychosis: Systematic review and meta-regression analysis of 110 studies. *PLoS ONE* **8** e55942.

Chapter 25: Early assessment of risks and their amelioration by the Stop Now And Plan (SNAP) model – National and international research

By Leena Augimeri

The Child Development Institute

The Child Development Institute (CDI; formerly called Earlscourt Child and Family Centre) is located in the Corsa Italia neighbourhood of Toronto. Founded over 100 years ago in 1913 by Reverend Peter Bryce, the 'Earlscourt home' was a haven for children unable to remain with their parents due to 'dire family circumstances'. By the 1970s, Earlscourt specialised in residential treatment and became recognised as a children's mental health centre. In the 1980s the Centre shifted its attention to evidence-based, family-focused community-based services and adopted a scientist-practitioner framework.

Kenneth Goldberg was the Executive Director of the former Earlscourt Child and Family Centre until he retired in 2004, when the Centre merged with the Crèche Child and Family Centre to form CDI. During his tenure, he encouraged a scientist-practitioner framework and insisted that programme evaluation be part of clinical programming. His leadership, along with the expertise of the Clinical Director at the time, Kathy Levene, set the stage for programmatic innovations. Even though Earlscourt was a small community-based children's mental health centre, it was strongly committed to evaluation and research. The goal was to improve the lives of children and families. As a result, in the early 1980s a small research unit was established. At that time Earlscourt hired a senior full-time research director, Dr Debra Pepler (now a professor at York University), and others over the years like Dr David Day (today a professor at Ryerson University), and Dr Chris Webster, one of the editors of the present book.

In 1985, after completing my undergraduate degree, and with support
from Dr Debra Pepler, I embarked on my professional career and joined
Earlscourt. I was hired as a researcher to be part of a multi-disciplinary team
led by Kenneth Goldberg to develop a new programme for young children
(aged 6–11) who were in conflict with the law. The programme was initially
called the 'Under 12 Outreach Project' (ORP) and today has become a model
intervention called SNAP® (Stop Now And Plan). The first of its kind in
Toronto (and worldwide), SNAP was designed to fill a major gap in children's
mental health services that had emerged following changes to juvenile justice
legislature in Canada. The passing of the Young Offenders Act in 1984 saw
the age of criminal responsibility raised from 7 to twelve. While this was
obviously an important step forward for vulnerable youths caught up in the
justice system, who could no longer be prosecuted for their actions, it also
highlighted a major lack of preventative mental health services to address
the pertinent needs of children with disruptive behaviour problems. This was
having a tremendous impact on a macro level, affecting not only life at home
but at school and across the entire community.

A void in appropriate services meant the full burden of these youths'
struggles was being carried by parents, teachers, peers, and in some cases
law enforcement. This is why, in 1985, the ORP was launched in partnership
with the Toronto Police Services, poised to address this growing need. In
1996, as a result of scientific evaluations, SNAP became gender specific and
moved from a time-limited intervention (approximately 3–4 months) to a
continued care model (up to age 18). In 2000, the programme was renamed
the SNAP Model (SNAP Boys and SNAP Girls) as a result of the clients
identifying it as such.

Through the dedication and perseverance of my colleagues, our programme
partners, and the children and families we set out to serve, this programme
has gone on to be recognised as the 'most fully developed intervention for
child delinquents to date' (Howell, 2001, p312) and 'the leading evidence-
based program for aggressive children with SVC [serious violent and
chronic] potential' (Howell *et al*, 2014, p46).

During my tenure with SNAP over the last 33 years I have had a rich and
fulfilling career, where I have also been able to complete my graduate studies
while building the SNAP model and establishing a dedicated unit within CDI
called the Centre for Children Committing Offences (CCCO) with support
from the McConnell Foundation. The CCCO is a dedicated unit specialising
in the middle years with a focus on gender specific interventions like SNAP,
risk/need assessment guides like the Early Assessment Risk Lists (EARLs)
and police-community referral protocols. Today I am the Director of SNAP
Scientific, Program Development & CCCO and leading the SNAP national

and international expansion initiatives. The Canadian expansion is a large scale national children's mental health implementation that will bring SNAP to 100 organisations (potentially reaching 140 different communities and 14,000 children) across Canada by 2022.

Two important points arise from this preamble: (1) it is owed to our clients, the children, families, and their communities, that the programmes we offer and develop are based on good practice, are routinely tested, and are proven to be effective; and (2) proper scientific research and evaluation activities need to be part of the organisation culture. My mission, well supported by my CDI organisation and colleagues, is to promote the scientist-practitioner framework within children's mental health. Having worked in the field for over three decades, I believe more than ever that we need continually to improve clinical practice from a culturally responsive and safety-inclined perspective, be accountable by ensuring we are not doing more harm than good, have proof that what we do has practical benefit, be cost effective, and help advance the field of children's mental health.

Intervention: the SNAP model

The SNAP model builds on the core principles noted above. It is a trauma-informed, gender-sensitive, multicomponent intervention that works within an eco-systemic framework; working with the individual child, family, school and community (e.g. child welfare, police, community-based services). The goal of SNAP is to increase emotional regulation, self-control and problem-solving skills; helping children stop and think before they act and make good choices 'in the moment'.

In following with the rich tradition of scientific research at CDI, and as noted previously, SNAP has been predicated from its very beginning on a scientist–practitioner framework. It became clear early in our journey that a strong evidence base must lie at the heart of SNAP, as we owe it to the individuals we work with to ensure only the best possible programming is delivered. SNAP research has integrated a multiple-systems approach. This has included the Criminal Justice System (CJS). The first randomised controlled trial (RCT) of SNAP, conducted in 1996, revealed that participation in the programme was associated with long-term, statistically significant reductions in parent-reported delinquent, externalising and internalising behaviour (Day & Augimeri, 1996). Further investigation, examining criminal justice records, revealed that the number of future criminal offences (obtained up to age 18) for children who received SNAP was reduced by almost half compared to children receiving a less intensive treatment (Augimeri et al, 2007). The goal of SNAP is to improve the life chances and well-being of vulnerable children susceptible for CJS and serious mental health issues.

Today, SNAP Boys and SNAP Girls (both undergoing replications across the country and internationally) continue to develop in the spirit of their original mission, as set out in 1985. Researchers at CDI (e.g. Augimeri *et al*, 2007; Augimeri *et al*, 2018; Day & Augimeri, 1996; Koegl *et al*, 2008; Pepler *et al*, 2010; Walsh *et al*, 2002) as well as external experts (e.g. Burke & Loeber, 2015; 2016; Farrington & Koegl, 2015; Granic *et al*, 2007; Lipman *et al*, 2008; Lewis *et al*, 2008; Woltering *et al*, 2011; 2015) have evaluated SNAP continuously[23] using a variety of methods (e.g. RCTs, neuroscience, quasi-experimental and cost benefit analyses) proving promising and effective findings. In 2018, WSIPP (Washington State Institute for Public Policy) conducted a stringent review of SNAP and found that the program produces benefits greater than costs; it received an 'evidence-based' rating.

Risk assessment: EARL-20B and EARLY-21G

Early on it became evident to clinical staff members that they had some responsibility to make projections about the risks the children might pose in the future. In due course, these notions were refined into the Early Assessment Risk Lists (EARL-20B for boys, and EARL-21G for girls) (Augimeri *et al*, 2001; Levene *et al*, 2001). Developed with leading experts at CDI in Toronto, these devices have demonstrated good validity and reliability. They are predictive of future CJS involvement (reviewed in Augimeri *et al*, 2017a; de Ruiter & Augimeri, 2012) and are used within SNAP programmes to inform treatment planning. At the time of writing, these schemes are undergoing revision.

Future directions for research and reach

The SNAP team recognise that for the programme to be as effective as possible, we need to understand the biology behind the behaviours that we observe, and the damaging emotional and cognitive patterns that we aim to change. Collaborations continue with external research institutions that have the capability of measuring neurobiological, endocrinological and psychophysiological markers of treatment success. We are continuing to co-operate with leading research institutions such as the Hospital for Sick Children and Centre for Addiction and Mental Health (CAMH) in Toronto. We also look to expand and build upon relationships with higher educational institutions in the United States and further afield.

---

23 As a result of the robust SNAP findings, it has received highest effectiveness designations from accredited sources that rate programmes in Canada (e.g. Public Safety Canada – Crime Prevention Inventory, Public Health Agency of Canada – Canadian Best Practices Portal) and in the United States (e.g. National Institute of Justice – Crime Solutions.gov, National Gang Center – Strategic Planning Tool).

Today, SNAP is engaged in a multi-year implementation strategy developed in 2012. At this time SNAP was selected by the LEAP–Pecaut Centre for Social Impact as their inaugural social innovation. This strategy introduces a new approach for bringing evidence-based services to Canadian communities. Through a venture philanthropy model, governments, foundations, businesses, individual donors and community partners work together to promote social innovations like SNAP that can help create massive social change within children's mental health. The strategy includes the infusion of business skills and planning in order to build capacity, fidelity and sustainable growth nationally and internationally (Augimeri *et al*, 2017a) and engagement in implementation science.

References

Augimeri LK, Koegl CJ, Webter & Levene K (2001) *Early assessment risk list for boys: EARL-20B, Version 2*. Toronto, ON: Earlscourt Child and Family Centre.

Augimeri LK, Farrington DP, Koegl CJ & Day DM (2007). The Under 12 Outreach Project: Effects of a community based program for children with conduct problems. *Journal of Child and Family Studies* **16** 799–807.

Augimeri LK, Walsh MM, Levene K, Sewell K & Rajca E (2014) Stop Now And Plan (SNAP) model. In: G Bruinsma & D Weisburd (Eds) *Encyclopedia of criminology and criminal Justice* (pp5053–5063). New York, NY: Springer.

Augimeri LK, Walsh M, Enebrink P, Jiang D, Blackman A & Kanter D (2017a) Gender-specific childhood risk assessment tools: Early Assessment Risk Lists for Boys (EARL-20B) and Girls (EARL-21G). In: RK Otto & KS Douglas (Eds), Handbook of violence risk assessment, 2nd edition. Oxford, UK: Routledge, Taylor & Francis.

Augimeri LK, Pepler D, Walsh M & Kivlenieks M (2017b) Addressing Children's Disruptive Behavior Problems: A thirty-year journey with SNAP (Stop Now And Plan). In: P Sturmey (Ed.) *Handbook of Violence and Aggression, Volume 2: Assessment, prevention, and treatment of individuals*. US: Wiley-Blackwell.

Augimeri LK, Walsh M, Donato A, Blackman A & Piquero A (2018) SNAP (Stop Now and Plan): Helping children improve their self-control and externalizing behavior problems. *Journal of Criminal Justice* **56** 43–49.

Burke J & Loeber R (2015) The effectiveness of the Stop Now and Plan (SNAP) Program for boys at risk for violence and delinquency. *Prevention Science* **16** (2) 242–253.

Burke J & Loeber R (2016) Mechanisms of behavioral and affective treatment outcomes in a cognitive behavioral intervention for boys. *Journal of Abnormal Child Psychology* **44** (1) 179–189.

Day DM & Augimeri LA (1996) Serving children at risk for juvenile delinquency: An evaluation of the Earlscourt under 12 outreach project (ORP). Report submitted to the Department of Justice. Toronto, ON: Earlscourt Child and Family Centre.

De Ruiter C & Augimeri LK (2012) Making delinquency prevention work with children and adolescents: From risk assessment to effective interventions. In: C Logan and L Johnstone (Eds) *Managing Clinical Risk* (pp199–223). London: Routledge.

Farrington DP & Koegl CJ (2015) Monetary benefits and costs of the Stop Now And Plan program for boys aged 6-11, based on the prevention of later offending. *Journal of Quantitative Criminology* **31** 263–287.

Granic I, O'Hara A, Pepler D & Lewis M (2007) A dynamic system analysis of parent-child changes associated with successful 'real-world' interventions for aggressive children. *Journal of Abnormal Child Psychology* **35** (5) 845–857. Printed On-Line: DOI 10.1007/ s10802-007-9133-4.

Howell JC (2001) Juvenile justice programs and strategies. In: R Loeber and D Farrington (Eds). *Child delinquents: Development, interventions and service needs* (pp305–321). Thousand Oaks, CA: Sage.

Howell JC, Lipsey MW & Wilson JJ (2014) *A handbook for evidence-based juvenile justice systems*. London, UK: Lexington Books.

Koegl CJ, Farrington DP, Augimeri LK & Day DM (2008) Evaluation of a targeted cognitive-behavioural programme for children with conduct problems – The SNAP® Under 12 Outreach Project: Service intensity, age and gender effects on short- and long-term outcomes. *Clinical Child Psychology and Psychiatry* **13** (3) 419–434.

Levene KS, Augimeri LK, Pepler DJ, Walsh MM, Koegl CJ, Webster CD (2001) *Early assessment risk list for girls: EARL-21G, Version 1, Consultation Edition*. Toronto, ON: Earlscourt Child and Family Centre.

Lewis MD, Granic I, Lamm C, Zelazo PD, Stieben J, Todd RM, Moadab I & Pepler D (2008) Changes in the neural bases of emotion regulation associate with clinical improvement in children with behaviour problems. *Development and Psychopathology* **20** 913–939.

Lipman EL, Kenny M, Sniderman C, O'Grady S, Augimeri L, Khayutin S & Boyle MH (2008) Evaluation of a community-based program for young boys at risk of antisocial behaviour: Results and issues. *Journal of the Canadian Academy of Child and Adolescent Psychiatry* **17** (1) 12–19.

Pepler D, Walsh M, Yuile A, Levene K, Vaughan A & Webber J (2010) Bridging the Gender Gap: Interventions with aggressive girls and their parents. *Prevention Science* **11** 229–238.

Walsh MM, Pepler DJ & Levene KS (2002) A model intervention for girls with disruptive behaviour problems: The Earlscourt Girls Connection. *Canadian Journal of Counselling* **36** 297–311.

Washington State Institute for Public Policy (2018) *Updated Inventory of Evidence-Based, Research-Based, and Promising Practices: For prevention and intervention services for children and juveniles in the child welfare, juvenile justice, and mental health systems*. Seattle, WA: Washington State Institute for Public Policy.

Woltering S, Granic I, Lamm C & Lewis MD (2011). Neural Changes Associated with Treatment Outcome in Children with Externalizing Problems. *Biological Psychiatry* **70** (9) 873–879.

Woltering S, Liao V, Liu Z-X & Granic I (2015) Neural rhythms of change: long-term improvement after successful treatment in children with disruptive behavior problems. *Neural Plasticity*, Article ID 873197 http://dx.doi.org/10.1155/2015/873197.

Chapter 26:
The Cambridge Study in Delinquent Development

By David P Farrington

The Cambridge Study in Delinquent Development (CSDD) is a long-term survey of the development of offending and antisocial behaviour in 411 London males from age eight to age 56 (see Farrington *et al*, 2013). The CSDD began in 1961 and has been intermittently funded by the Home Office and the Department of Health. It was begun by Professor Donald West in 1961, and Professor David Farrington joined in 1969, taking over the direction of the CSDD in 1982. The latest interviews were carried out in collaboration with Professor Jeremy Coid.

Aims

The original aim of the CSDD was to describe the development of delinquent and criminal behaviour in inner-city males, to investigate to what extent this could be predicted in advance, and to explain why juvenile delinquency began, why it did or did not continue into adult crime, and why adult crime often ended as men reached their 20s. The main focus was on continuity or discontinuity in behavioural development, on the effects of life events on development, and on predicting future behaviour. The CSDD was not designed to test any one particular theory about delinquency but to test many different hypotheses about the causes and correlates of offending, and many different mechanisms and processes linking risk factors and antisocial behaviour.

Characteristics of the sample

At the time they were first contacted in 1961-62, the boys were all living in a working-class area of South London. The sample was chosen by taking all the boys who were then aged eight to nine and on the registers of six state primary schools within a mile of a research office that had been established. Therefore, the boys were not a probability sample drawn from a population, but rather a complete population of boys of that age in that area at that time (see Farrington, 2003).

Most of the boys (357, or 87%) were of white British origin, being brought up by parents who had themselves been brought up in England, Scotland or

Wales. On the basis of their fathers' occupations, 94% of the boys could be described as working-class (categories III, IV or V on the Registrar General's scale, describing skilled, semi-skilled or unskilled manual workers), in comparison with the national figure of 78% at that time. The majority of the boys were living in conventional two-parent families; at that time only 6% of the boys had no operative father and only 1% had no operative mother. This was, therefore, overwhelmingly a traditional, white, urban, working-class sample of British origin.

Data collected at different ages

The boys were interviewed and tested in their schools by psychologists when they were aged about eight, 10 and 14. They were then interviewed in our research office at about 16, 18 and 21, and in their homes at about 25, 32 and 48, by young social science graduates. At all ages except 21 and 25 (when subsamples were interviewed), the aim was to interview the whole sample (see Farrington, 2003).

Interviews with the boys' parents were also carried out by female psychiatric social workers who visited their homes. These took place about once a year from when the boys were aged eight until when they were aged 14-15 and were in their last year of compulsory education. The primary informants were the mothers, although many fathers were also seen. In addition, their teachers completed questionnaires when the boys were aged about eight, 10, 12 and 14. Also, searches of criminal records were carried out of the boys themselves, of their biological mothers, fathers, brothers and sisters, and later of their wives and female partners, and of their children.

Although the most interesting individuals in any research on offending tend to be the hardest to locate and the most unco-operative, we have always managed to trace and interview a very high proportion of the sample: 389 out of 410 who were alive at age 18 (95%) and 378 out of 403 who were alive at age 32 (94%), for example. By age 48, 17 of the men had died, of whom 13 had been convicted – it is a problem for criminological researchers that the most interesting (i.e. antisocial) people tend to lead exciting, risk-taking lives, and tend to die early. Of the remaining 394 men who were still alive, 365 (93%) were interviewed at age 48; five men could not be traced and 24 refused.

Between 2004 and 2013, 551 adult children of these males (84% of a target sample of 653) were interviewed at the average age of 25; 291 of the 343 sons (85%) and 260 of the 310 daughters (84%). Of the remainder, 39 children refused, 33 parents refused, 13 children could not be traced, 14 were elusive (agreeing or not refusing but never being available to interview), and three were aggressive or problematic. In the interests of clarity, the original 411 males are termed 'generation 2' (G2), their parents are termed 'generation 1' (G1), and their children are termed 'generation 3' (G3) (see Farrington *et al*, 2015).

Criminal careers

Natural history of offending

By the age of 56, 42% of the G2 males had been convicted of offences, most commonly thefts, burglaries and the unauthorised taking of vehicles, although there were also quite a few offences of violence, vandalism, fraud and drug abuse. The average criminal career contained 4.9 convictions and lasted 9.8 years, from age 19.7 to age 29.5 (see Farrington *et al*, 2013).

We found that the peak age of increase in the prevalence of convictions was 14, while the peak age of decrease was 23. These times of maximum acceleration and deceleration in prevalence draw attention to periods in male lives when important life changes are occurring that influence offending. Perhaps the most important social influence changes from parents to male peers around age 14 and from male peers to female partners around age 23, on average.

Persistence in offending

The majority of those who were convicted as juveniles were reconvicted as young adults. Furthermore, the G2 males who were first convicted at the earliest ages tended to become the most persistent offenders, in committing large numbers of offences at high rates over long time periods. The 'chronic offenders' up to age 56 were defined as the 28 men (7% of the sample) who committed half (51%) of all officially recorded offences. The chronics each had at least 10 convictions, and they had especially long criminal careers (from age 13.8 to age 37.5 on average) characterised by high rates of offending. Because they are so few and account for so much of the crime problem, the chronics are important targets for prevention and treatment.

Offending by family members

We also studied the conviction careers of the men's families. Each family of origin had 5.5 persons on average (mother, father and 3.5 children) and on average 1.5 of them were convicted, or 600 persons out of 2,200 searched. Two-thirds of the families (64%) contained at least one convicted person, but only 6% of families accounted for half of all convictions (see Farrington *et al*, 2009). Therefore, offending was concentrated in a relatively small number of families.

Self-reported offending

During the interviews, the G2 males were asked to self-report offences that they had committed that had not necessarily come to the notice of the police. The most important interviews were at ages 14, 18, 32 and 48. During these four age ranges, almost all of the males (93%) said that they had committed at least one of eight types of offences (burglary, theft of motor vehicles, theft from motor vehicles, shoplifting, theft from machines, assault, drug use and vandalism), which account for the majority of all conviction offences. However, only 29% had been convicted for one of these offences during the same age ranges.

Based on the commission of 8 offences, the average age of onset was much earlier according to self-reports (10.3, compared with 19.1 according to convictions). Similarly, the average age of desistance was much later in self-reports (35.2, compared with 25.1 according to convictions). The probability of a self-reported offence leading to a conviction was highest for burglary and theft of vehicles (both 28%) and lowest for fraud and theft from work (both 1%; see Farrington et al, 2014).

Risk factors

We found many risk factors that predicted a high probability of offending. This article concentrates on risk factors measured in childhood, that predict convictions for violence for both G2 males and G3 males (see Farrington 2018).

Childhood predictors

The strongest family predictors of violence by G2 males were convictions of the G1 parents, harsh discipline, poor parental supervision, parental conflict, and coming from a disrupted family (separation from a biological parent). The strongest individual predictors were high troublesomeness (rated by peers and teachers), high daring (taking many risks), high dishonesty (rated by peers), high hyperactivity (lacks concentration or restless in class, rated by teachers) and low intelligence. The strongest socio-economic predictors were low family income, large family size, low socio-economic status, and poor housing.

The strongest family predictors of violence by G3 males were convictions of the G2 parents, physical punishment and poor parental supervision. The strongest individual predictors were suspension from school, frequent truancy and high risk-taking. The strongest socio-economic predictors were poor housing, large family size and low take-home pay of the family breadwinner.

Generally, the same risk factors were important for both generations of males. When the same 20 risk factors were used to predict convictions up to age 21, the strength of relationships for G2 males correlated .80 with the strength of relationships for G3 males (Farrington et al, 2015). The most important independent predictors in both generations were convicted parents, high daring or risk taking, and a disrupted family. Similarly, in international comparative research, the same risk factors were important predictors in both the CSDD and the Pittsburgh Youth Study (Farrington & Loeber, 1999). Generally, risk factors for offending are highly replicable over time and place, at least in Western industrialised countries.

Mechanisms and processes

We have made several attempts to go beyond the identification of risk factors to test alternative theories about mechanisms and processes relating risk factors to offending. For example, we tested different explanations of the relationship between disrupted families (broken homes) and delinquency and found that, while G2 males from broken homes (permanently disrupted families) were more delinquent than G2 males from intact homes, they were not more delinquent than G2 males from intact high conflict families. Therefore, the loss of a parent was not the key factor. Overall, the most important factor was what happened after the family break. G2 males who remained with their mother after the separation had the same delinquency rate as G2 males from intact low conflict families. G2 males who remained with their father, with relatives or with others (e.g. foster parents) had high delinquency rates. Therefore it was not true that broken homes always had undesirable consequences (see Farrington et al., 2009).

Life events

Effects of life events

In a longitudinal survey, it is possible to investigate the effects of specific life events on the development of delinquency, by comparing before and after measures of offending. For example, the effects on delinquent behaviour of being found guilty in court were studied. If convictions have a deterrent or reformative effect, a boy's delinquent behaviour should decline after he is convicted. On the other hand, if convictions have stigmatising or contaminating effects, a boy's delinquent behaviour should increase after he is convicted. These hypotheses were tested by studying self-reports of delinquency before and after a boy was first convicted. The results suggested that first convictions had undesirable delinquency-amplifying effects on G2 males (see Farrington, 2003).

Another investigation of the effect of a specific event on offending focussed on unemployment. The key question was whether the G2 males committed more offences (according to official records) during their periods of unemployment than during their periods of employment. The results showed that the G2 males did indeed commit more crimes while unemployed than while employed. Furthermore, the difference was restricted to offences involving financial gain, such as theft, burglary, robbery and fraud. There was no effect of unemployment on other offences, such as violence, vandalism and drug use. These results suggest that the G2 males committed more offences while they were unemployed primarily because they lacked money at these times and were trying to get money.

Factors encouraging desistance

An important life event that encouraged desistance was moving out of London. Most families who moved out were upwardly mobile families who were moving to prosperous suburban areas in the Home Counties, often buying their own houses rather than renting in London. It was clear that both the official and self-reported offending of the G2 males decreased after they or their families moved out of London, possibly because of the effect of the move in breaking up delinquent peer groups.

It is often believed that marriage is one of the best treatments for male offending. When we asked the G2 males in their 20s why they had stopped offending, they often mentioned marriage and the influence of women, as well as the fact that they did not hang around so much with delinquent friends. Before-and-after analyses showed that getting married led to a decrease in conviction rates compared with remaining single, whereas separation from a wife led to an increase in conviction rates compared with staying married (see Farrington, 2003).

Life success

Measuring life success

We looked at life success among the G2 males at ages 32 and 48, measured on 9 criteria, including their employment and accommodation histories, cohabitation, alcohol and drug use, convictions and self-reported offending, anxiety/depression and violence. The vast majority were rated as successful at age 32 and this improved further by age 48 (see Farrington *et al*, 2009).

Life success of offenders

The convicted males were divided into 47 desisters who were convicted only before age 21, 31 late-comers to crime who were convicted only at age 21 or older, and 65 persisters who were convicted both before and after age 21. The key question that was addressed is to what extent these categories of offenders were successful in different aspects of their lives at age 48. The good news is that the majority of all groups were considered to be leading successful lives: 95% of unconvicted men, 96% of desisters, 84% of late onset offenders, and 65% of persisters.

The most important finding is that desisters were not significantly different from unconvicted men in 8 out of 9 areas or in their total success score. Therefore, as with smoking, those who give up offending eventually become similar to non-offenders.

Late onset offenders were significantly different from unconvicted men in their alcohol and drug use. Interestingly, among the best predictors of late onset offenders were nervousness and having few friends at age 8-10, teacher-rated anxiety at age 12-14, high neuroticism at age 16 and not having had sexual intercourse by age 18. It seems that the protective effects of social inhibition in adolescence may wear off after age 21 when men leave home.

Intergenerational transmission

Most recently, the intergenerational transmission of offending has been studied between G2 males and G3 males. There was significant intergenerational transmission of convictions; 43% of G3 sons of G2 convicted males were convicted, compared with 18% of G3 sons of G2 unconvicted males (Farrington *et al*, 2017). Intergenerational transmission was strongest for burglary, possessing an offensive weapon, and threatening behaviour. There was also significant intergenerational transmission of self-reported offending (Farrington *et al*, 2018), and this was strongest for burglary, assault and marijuana use. The intergenerational transmission of convictions was mediated by socio-economic deprivation, poor child-rearing, disrupted families and an anti-establishment attitude. The intergenerational transmission of self-reported offending was mediated by socio-economic deprivation and an anti-establishment attitude.

Policy implications

The main policy implications of the CSDD are relevant to risk assessment and risk-focussed prevention. Risk assessment tools such as the EARL-20B (Early Assessment Risk List for Boys), which aims to identify children who are at risk of reoffending, are based on international co-operation with longitudinal surveys such as the CSDD and the Pittsburgh Youth Study that have discovered the most important risk factors for offending. While risk assessment and risk-focussed prevention are relevant to the onset and persistence of offending, the CSDD also has policy implications for desistance (e.g. in showing the beneficial effects of employment, marriage and moving house).

Risk-focussed prevention suggests that, in order to reduce offending, the key risk factors should be identified, and programmes should be implemented to tackle these risk factors. Based on the CSDD, it might be suggested that early prevention experiments are especially needed that target four important risk factors: low school attainment, poor parental child-rearing behaviour, impulsiveness and poverty (see Farrington, 2015).

Because of the link between offending and numerous other social problems, any measure that succeeds in reducing crime will probably have benefits that go far beyond this. Early prevention that reduces offending would probably also reduce drinking, drunk driving, drug use, sexual promiscuity and family violence, and perhaps also school failure, unemployment and marital disharmony.

It is clear from the CSDD that the most persistent offenders start early, have long criminal careers, and have difficulties in many aspects of their lives. Furthermore, we know that persistent offenders tend to produce the next generation of delinquent children. It is important to target children at risk with prevention programmes in childhood in order to break this cycle of intergenerational transmission.

References

Farrington, D. P. and Loeber, R. (1999) Transatlantic replicability of risk factors in the development of delinquency. In Cohen, P., Slomkowski, C. and Robins, L. N. (Eds.) *Historical and Geographical Influences on Psychopathology*. Mahwah, N.J.: Lawrence Erlbaum (pp. 299 329).

Farrington, D.P. (2003) Key results from the first 40 years of the Cambridge Study in Delinquent Development. In Thornberry, T.P. and Krohn, M.D. (Eds.) *Taking Stock of Delinquency: An Overview of Findings from Contemporary Longitudinal Studies*. New York: Kluwer/Plenum (pp. 137-183).

Farrington, D. P., Coid, J. W. and West, D. J. (2009) The development of offending from age 8 to age 50: Recent results from the Cambridge Study in Delinquent Development. *Monatsschrift fur Kriminologie und Strafrechtsreform (Journal of Criminology and Penal Reform)*, **92**, 160-173.

Farrington, D. P., Piquero, A. R. and Jennings, W. G. (2013) *Offending from Childhood to Late Middle Age: Recent Results from the Cambridge Study in Delinquent Development*. New York: Springer.

Farrington, D. P., Ttofi, M. M., Crago, R. V. and Coid, J. W. (2014) Prevalence, frequency, onset, desistance and criminal career duration in self-reports compared with official records. *Criminal Behaviour and Mental Health*, **24**, 241-253.

Farrington, D. P. (2015) The developmental evidence base: Prevention. In Crighton, D. A. and Towl, G.J. (Eds.) *Forensic Psychology* (2nd ed.). Chichester: Wiley (pp. 141-159).

Farrington, D. P., Ttofi, M. M., Crago, R. V. and Coid, J. W. (2015) Intergenerational similarities in risk factors for offending. *Journal of Developmental and Life-Course Criminology*, **1**, 48-62.

Farrington, D. P., Ttofi, M. M. and Crago, R. V. (2017) Intergenerational transmission of convictions for different types of offences. *Victims and Offenders,* **12**, 1-20.

Farrington, D.P. (2018) Origins of violent behavior over the life span. In Vazsonyi, A.T., Flannery, D.J., and DeLisi, M. (Eds.) *The Cambridge Handbook of Violent Behavior and Aggression* (2nd ed.). Cambridge: Cambridge University Press (pp. 3-30).

Farrington, D.P., Ttofi, M.M. and Crago, R.V. (2018) Intergenerational transmission of self-reported offending in the Cambridge Study in Delinquent Development. In Eichelsheim, V. I. and Van de Weijer, S. G. A. (Eds.) *Intergenerational Continuity of Criminal and Antisocial Behaviour: An International Overview of Studies.* Abingdon, UK: Routledge (pp. 115-136).

Chapter 27:
In search of data that can inform clinical, policy and legislative changes and public education in forensic mental health: The National Trajectory Project

By Anne G Crocker, with the National Trajectory Team:
Tonia L Nicholls, Michael C Seto, Yanick Charette,
Malijaï Caulet, Catherine Wilson, Jamie Livingston
& Leila Salem

> 'But the insane criminal has nowhere to call home: no age or nation
> has provided a place for him. He is everywhere unwelcome and
> objectionable. The prisons thrust him out; the hospitals are unwilling
> to receive him; the law will not let him stay at his house; and the public
> will not permit him to go abroad. And yet humanity and justice, the
> sense of common danger, and a tender regard for a deeply degraded
> brother-man, all agree that something should be done for him'.
> (Edward Jarvis, 1857)

The field of forensic mental health has grown over the past 25 years and
has also developed important international conferences, associations and
journals to share knowledge between scientists, clinicians, administrators,
policy makers and lawmakers. There remains, however a dearth of
literature and large multisite studies to inform clinical, organizational,
policy and legislative change at national and international levels, above
and beyond applying results of grouped risk data to individual persons.
More than twenty-five years ago, Hodgins *et al* (1992) undertook the largest
national descriptive study of individuals found Not Guilty by Reason of
Insanity in Canada. In the US, the MacArthur Community Violence study
identified key violence risk factors across five sites, and in particular

underlined the importance of substance use above and beyond mental illness (Monahan & Steadman, 1994). More recently, Priebe *et al* examined trends in mental health care across nine European countries (2005; 2008). These are selected studies that exemplify the key components necessary to address the needs of the forensic population and ensure public safety:

1. the makeup of forensic populations
2. violence risk factors in community settings
3. mental health service use trends and demands.

With the multiplicity of media outlets and sensationalist forensic mental health cases, there is a need to collect and disseminate accurate population-level trends and characteristics to inform the public and the media, as well as decision and policy-makers.

Over the past 20 years, there has been an international trend towards increasing demand for forensic mental health services, and Canada is no exception (Jansman-Hart *et al*, 2011). The National Trajectory Project (NTP: https://ntp-ptn.org) is the most extensive study conducted about individuals found Not Criminally Responsible on Account of Mental Disorder (NCRMD) and the Review Board process in Canada (Charette *et al*, 2015; Crocker *et al*, 2015; Crocker *et al*, 2015a, 2015b; Nicholls *et al*, 2015) following significant Canadian legislative changes in 1992.

Below are some of the highlights of this comprehensive file review of 1,800 men and women found NCRMD across British Columbia, Ontario and Québec (the three most populous provinces in Canada) between 2000 and 2005 and followed-up until 2008. There were interprovincial differences in the rates of NCRMD verdicts. On average, over the five-year period reviewed, there were 6.08 NCRMD verdicts per 1,000 criminal court decisions in Quebec, 0.95 in Ontario and 1.34 in British Columbia (Crocker *et al*, 2015) and the trend was maintained over time. In addition to interprovincial differences regarding the makeup and outcomes of NCRMD individuals through the Review Board system, some of the key findings of the study are highlighted here:

■ Who are the persons found NCRMD? (Crocker *et al*, 2015)

   ▪ Men represented 84% of persons found NCRMD.

   ▪ Nearly three quarters of persons found NCRMD had a psychotic spectrum disorder and a quarter had a mood disorder as their primary diagnosis.

   ▪ More than one-third had a co-morbid substance use disorder.

- Women found NCRMD were more likely to suffer from a mood disorder and more likely to be older than their male counterparts (Nicholls *et al*, 2015).

- Three-quarters of individuals with an NCRMD finding had a prior mental health hospitalisation and half had no criminal history.

■ What offence led to the NCRMD verdict? (Crocker *et al*, 2015)

- Less than 10% of NCRMD verdicts followed a severe violent offence (murder, attempted murder or sexually based offence).

- One third of individuals were found NCRMD for some form of assault and one third for uttering threats.

- More than a third of victims were family members, and 23% a mental health care worker or police officer.

■ How are decisions about release made?

- Dynamic factors, behavior between hearings and mental health factors in particular, were found to be heavily weighted by the Review Boards in their decision-making (Crocker *et al*, 2014; Wilson *et al*, 2016).

- Factors relevant to community reintegration, such as the risk items of the HCR-20, are rarely thoroughly discussed in clinicians' reports to Review Boards and in Review Boards' justifications for dispositions (Wilson *et al*, 2015).

■ What are the perceptions of Review Board processes by individuals found NCRMD?(Livingston *et al*, 2016)

- Some participants noted that Review Board hearings tend to focus on the negative attributes of people found NCRMD and ignore strengths.

- Results suggest that many participants perceived that the NCRMD verdict leads to more control and surveillance than court-imposed sentences.

- Individuals found NCRMD generally perceived that they were treated respectfully and fairly during Review Board hearings.

■ What about re-offending and rehospitalisation?

- Recidivism rates of individuals found NCRMD were lower than recidivism rates typically reported for mentally ill or non-disordered incarcerated offenders (Bonta *et al*, 2014; Bonta *et al*, 1998; Villeneuve & Quinsey, 1995).

- Primary diagnosis did not influence risk of reoffending, but substance abuse, the presence of a co-occurring personality disorder, and a prior conviction or finding of NCRMD were relevant factors that increased risk (Charette *et al*, 2015).

■ Individuals found NCRMD placed in independent housing following a conditional discharge from the Review Board were more likely to commit a new offense and to be readmitted for psychiatric treatment compared with those housed in supportive housing (Salem *et al*, 2015).

Summary

■ Given three quarters of NCRMD individuals were previously known to the general mental health system, there are opportunities for prevention and earlier intervention.

■ When compared to correctional populations with or without mental illness, NCRMD accused display lower rates of recidivism.

■ There is a need to decrease the gap between evidence and clinical practice regarding use of risk assessment instruments.

■ Forensic services and Review Boards seem to be doing a good job relative to the challenging population they work with: the NCRMD system both protects the public and oversees the rehabilitation of persons found NCRMD.

■ The NTP provides evidence to inform legal and clinical practices and policies. It also provides an opportunity to orient future research such as understanding key factors in community reintegration and long-term outcomes of forensic patients, effects of legislative changes on services and trajectories of patients, how to improve the implementation and use of risk assessment and management tools in mental health services, cost-effectiveness of forensic mental health programs and interventions, etc.

We need to continue to organise and collect data that provide the trends and accurate pictures of forensic mental health populations and services across countries, over time, and when significant mental health care and justice changes take place (Crocker *et al*, 2017). This will help plan for the development of inpatient and community resources, to create policy that is fair and equitable to our patients while still ensuring the safety of the public, allocate appropriate resources and allow for periodic changes in laws and mental health policies.

References

Bonta J, Blais J & Wilson HA (2014) A Theoretically Informed Meta-Analysis of the Risk for General and Violent Recidivism for Mentally Disordered Offenders. *Aggression and Violent Behavior* **19** (3) 278–287.

Bonta J, Law M & Hanson K (1998) The prediction of criminal and violent recidivism among mentally disordered offenders – a meta-Analysis. *Psychological Bulletin* **123** (2) 123–142.

Charette Y, Crocker AG, Seto MC, Nicholls TL & Caulet M (2015) The National Trajectory Project of Individuals found Not Criminally Responsible on Account of Mental Disorder in Canada. Part 4- Criminal Recidivism. *Canadian Journal of Psychiatry* **60** (3) 127–134.

Crocker AG, Charette Y, Seto MC, Nicholls TL, Côté G & Caulet M (2015) The National Trajectory Project of Individuals found Not Criminally Responsible on Account of Mental Disorder in Canada. Part 3- Trajectories and outcomes through the forensic system. *Canadian Journal of Psychiatry* **60** (3) 117–126.

Crocker AG, Livingston JD & Leclair MC (2017) Forensic mental health systems internationally. In: R Roesch & AN Cook (Eds.) *Handbook of Forensic Mental Health Services* (pp3–76). Taylor & Francis/Routledge.

Crocker AG, Nicholls TL, Charette Y & Seto MC (2014) Dynamic and Static Factors Associated with Discharge Dispositions: The National Trajectory Project of Individuals Found Not Criminally Responsible on Account of Mental Disorder (NCRMD) in Canada. *Behavioral Sciences & the Law* **32** (5) 577–595.

Crocker AG, Nicholls TL, Seto MC, Charette Y, Côté G & Caulet M (2015a) The National Trajectory Project of Individuals found Not Criminally Responsible on Account of Mental Disorder in Canada: Part 2–The people behind the label. *Canadian Journal of Psychiatry* **60** (3) 106–116.

Crocker AG, Nicholls TL, Seto MC, Charette Y, Côté G & Caulet M (2015b) The National Trajectory Project of Individuals found Not Criminally Responsible on Account of Mental Disorder in Canada. Part 1– Context and Methods. *Canadian Journal of Psychiatry* **60** (3) 95–105.

Hodgins S, Webster CD & Paquet J (1992) *The Canadian database: Patients held on lieutenant-governors' warrants*. Ottawa: Research and Statistics Divisions, Department of Justice Canada.

Jansman-Hart EM, Seto MC, Crocker AG, Nicholls, T. L., & Côté, G. (2011). International trends in demand for forensic mental health services. *International Journal of Forensic Mental Health* **10** (4) 326–336.

Jarvis E (1857) Criminal insane: Insane transgressors and insane convicts. *Journal of Insanity* **13** (3) 195–231.

Livingston JD, Crocker AG, Nicholls TL & Seto MC (2016) Forensic Mental Health Tribunals: A Qualitative Study of Participants. *Experiences and Views* **22** (2) 173–184.

Monahan J & Steadman HJ (1994) *Violence and Mental Disorder: Developments in risk assessment*. Chicago, IL: University of Chicago Press.

Nicholls TL, Crocker AG, Seto MC, Charette Y, Côté G & Wilson CM (2015). The National Trajectory Project of Individuals Found Not Criminally Responsible on Account of Mental Disorder in Canada. Part 5- How essential are gender-sensitive forensic psychiatric services? *Canadian Journal of Psychiatry* **60** (3) 135–145.

Priebe S, Badesconyi A, Fioritti A, Hansson L, Kilian R, Torres-Gonzales F, Wiersma D (2005). Reinstitutionalisation in mental health care: Comparison of data on service provision from six European countries. *British Medical Journal* **330**, 123–126.

Priebe S, Frottier P, Gaddini A, Killian R, Lauber C, Martinez-Leal R, Wright D (2008) Mental health care institutions in nine European countries, 2002 to 2006. *Psychiatric Services* **59** (5) 570–573.

Salem L, Crocker AG, Charette Y, Seto MC, Nicholls TL & Côté G (2015) Supportive housing and forensic patient outcomes. Law and Human Behavior 39 (3) 311–320.

Villeneuve DB & Quinsey VL (1995) Predictors of General and Violent Recidivism among Mentally Disordered Inmates. *Criminal Justice and Behavior Criminal Justice and Behavior* **22** (4) 397–410.

Wilson CM, Nicholls TL, Charette Y, Seto MC & Crocker AG (2016) Factors associated with Review Board decisions following rehospitalization among discharged individuals found Not Criminal Responsibility. *Behavioral Sciences and the Law*.

Wilson CM, Nicholls TL, Crocker AG, Charette Y & Seto MC (2015) What Factors are Mentioned by Forensic Review Boards in their Reasons for Disposition Decisions? Paper to be presented in TL Nicholls (Chair), The National Trajectory Project: An exploration of public policy, Aboriginal issues, Review Board hearings an. Annual conference of the American Psychology-Law Society, San Diego, USA.

Section 7

Ars Forensica –
Applying mortar between the scientific bricks

Chapter 28:
A framework for career development

By Quazi Haque and Chris Webster

We editors are fortunate to have at hand accomplished contributors who have been able to condense complex issues into concise chapters without in any way trivialising them. Each chapter thus contains a relatively small number of important scientific references, which should be seen as a springboard toward wider reading in the area. While being parsimonious with references, our colleagues have also offered ideas on further reading and other influences that have shaped their interests in the field of risk assessment and forensic mental health more generally. Furthermore, what comes through from such a task is an appreciation that our colleagues have also profited from a broader reading which encompasses not just well designed research studies that have reached the highest echelons of scientific publications, but also influences from more local cases studies, related academic fields (such as sociology and anthropology), and even from non-scientific fictional literature.

A knowledge and experience circuit

In Figure 28.1 we have attempted to format the range of knowledge, skills and experiences that are useful when commencing and maintaining a career in forensic and correctional mental health. We have placed core competencies in the centre of the diagram. In doing this, we emphasise the skills in which forensic and correctional mental health practitioners *must* exhibit proficiency (e.g. diagnostic formulations, assessing competence to stand trial, ensuring consent-to-treatment issues have been dealt with properly, writing reports, testifying before courts and tribunals, refining security measures, and so on). We stress that many highly capable practitioners are kept very busy and productive without stepping far outside this core.

Many clinicians will hold essential competencies in the use of pharmacological treatments for the treatment of mental health conditions. This is a vast subject which is better addressed in other specialist texts, such as by Joel Paris (2010) or Stephen Stahl's book series (2016). Paris makes a strong case that many current psychotropic agents are highly effective and have advanced the treatment of certain disorders. Many patients, however, experience bad results when treatments are over-used, prescribed outside of evidence-based indications, or simply given to the wrong patients. Stahl highlights the need for clinicians to have a working familiarity with neural circuits and neurochemistry to support their prescribing practice.

But we also draw attention to the fact that by itself, this work, day in and day out, can be very draining (see reference to Pat Barker's *Regeneration* mentioned in Chapter 30). For that reason we have placed a dot in the very centre of this diagram. The dot stands for the need to maintain personal health while conducting this potentially debilitating work[1]. We are here referring to the importance of seeking sources of inspiration (as from the theatre, moving pictures, music, religious studies, family, creative writing, and so on).

In the next ring of the diagram we place Specialised Clinical Practice (top). By this we mean only that many a mental health professional, in addition to dealing with 'general' practice, can and perhaps should develop a particular interest (e.g. intimate partner violence, intellectual deficit, sex offending, etc). Since risk assessment and management forms such a big part of forensic and correctional mental health work, many practitioners find it convenient and helpful to focus on this central topic (right). Since, as is stressed in this book, the field does not advance far without figuring out the strengths and limitations of prior clinical work, some colleagues take on responsibility for organising or participating in follow-along research (see Chapters 24-27, this volume). This is covered in Figure 28.1 (middle ring, bottom). Good though it undoubtedly is to be a competent clinician, it helps the field greatly if those skills can be shared. By this we mean developing expertise in educating others (middle ring, left).

We turn now to the outer circle. At the top, we place Programme Development and Evaluation. Sad to say, the great bulk of programmes, both inpatient and community, are never evaluated for effectiveness (see Chapter 11). This is, of course, not to say that such programmes accomplish nothing; only that that in all likelihood they could achieve more if properly studied. The matter of achieving diagnostic precision is included in the diagram (upper right). It is not that DSM and ICD classifications are fixed for all time. They are in constant need of revision. There is work to be done on behalf of professional bodies which promulgate these schemes. In many respects, forensic and correctional psychiatric services can be ideally situated to undertake basic biomedical, neurological, neuropsychiatric, neuropsychological and other kinds of related research (outer circle, right).

---

1   In Canada, a very prominent forensic psychiatrist, Dr John Bradford, has described his own experiences with Post-Traumatic Stress Disorder as published online in the Ottawa Citizen and related accounts on the internet.

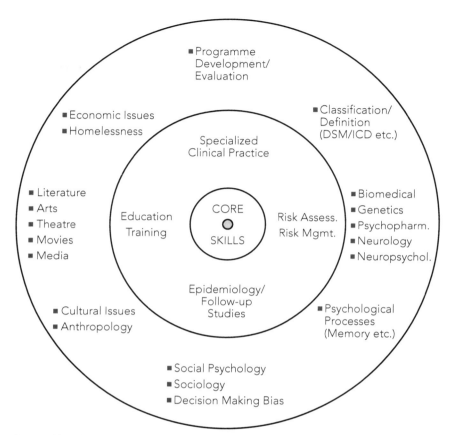

Figure 28.1: Forensic Careers – a knowledge and experience circuit

Always assuming that ethical requirements are met and that any intrusions do not disadvantage patients, organised research can improve the quality of assessments and treatments. Psychological processes are in need of study. It is important to know how biases do or do not enter evaluations (Chapter 6), how memory distorts under certain conditions, why eyewitness testimony is not necessarily reliable, how false memories can be inadvertently inculcated, and so on (lower centre-right). Since so much decision-making is shared among practitioners in contemporary forensic mental health services, it is necessary to figure out how colleagues can best work together in the interests of individual patients and the courts and tribunals (bottom). Grave harm can ensue if cultural differences are not taken into account during the course of evaluations (e.g. Chapter 18, this volume). The content of courses taken years ago in anthropology may, for some colleagues, come in handy as a starting point for new considerations (lower left). The outer ring in our diagram (left) appeals to the importance of pursuing the arts generally, the topic of the following two chapters. Finally, some colleagues feel impelled, as they should, to devote energy to thinking about an area that interlinks in so many ways with psychiatry and the criminal law – namely, homelessness (upper centre left).

In viewing Figure 28.1, it is helpful to realise that the middle and outer circles can be rotated separately. In this way, professionals can find the pathway that best suits their current ambitions, always recognising that such pathways will very possibly change as new challenges and opportunities present themselves.

References

Cobb C (2013) 'Tough Forensic Guy John Bradford Opens up about his PTSD'. *Ottawa Citizen* **11th November.**

Paris J(2010) *The Use and Misuse of Psychiatric Drugs: An evidence-based critique.* Wiley-Blackwell.

Warburton K & Stahl S (2016) *Violence in Psychiatry.* Cambridge University Press.

Chapter 29:
Leading hands-on group discussions in forensic mental health services – A poetic twist

By Chris Webster

> *Much madness is divinest sense*
> *To a discerning eye;*
> *Much sense the starkest madness.*
> *'Tis the majority*
> *In this, as all prevails.*
> *Assent, and you are sane;*
> *Demur, - you're straightway dangerous,*
> *And handled with a chain*

Emily Dickinson

William Seighart is a well-known English businessman, philanthropist and writer. He tells his readers that from time to time he suffers from depression. He finds, though, that his moods oftimes can be dispelled by matching his discomforts to exactly the *right kind of poetry*. It occurred to him that he might not be alone in finding the muse to offer relief[24]. Accordingly, he has produced a small book called *The Poetry Pharmacy* (2017). He isolates 'feelings of inadequacy', 'apathy', 'depression', 'loss of sense of self' and so on. He then sets about finding the right poem to match that condition. The book is cleverly constructed with the poems laid out on the right-facing page. On the left-facing page he explains to the reader why his selected poem is apt to the particular psychological state of ill-being[25]. Sieghart's own writing, though, is able to stand on its own almost aside from the poems he is extolling. This is a sophisticated

---

24 Readers may know that the British empiricist philosopher John Stuart Mill, as a young man, dug himself out of a deep depression by turning to Wordsworth's poem 'Lines composed a few miles above Tintern Abbey'.

25 The author of this piece was intrigued to note the parallel between Sieghart's form of organisation and that used in V2 of the HCR-20 (i.e. coding instructions for items on the right hand page; literature review for those items on the left).

analysis. Present readers should not think for a moment that he is urging abandonment of conventional approaches to the treatment of mental and personality disorder (i.e. including psychopharmacological). What he is offering is an *adjunctive* avenue. The book's subtitle puts it well: *Tried-and-True Prescriptions for the Heart, Mind and Soul*[26]. It is also worth noting that the poems he has selected tend to be short. Those mentioned here average under 14 lines. It is to be noted, that this chapter is pitched around the idea of a 'reading list'. Mr. Sieghart's book provides exactly that.

In what follows I have extracted short quotations, not from the poems themselves, but from William Sieghart's comments about those works. And, for the convenience of the reader, I have organised the poems I have lifted[27] from his book according to the organisation of V3 of the HCR-20. The result is a kind of reformulation or refocusing of the basic HCR-20 into an intervention-oriented scheme[28]. Although *The Poetry of Pharmacy* concentrates mainly on depression and anxiety, and does not take psychosis and like conditions into account, this is not viewed as too severe a limitation for present purposes.

Items

H1 Violence History

> *'Letting go of the past takes work, and it may be a process that takes a lifetime.'* (p22)

Prescribed for: Emotional baggage
Also for: Psychological scarring, trauma, trust issues
Poem prescribed: *Burlap Sack* by Jane Hirshfeld (15 lines)

---

26 At an earlier stage of my career, I co-led a weekly discussion group for forensic inpatients. The other leader was Dr Fred Jensen, the service's Clinical Director. We aimed to make our meetings less counter-productive than those described so cleverly by Margaret Gibson in her 'Butterfly Ward' (1994). All the same, we did at times need to cast about for a suitable topic for discussion among us all. Had *Poetry Pharmacy* been available I would have tried it out. It amuses me to think of the *practical* value of poetry.

27 This idea is not entirely original. As noted in Chapter 11, in 2001 we published a 'Companion Guide' to the HCR-20. The various authors were given the task of explaining not so much how, say, 'lack of insight' is to be assessed, but how self-awareness or self-knowledge is to be inculcated.

28 It is a surprise, in reading *Poetry Pharmacy*, to meet again old friends – poems perhaps not imbibed since schooldays. Presumably, way back then, wise teachers drummed lines into our developing heads. Their hope, perhaps, might have been that these compressed notions of thought would help guide us through life and help us over its difficult moments.

H2 Other Antisocial Behaviour History

'It's terribly easy when things go wrong, and when we're at our angriest, to blame the ones we love by default ... we should ask ourselves and those around us, "How can I be more kind?"' (p102)

Prescribed for: Unkindness
Also for: Cruelty, intolerance, bickering in relationships, self-obsession
Poem prescribed: *It Happens all the Time in Heaven* by Hafez (translated by Daniel Ladinsky) (19 lines)

H3 Relationships History

'The journey from the bleakness of heartbreak to full recovery is long and arduous, and it is far from straight ... Sometimes, all we really need is for someone to give us permission to feel as we feel.' (p126)

Prescribed for: Heartbreak
Also for: Break-ups, romantic obsession, overreaction to loss
Poem prescribed: *Recension Day* by Duncan Forbes (14 lines)

H4 Employment History

'Are you idly wistful for another life, as every other of our perennially dissatisfied species is? Are there ambitions you gave up long ago that still haunt you?' (p38)

Prescribed for: Dissatisfaction with life
Also for: Existential angst, failure, lack of job fulfilment, falling out of love, wasted potential
Poem prescribed: *The Price* by Stuart Henson (14 lines)

H5 Substance Use

'...there's a reason that Alcoholics Anonymous recommend recovery be approached one day at a time. Breaking things down into bite-sized chunks doesn't just make them more manageable: it also provides us with many more chances to start again if we fail.' (p4)

Prescribed for: Compulsive behaviour
Also for: Addiction, obsession, self-destructiveness
Poem prescribed: from *New Every Morning* by Susan Coolidge (5 lines)

H6 Mental Disorder

'…if you can remind yourself that the world may not be as bad as it seems, then escape is possible. Cling to that hope. Drag yourself to the surface. Sometimes, it will make you feel better.' (p104)

Prescribed for: News overload
Also for: Depression, disillusionment, general malaise, pessimism
Poem prescribed: *Sometimes* by Sheenagh Pugh (12 lines)

H7 Personality Disorder

'We will always have that chance to be reborn into positivity and change. Grab it. Begin afresh, afresh, afresh.' (p32)

Prescribed for: Stagnation
Also for: Apathy, depression, despair, grief
Poem prescribed: *The Trees* by Philip Larkin (12 lines)

H8 Traumatic Experiences

'Grief is surgery. It consumes you, for a while; it puts you under. But once your scars have knitted together, you realize that all that pain was necessary. It is a healing process, despite the fact that it must begin with violence.' (p134)

Prescribed for: Maturing grief
Also for: Despair, heartbreak, loss
Poem prescribed: *Into the Hour* by Elizabeth Jennings (18 lines)

H9 Violent Attitudes

'…it may be our thoughts, and not the reasons for them, that do the most damage…' (p48)

Prescribed for: Failure to live in the moment
Also for: Fretfulness, regret, self-recrimination, worrying
Poem prescribed: *Golden Retrievals* by Mark Doty (14 lines)

H10 Treatment or Supervision Response (Past)

'When people rediscover the thread that runs through their story, it is often a revelation.' (p14)

Prescribed for: Purposelessness
Also for: Apathy, nihilism
Poem prescribed: *The Way It Is* by William Stafford (10 lines)

C1 Insight

'The trick, when you're staring down the barrel of your own stupidity, is to gather up the horror of it all, to understand it and to accept it.' (p62)

Prescribed for: Making mistakes
Also for: Regret, living in the past, self-recrimination, self-loathing
Poem prescribed: *The Mistake* by James Fenton (20 lines)

C2 Violent Ideation or Intent

'...but this poem helps me to calm my mind and my breathing, and drift into unconsciousness.' (p2)

Prescribed for: Anxiety
Also for: Fear for children, fear for the future, sleeplessness, stress, worrying
Poem prescribed: *The Peace of Wild Things* by Wendell Berry (11 lines)

C3 Major Mental Disorder

'One flash of sunlight can be all it takes to give us the sense of possibility that can change everything.' (p16)

Prescribed for: Need for reassurance
Also for: Anxiety, depression, general fear, fear of mortality, pessimism
Poem prescribed: *Everything is Going to be All Right* by Derek Mahon (12 lines)

C4 Instability

'If ... we maintain equanimity in the face of our true selves, we can learn to accept ourselves for who we really are – darkness and all.' (p70)

Prescribed for: Emotional repression
Also for: Guilt, avoidance of pain, unhealthy coping mechanisms
Poem prescribed: *The Guest House* by Rumi (translated by Coleman Barks) (18 lines)

C5 Treatment and Supervision (Present)

'Of course, we could choose to patch over our cracks, to build up our walls and our roofs until the wind can't shake us. But would it be worth it, if in so doing we also shut out all chance of new feeling, new light? Sometimes it is good to be shaken.' (p8)

Prescribed for: Psychological scarring
Also for: Emotional baggage, feelings of brokenness, cynicism, fear of vulnerability, self-isolation
Poem prescribed: *Although the Wind* by Izumi Shikibu (translated by Jane Hirshfield with Mariko Aratani) (5 lines)

R1 Professional Services and Plans

'When you really think about it, it's a wonderful thing that our lives are so rich with different possibilities.' (p78)

Prescribed for: Fear of the unknown
Also for: Fear for the future, fear of uncertainty
Poem prescribed: *What If This Road* by Sheenagh Pugh (14 lines)

R2 Living Situation

'Even if your surroundings are grim and brutal, even in a darkened room or right in the middle of a miserable urban expanse, you can still find beauty in the world around you.' (p100)

Prescribed for: Longing for beauty
Also for: Glumness, depression, purposelessness, ugly surroundings
Poem Prescribed: from *Endymion* by John Keats (24 lines)

R3 Personal Support

'There will always be someone who wants to liven up their commute with a mental image of us, wrinkled knees and all. The trick is simply to find them, and then have the courage to show them what we've got.' (p12)

Prescribed for: Glumness
Also for: Fear of being unloved, loss of perspective, weariness, feelings of unattractiveness
Poem prescribed: *Celia Celia* by Adrian Mitchell (4 lines)

R4 Treatment or Supervision Response (Future)

'You can start the day hopeless and end it knowing that everything is going to be OK. Life can change very, very quickly, often turning on moments or causes that you would never have expected.' (p6)

Prescribed for: Depression
Also for: Hopelessness, intractable misery
Poem Prescribed: *Everyone Sang* by Siegfried Sassoon (10 lines)

R5 Stress or Coping

'In the long run, menial tasks are also a great cure for directionlessness ... In their mundanity and repetitiveness these tasks give you a rhythm, which in turn becomes a king of structure, which, ultimately, will give you the ability to cope.' (p20)

Prescribed for: Feeling of unreality
Also for: Apathy, boredom, messiness, purposelessness, need for self-care
Poem prescribed: *Of Gravity and Light* by John Burnside (18 lines)

References and further reading

Dickinson E (1994) *The Selected Poems of Emily Dickinson*. Hertfordshire, England: Wordsworth Editions.

Douglas KS, Webster CD, Hart SD, Eaves D & Ogloff JRP (Eds) (2001) *HCR-20 Violence risk management companion guide*. Burnaby, Canada: Mental Health, Law, and Policy Institute, Simon Fraser University.

Gibson M (1994) *The Butterfly Ward*. Originally published 1976. Toronto, Canada: Harper/Collins.

Mill JS (1966) *Autobiography of John Stuart Mill*. Originally published 1924. New York: Columbia University Press.

Sieghart W (2017) *The Poetry Pharmacy: Tried-and-true prescriptions for the heart, mind, and soul*. UK: Particular Books, Penguin

Webster CD, Douglas KS, Eaves D & Hart SD (1997) *HCR-20: Assessing risk for violence, Version 2*. Burnaby, Canada: Mental Health, Law and Policy Institute, Simon Fraser University.

Wordsworth W (1798) *Lines Composed a Few Miles above Tintern Abbey, on Revisiting the Banks of the Wye during a Tour*. Poetry Foundation.

Chapter 30: Risk Rules – Seeing through brick walls faced by clinicians, researchers and administrators

By Chris Webster & Quazi Haque

'Thank you for your attention. You may very well choose to dismiss what I have said as the vapourings of a literary man, a member of a small and notoriously visionary profession, but one which has sometimes shown an ability to see through a brick wall, which so far science has not tried to do. Psychiatry, which pretends to be a science but which at its best is a form of art, might give it a try.' (p311) (Robertson Davies, 1985, *Murder as it Looks to a Literary Man*)

A holistic biopsychosocial approach toward assessment, formulation and treatment reaps dividends for clients as well as professionals. The evolution of positive psychology and the development of techniques such as mindfulness, biofeedback and more recent technological advances in the delivery of mental health treatment, offer enhanced opportunities for clients to participate in how they receive their own treatment. This area has already been covered to a certain extent by Simpson (Chapter 20) and Haque (Chapter 21). As well, the previous chapter by one of us (CDW) pitches the idea that poetry, selected carefully, can sometimes get across ideas that are otherwise hard to convey.

Literary influences

Literature can highlight the motives and actions of patients and professionals existing within the mental health, forensic and correctional systems. For the most part, these fictions are based on 'real' events that actually occurred at specific times under particular circumstances. It needs to be held in mind that the work of the various writers summarised below is more *grounded* than might at first be thought. Reading of this kind adds tones and textures. These subtleties can be helpful when it comes to appraising why an individual makes a choice to act with violence[1]. And it often provides a cautionary tale to those who are believed to be in the best position to intervene and provide care. For this reason, we would like to offer our selective and personal reading list with the reader. We have also been sufficiently brazen to highlight one particular theme, or 'risk rule', for each book or short story while acknowledging the layers of complexity contained across this mind-stretching collection.

We conclude with a filmography (Appendix, p275), which we hope lists movies that are empathic and fair depictions of psychiatric illness in its myriad forms. We have been at pains to list films that provide other than damaging and distorted portrayals of the experience of mental disorder.

1. Searching for patterns

James Brussel (1968) *Casebook of a Crime Psychiatrist*

Famously, Brussel, in his search for 'the mad bomber' of New York, said, 'Chances are he will be wearing a double-breasted suit. Buttoned.' And, of course, that was how George Metesky was attired when he was eventually arrested. It is tantalising to think that, to some degree at least, psychiatrists and colleagues in related fields might be able to proffer accurate forecasts on the basis of the perpetrator's psychological and psychiatric characteristics. It was indeed this prospect that drew, many years ago, one of our present contributors to the field. No doubt this colleague, as he qualified himself in training, found other challenges and opportunities as he moved along. He may have realised that this was not an easy sub-speciality to enter. As Brussel notes, the police tend not to be welcoming toward 'outsiders' even as they struggle, sometimes against mounting public pressure, to prevent further violence from someone 'on the loose'. It is a lot easier to deal with persons who have already been apprehended and are safely stowed in custody.

Brussel explains how 'profiling' works. To do this he relies on the Metesky and other cases. He makes the point that forensic psychiatrists, working collaboratively with police services, often help by *ruling out* suspects who, at first blush, seem likely to be implicated in the crime under investigation. And readers of the casebook soon realise that Brussel makes no claim that he or other colleagues can 'get it right' more than a fraction of the time. Yet this is no reason to think that some colleagues in

---

1 We, the editors, cannot refrain from remarking that, though they tend to read a number of mental health reports in the course of a week, few of these are actually interesting or compelling to read. They tend to be formulaic, contain much redundant information and be devoid of the aforementioned 'texture' which can do so much to bring the issues into focus.

the forensic arena cannot make thoughtful contributions when it comes to apprehending persons suspected of having committed very serious crimes. Psychiatrists, clinical psychologists and other mental health professionals are exposed to a variety of cases during training. They file these instances into 'banks'. These banks are organised, in part, by schemes like the DSM and the ICD. Without wishing to pretend to be able to peer further into the brain structure and function of our colleagues, it is possible here to assert that they come to possess 'orienting maps', which lay persons do not. For sure, we know more than most about the way most psychiatric conditions unfold over time and under which particular circumstances.

Risk Rule: Patience and persistence usually triumphs over periodic panache.

2. Law and ethics

Harper Lee (1960) *To Kill a Mockingbird*

Richard Schneider (Chapter 2) considers law to be an entity that is continuously developing, evolving and morphing in order to be responsive to changing societal demands. Atticus Finch comes to understand this as he stands alone in defending a black man (Tom Robinson) against a false charge of rape. Atticus, a widower, has the responsibility of raising his two children. The kids, Scout and Jem, are perfectly 'normal', meaning they are adventurous and high-spirited. One thing that arouses their curiosity is the presence of the neighbour. 'Boo' Radley (Arthur) never leaves the house. The kids spy on him. In the course of defending Tom Robinson in court, Atticus offends Bob Ewell (the father of the girl against whom the alleged rape was supposed to have been perpetrated). Later in the story Scout and Jem are attacked at night. They escape, all thanks to 'Boo' who had been shadowing them. He kills Ewell. This having happened, Atticus expects the law to unfold, for Arthur ('Boo') to be charged. Atticus is, after all, a by-the-book lawyer. But the Sheriff, Heck Tate, will have none of it. He obliges Atticus to 'stay his hand', arguing that customary though this might be in most cases, a court appearance, even if perfunctory, would destroy the fragile 'Boo'. For ethical reasons, the law had to be given a twist. Overly mechanical application of the criminal law can result in considerable unfairness.

Risk Rule: 'It ain't no sin if you crack a few laws now and then, just so long as you don't break any.' (Mae West)

3. Mental disorders and violence

Graham Greene (1981) *Doctor Fischer of Geneva or the Bomb Party*
Graham Greene's book provides an example of how presentations of
troubled individuals may not fall neatly into operationalised diagnostic
criteria. Greene is particularly skilled at creating troubled characters
cast in intricate social webs (for example, Henry Scoby in *The Heart of the
Matter* and Pinky in *Brighton Rock*). In the *Bomb Party*, the narrator is a
widower in his 50s who falls in love with a younger woman, Anna-Luise.
She has an enormously rich father who goes by the title of Doctor Fischer.
What kind of doctor he is, no one knows. He lives by a lake in a huge,
luxurious house, having made his money from the invention of a toothpaste.
The book's action centres on Dr Fischer's personality and conduct. He has
assembled around him a group of very wealthy sycophants, who provide for
him a means of 'experimentation'. He offers them huge prizes but to obtain
those gifts they must risk being blown up.

The narrator is drawn toward Dr Fischer, particularly after the death of
Anna-Luise. We, the reader, are left trying to understand what prompts the
doctor's effort's to humiliate and destroy others. Fischer's presentation is not
unlike many evaluations which professionals must undertake – emotions and
behaviours within the realms of common human experience, such as hate,
fear, shame, pride, contempt, cruelty and courage, which become amplified
and distorted through the experience of mental illness. A superficial reading
of the novel might tempt a professional reader to offer up a diagnosis of
Personality Disorder for Doctor Fischer. But in this case, depression needs to
be considered. For a fuller account, see Webster & Ben-Aron (1985). Readers
are also directed to *Crime and Punishment* (Dostoevsky, 1866, see MS
Webster, 1981) which portray so well the frequently observed but complex
relationships between poverty, mental illness and violence.

*Risk Rule: There's more to it than what meets the eye – Psychiatric conditions
can sometimes be hard to untangle and often need time to declare themselves.*

4. Psychopathic personality disorder

Sinclair Lewis (1935) *It Can't Happen Here*
This uncannily far-seeing novel is built around the idea that fascism could
take over in the United States. Although Hitler and Mussolini were hard
at work building their movements in 1930s Europe at the very time he
was writing the book, WWII was still a few years away. Lewis lays out a
future of political ruthlessness, anti-Semitism, nationalism, the creation of
concentration camps and the suppression of democratic principles through

the invocations of military and quasi-military force. Lee Sarason, who would likely score near the top on a Hare PLC-R examination, becomes president in a coup. He leads a self-indulgent lifestyle with his young male cronies. He has no regard for the day-to-day plight of his citizens. As in *To Kill a Mockingbird*, readers are treated to a vision of a whole society gone mad. Literature seems especially well suited to pointing out that psychopathy is not a unitary construct. The two assailants in Truman Capote's *In Cold Blood* give an accurate representation of the impulsive, chaotic and antisocial aspects of the condition. Evelyn Waugh is a dab hand at elucidating these kinds of characters (e.g. Basil Seal in *Put Out More Flags*, 1942).

Risk Rule: Some people can't ever get it right – The condition of psychopathy is not a unitary construct and can appear in various guises.

5. Trauma

Pat Barker (1991) *Regeneration*

Regeneration is based on the real-life Dr William Rivers. At the start of WWI, Rivers is a neurology researcher at Cambridge University. From this cosy spot he is yanked into a Captain's uniform and sent to Scotland. There, in a country-mansion converted to a wartime mental hospital, he has to treat traumatised soldiers. This he does with more than passing success. Indeed, he becomes, in a sense, an ideal psychiatrist. He knows how to help the men he is called upon to serve. But at a certain point, his superior recognises that Rivers himself is becoming emotionally overwhelmed by the work and he orders him to take time away from the job. This story reminds us all that, while we are taught to consider the possible effects of trauma on our patients, room must also be left to consider the effects of these unavoidable incursions on our own psychological well-being.

Risk Rule: Support the home team – Look after yourself, look after your colleagues.

6. Bias

Vladimir Nabakov (1972) *Transparent Things*

Hugh Person is an American working in Switzerland. Although he has a Ph.D. in literature he does drudgery-type editing work for a publisher. Early on in the novel, Nabakov discloses that Hugh has trouble sleeping and that on one occasion he wrecked a bedside lamp while asleep. In due course, Hugh falls in love with a high-spirited, athletic young woman, Armande. They marry. While asleep, he does to her what he did to the lamp. He is found by the court not to be responsible for the murder. Later, he is committed to prison and hospital. Eventually, he is released and he returns to America. In due course, he decides to make a sentimental trip back to Switzerland. He takes a room in a hotel in which he and his wife had once stayed. Next day, in the hotel lobby, he meets a man who, in passing, happens to remark that people like Hugh should never be allowed to re-join society. Hugh has to deal with this. The story, ending with the chance encounter in the hotel lobby, shows how difficult it can be for former forensic patients ever to evade social biases. Hugh figures he has 'served his time', that, though he remains deeply regretful about the murder of his beloved Armande, he ought, in fairness, be allowed to move on with his life.

Risk Rule: Charity begins at home – Take every opportunity to challenge stigma against the mentally ill.

7. Accuracy

Alice Munro (2009) *Child's Play*

Marlene is around 12. She lives an ordinary small-town life with her parents. From time to time another girl visits the town. Verna is mentally challenged. Despite her mother's urging her to be friendly with Verna, Marlene persists in her dislike. Later, Marlene goes to a summer camp. There she chums up with another girl called Charlene. They become fast friends very quickly. The staff refer to them as 'the twins'. Toward the end of their stay, the pair finds out that Verna is to be coming to the camp. Marlene has already filled Charlene's head with antipathy toward Verna. One day the three girls are swimming in the lake. They are in close proximity. A speedboat roars by. It creates a large wave. Marlene and Charlene laugh as they are tumbled over. But Verna is slow to recover. Without so much as a word between them, they reach out and hold Verna under. Verna drowns. Camp breaks up. Marlene and Charlene leave without any discussion of what had happened. The incident is, of course, written off as an accident.

The story traces the effects of this tragedy on both girls as they grow into adulthood separately harbouring their secret. The story is instructive because it strengthens the point made in the preceding paragraph – mainly, 'facts' at the time of subsequent formal evaluations tend to be missing or obscured. But a second point is this: the murder occurred as a result not of one girl acting alone but the two girls acting synergistically. The action took place without direct discussion. It all occurred in a second or two. To be sure, the girls had previously built a general 'case against' Verna. Yet while the ground had been tilled and the seed planted, there was no specified plan to harvest. The crime was opportunistic, borne of an over-heated symbiotic relationship. In Chapter 7 we make the point that it is difficult to make accurate projections of possible future violence. There are many reasons for this. One such reason is that assessors all too frequently are not in possession of a detailed, precise description of what actually happened in the first place to provoke the attention of the police or other authorities. Too often, clinicians are playing with half a deck. This idea comes up very strongly in Munro's story (for a full account, see Webster & Bélisle, 2014).

Risk Rule: When you bark up a tree, make sure it's the right one – Take as many perspectives as possible into account during assessment.

8. Actuarial Prediction

Giles Foden (2009) *Turbulence*

In this novel, brainy young meteorologist Henry Meadows recounts his involvement during one 'peculiar wartime winter' in a secret project to predict the atmospheric conditions that will allow the D-Day invasion (Operation Overlord) to proceed with maximum efficiency. Meadows is sent to Scotland. There his task is to extract information from a former, very eccentric, pacifistic meteorologist called Ryman. Meadows is in specific quest for the 'Ryman number'. It is believed by the high-ups that the Ryman number will enable them to select the best possible day and time to set Overlord into motion. Meadows has access to all kinds of measures having to do with the weather. It is a matter of comprehending 'turbulence'. For Meadows, turbulence is 'a predictable process seen from one perspective that becomes disordered and unpredictable viewed from another, or when observed over a different time period' (pp38–39). Given the size of the Allied operation and the strength of the German defences in Normandy, it was vital that the timing for Operation Overlord be as near-optimal as possible. It was a matter of getting moonlight to co-operate with absence of wind and rain.

With many a twist and turn, the story falls into place. Meadows finds the small window of opportunity and is able to advise his superiors as to when best to strike. He is able to do this because of sophisticated measures in place and his ability to co-ordinate and benefit from an array of statistical data.

For present purposes, the story helps readers to understand how difficult it can be to predict complicated physical events like the weather. Small wonder, then, it is so hard to predict violent acts – especially when mental disorders are involved. This is exactly the point John Monahan and Henry Steadman made several years ago (1996). A more straightforward account of weather prediction in the D-Day landing can be found in JM Staggs' (1971) *Forecast for Overlord, June 6 1944.*

Risk Rule: Measure twice, cut once – Decision making proceeds best when accurate and relevant measures are taken into account.

9. Prevention

Anton Chekov (1892) *Ward No 6*

The main actor in Chekov's story is a doctor, Andrei Yetmych. Not much to his liking, Dr Yetmych ends up practicing in a remote Russian community. Among his other medical responsibilities in the hospital lies the command of Ward 6. Although banished from city life, he nonetheless starts his appointment with enthusiasm. He sees the patients, prescribes the pills, he reads the latest journals. He fantasises about becoming acknowledged not only as a great scientist but a renowned philosopher. He has trouble reconciling his self-proclaimed brilliance with the fact that he is so far from the mainstream, surrounded by fools and incompetents.

Ward 6 is for the insane. It contains but five desperate inmates. These unfortunates are presided over by Nikita. Nikita was selected for the job on the basis of his army experience and the size of his fists. With these fists he rules the roost. Gradually, over time, the bright but lazy doctor comes to ruminate on how, despite his clear intellectual superiority, he has come to land up in such a position in such a place. That he comes to do little actual work does not much matter. His underlings pick up the slack. He also starts to drink more than is wise. What he fails to realise is that subordinates can have ambitions too. These juniors can contrive – as happened in this instance – a situation in which his basic competence could be investigated.

In due course he is dismissed. Later he is summoned to the hospital on a pretext. He assumes he is being invited to offer consultation in regard to some patient. Once at the hospital he is kept there and confined to the tender care of Nikita in Ward 6. Dr Yetmych comes to learn that, fine though philosophy may be, it pays to think of practical matters, that his misery could have been prevented had he kept a closer eye on what was occurring among his staff members under his very nose. The salutary tale should remind those of us who work with patients that we have responsibilities not only to our patients, but to our colleagues. The story gets across the point that our patients need the benefit of intellectual effort being applied to them and their circumstances in direct, practical ways.

Risk Rule: Don't trip on the kerb before crossing the road – Remain focused on caring for individual patients and members of your staff.

10. Serial measurement

Mikhail Bulgakov (1925) "Morphine" in A Country Doctor's Notebook

Young Dr Bromgard arrives at a small country town to assume a new practice. No sooner has he arrived than he receives word that Dr Polyakov, a colleague at a hospital some distance away, has fallen gravely ill. Before Bromgard can go to his friend's aid, Polyakov is brought to his own hospital with a self-inflicted gunshot wound. Barely conscious, Polyakov gives Bromgard his journal before dying. What Bromgard uncovers in the entries is Polyakov's uncontrollable descent into an unrelenting morphine addiction – started with an injection to soothe his back pain. The diary explains the thrill of the drug. The feverish final entries describe his ineluctable path to his death. It is the diary, with its serial entries, which helps the reader understand what took place and why. Much is made these days of the role of narrative in psychological assessment (see Wilson, 2011).

Risk Rule: A stitch in time saves lives – Patient self-reports of harm can be revelatory, and sometimes require swift action.

11. Structured Professional Judgment

Marcus Aurelius (160-180AD) *Meditations*

Derek Eaves was strongly influenced by the works of Marcus Aurelius. Ideas within works such as *Meditations* promote principles of self-development and adherence to one's values. In a more general way, Aurelius argued for maintaining flexibility of approach. He wanted to ensure sufficient balance creatively to make the best out of situations when different perspectives are taken by others. When such principles are applied to the field of risk assessment and treatment, we suggest being wary of self-professed experts who claim to know the 'one big thing' and are highly confident in their abilities to forecast events over the long term. From our experience it is better (and probably more accurate) to take a wider knowledge-based approach that is more humanistic and perhaps more modest in stance. Professional skill and peer support is required to avoid over-reliance on powerfully argued single points of view. Effective inter-disciplinary teams will often bring to bear multiple perspectives when facing a rehabilitation challenge with a client. The task is to figure out which perspective, or indeed perspectives, are seemingly most appropriate at each particular stage of rehabilitation.

Risk Rule: Bad workmen may blame their tools; terrible ones don't use any – Tread the path that has been trod before by using approaches supported by evidence.

12. Implementation

Margaret Gibson (1976) *The Butterfly Ward*

In *The Butterfly Ward* we meet Ada who is a long-time resident in a mental hospital. Years ago she suffered a lobotomy. Whereas pre-surgery Ada had a good vocabulary and an ear for poetry, she is left with little but childhood rhymes. These days she keeps a spiral-bound diary in which she maintains a calendar. She can tell anyone the day's date. It is her big accomplishment. There is a ward meeting. On this day the meeting is to be chaired by a young doctor-in-training. The meeting gets somewhat out of hand and Ada is insulted by another patient. The meeting has to be brought to a conclusion by the head nurse. Later, Ada is found in the dormitory singing softly to herself. At the other end is the body of the woman who demeaned her. Ada has used her metal spiral binding from her diary for a purpose unforeseen by the staff.

The story points up the fact that inpatient units can be dangerous place in which to live. Care is needed to minimise the presence of 'sharps'. More importantly, the story emphasises the idea that staff members have a big responsibility in these matter. The young doctor was seemingly ill-prepared for the role of implementing a therapeutically oriented ward meeting. The meeting, supposed to improve the social climate on the unit, did exactly the reverse.

Risk Rule: Scout's Motto – Be prepared (and be planful, be respectful, and be courteous) – Therapeutic gains can unravel fast when your patients are not kept appropriately up to speed.

13. Strengths

Charlotte Perkins Gilman (1928) *Making a Change*

In *Making a Change*, the younger Mrs Gordins is cast as the mother of an infant. She lives with her husband, Frank, and her mother-in-law, the elder Mrs Gordins. The young woman is having a tough time adjusting to motherhood. The baby's crying upsets her and she does not have the knack of soothing it. She misses her work as a music teacher. Frank, her husband, is preoccupied with his job. He leaves each morning with a spring in his step. He does not really notice that his wife is seriously depressed. The elder Mrs Gordins notices everything – particularly the fact that her daughter-in-law does not cope well with the baby. Changes need to be made. Her chance comes one day when she smells gas in the apartment. The odour she traces to the main bedroom. The door is locked. Undeterred, she effects a rescue. A bond between the two women is strengthened. Moreover, the elder Mrs Gordins now has an opportunity to set the family on a different course. She establishes a day-care on the roof of the building and takes great joy in managing it. The family income increases substantially. The younger Mrs Gordins is able to return to the teaching work she has so greatly missed. All this is done behind Frank's back. When Frank later comes to realise what has been done by his marvel of a mother, he cannot but be grateful.

The story shows how, with skill, patience and determination, seemingly 'hopeless' situations can be turned around. To us, the editors, Mrs Gordins is the kind of social worker or community nurse we are often lucky enough to meet. These are colleagues who can figure out what they have to work with, can share some of the burden, can grab what additional resources are needed, and get on with the job.

Risk Rule: A problem shared is a problem halved – When strengths are harnessed it makes it easier for people to get through hard times.

14. Intimate partner violence

Leo Tolstoy (1890) *The Kreutzer Sonata*

We meet Mr Pozdnyshev in a railway carriage. At first he holds himself apart from his coach-mates. But gradually he gets drawn into conversation. There is discussion about the education of women, whether or not love can last forever, and other such topics. Eventually Mr Pozdnyshev, evidently a member of the nobility, opens up. To everyone's surprise he declares that earlier he had killed his wife. He describes how well the marriage had worked, at least from his point of view, but eventually his wife tired of producing children and sought consultation from a doctor as how best to avoid these additions to their already large family. Although Mr Pozdnyshev disagreed with the doctor's advice, his wife was happy to gain a modicum of freedom. Yet, as it turned out, she developed an interest in her music teacher. Pozdnyshev, travelling on business, got the idea that things at home may have got out of hand. So he returned home abruptly. There, he surprised his wife and the teacher. The teacher fled, but an enraged Pozdnyshev stabbed his wife fatally.

It is in the carriage that Mr Pozdnyshev is able to unburden himself and to explain, at least to a degree, how he has managed to come to terms with his dreadful, indulgent act. He has, as we might say, 'gained insight'. In part, he traces the eventual murder to his childhood. He reflects on how he was encouraged to discount and diminish women from the beginning. Tolstoy also puts some meat on the DSM-5 Obsessional Jealousy potatoes. He shows how pathological jealousy develops (see DSM-5, p264 where it says merely that obsessional jealous is '…characterized by non-delusional preoccupation with a partner's perceived infidelity').

This novel caused a stir on its initial publication. It challenged the basic order that men and women can live in basic harmony and that, generally speaking, marriage is a fine thing. The full written story by the author is valuable to mental health, forensic and correctional professionals. It emphasises how rapidly emotions can change and how two persons in an intimate relationship can bring out the worst in one another. Mr Pozdnyshev literally works himself into such a state of paranoia that the murder of his wife seems more-or-less inevitable. The reader gets the impression that Mr Pozdnyshev is telling the truth. There is nothing deceptive in the story. The fact that the story is told to perfect strangers adds credibility to the account. There is no prosecutor or defence attorney trying to elicit some re-construction helpful to the accused or to the state. In this way we are presented with the kind of *unbiased* picture seldom offered in formal courts and tribunals.

Risk Rule: Beware the fixed idea – Morbid jealousy is a symptom to be treated vigorously.

15. Sexual offending

Barbara Gowdy (1992) *We so Seldom Look on Love*

We are very used to accounts of male sex offenders. Few readers of this volume will not have encountered Mr Humbert in Nabakov's *Lolita*, for example. For that reason we chose here to centre on an account of a female sex offender. Barbara Gowdie supplies an engaging story. As a girl the protagonist is obsessed with death. She buries small animals. And she comes to think she has stumbled across a form of 'secret activity' (life itself) that others would be delighted to experience if only they could have the chance. By 16 she knows what she wants: men. Dead men, to be precise. And so she gets a job in a mortuary.

In due course we are introduced to Matt, a medical student. She tells him straight-out that she is a necrophile and provides a lot of detail about her preferred activities in the morgue. Matt and she have sex, but this unsettles her. She figures that she's incapable of falling in love with a man who is not dead (p146), that she did not have the capability of turning off her urges. Matt announces that he is planning to commit suicide. She rushes over to his place. Matt is not dead. He is naked, standing on a step ladder with a noose around his neck. He kicks away the step ladder. At long last she gets him the way she has always wanted him. Gowdie treats us to an account of the gradual strengthening over time and circumstance of an attitude, an idea, a drive. Her story helps us understand how unusual, out-of-the-ordinary urges are developed and sustained. We come to realise how, once ensconced, these urges are very difficult to divert.

Risk Rule: Be careful what you urge for – Sexual impulses can be very strong and are sometimes expressed in strange and destructive forms.

16. Intellectual disability

Eric Blair (1927) *The Brothel Boy: A fragment of a manuscript*

Norval Morris, an influential sociologist, brought to light this short story by Eric Blair (George Orwell). He bought it in handwritten form while travelling in Burma. The subject of the story is a young, mentally-handicapped boy who works in a brothel. There he does routine janitorial chores around the place. At a certain point he decides to do to a young girl what he has seen other men do to her and her co-workers. But he is unaware of the niceties normally required in the complicate business of sex. He rapes her. In the process she bangs her head. The villagers beat the boy. The girl dies. The problem then for a young British administrator is figuring out what he should do next. It does not seem right to order the boy hanged. The boy had not understood the implications which would flow from his disastrous act against the girl. Nonetheless, with great reluctance, he has to bow to mob rule and have the boy put to death. Most modern countries have laws which protect persons like the brothel boy. Yet it remains the fact that the media oftentimes needs help from mental health professionals to explain that, despite having committed serious injury or death, many people can be helped to live a safe and productive life.

Risk Rule: One size does not fit all – Persons with intellectual disability (and other mental disorders) need special care and protection, especially when facing legal proceedings.

17. Gender

Joyce Carol Oates (1994) 'Extenuating Circumstances' in *Haunted: Tales of the Grotesque*

Oates' work is famous for its attention to violence perpetrated by men upon women, but she is equally powerful when representing the female as aggressor. In this tale, a woman, initially full of hope, has a child. The boy is two. She is on her own, her husband having deserted her. Although the husband does send some support payments through his lawyer, she is on her own emotionally and financially. Even her mother has backed out. Her job is to tend to the boy. Her circumstances are dismal. She can't pay the rent. Unaccountably, she still yearns for the man who has deserted her. It is the accumulation of small things that erodes what shreds of confidence remain. It is hot, very hot. It has not rained in ages. There are insects. There is incessant noise from machinery. There is the dust. She is lonely.

She can't sleep. Hope has run out. She is gaining weight. She has cramps. She is uncomfortable. She is reaching the limits of her endurance. And on top of all this, there is the boy's whining, his crying. One day it chances that the little lad near scalds himself to death by upending a pot of water reaching the boil on top of the kitchen stove. She averts a serious accident. Yet this very incident gets the young mother to thinking. Can accidents be made to happen? And so it came to pass that it did happen. The boy neither screamed nor struggled. His mother wrapped his body in his comforter and left. This story illustrates well how extreme violence can arise quickly, without much if any premeditation. It also shows how often it is not only a single thing that drives a person to commit such a crime, but rather the accumulation of many factors working in conjunction.

Risk Rule: Straws do break camels' backs – Women face challenges rarely faced by men, such as unremitting responsibility for child care.

18. Cultural influences

Richard Wagamese (2012) *Indian Horse*

This is a Canadian story, but it could be American, Australian, Finnish… Indeed, what is outlined in this story can be found in any culture in practically any part of the world. It is one culture playing out against another. As mental health professionals we see in our clinics and services our share of people who have been dispossessed, who are in particular need of support and protection. Wagamese's story starts off with an indigenous family trying to evade the Canadian authorities. It is set in a time when the government of the day believed that it was in the best interests of Native children to have them placed in residential schools. The idea was to separate the children from their languages and to make them suitable for lives as 'ordinary' Canadians. Although the last of the schools was shut down in 1996, residual, unaddressed effects remain. In the story, the boy, Saul Indian Horse, is eventually 'captured' and sent to a residential school. There, like all the other children, he is utterly miserable. But a new young priest joins the staff. The Father soon recognises that the boy has talent as a skater, a hockey player. The priest devotes a lot of attention to teaching him the game. Saul excels. He does well playing for local teams. Eventually, the priest is able to get him out of the school by having him more or less adopted by a 'hockey-mad' Indigenous family. In this environment the boy develops further his skills and plays competitive hockey to a high level. Yet the tension when the native boys play against white boys is palpable. They are subjected to many indignities. In the end, his life unravels. He leaves the family and becomes an itinerant labourer with a drinking problem. Eventually, he gets some professional help. The dénouement for the reader comes when it is revealed that it was the repeated sexual improprieties of the skater-priest who set the boy's life into the downward spiral suffered by so many alumni of the residential school system.

This story links to Douglas Boer's Chapter (18). It reminds mental health professionals that, for persons who have been cruelly abused, the usual clinical methods may not work especially well. It takes some doing, as this story illustrates, to help victims get to a point where they can relinquish their stories. It took Saul a long time to reach this stage and it was accomplished in part through the support he received upon return to his adoptive family.

Risk Rule: Turn on the lights in dark places – Be vigilant toward abusive power differentials, especially in institutions.

19. Group-based violence and terrorism

William Golding (1954) *Lord of the Flies*

Most readers will be acquainted with this novel. Indeed, many will have been *required* to have read it as schoolchildren. Golding is interested in exploring the basis of human nature, warts and all. For his platform he uses the idea of children, of varying ages, cast on an otherwise uninhabited island. It becomes apparent that, if they are to survive with hope of eventual rescue, some degree of order needs to be established. It falls to Ralph, maybe 12 years old, to establish basic rules. In this task he is assisted and advised by 'Piggy'. Piggy, fat and very short-sighted, is well used in his back-home existence, to being taunted and humiliated. Yet he has good sense. Early on, he points out to Ralph that they need a means of summoning other children who may have survived. He spots a conch shell and knows it can be used as a trumpet. Soon, they assemble a large group of kids.

Within the overall contingent a faction emerges led by Jack. The children in this sub-group are members of a choir. They appear in the beginning dressed in their chorister uniforms. They march military-style on the beach under Jack's command. At an early meeting Ralph asserts himself as the overall leader. There are many 'administrative tasks' for Ralph to deal with – the boys need protein to eat, they need shelter, and they need to have a way to announce their presence to any ship that might happen by. Ralph struggles bravely with this weight of responsibility. But Jack's faction, which takes on the role of hunting, becomes progressively more elemental, more violent. In the end, just as Ralph is about to fall prey to the hunters, the band is rescued by a passing naval vessel.

This story, though seemingly distant from the central issues dealt with in this book, is, in fact, perfectly relevant. Ask any seasoned hospital administrator about 'how things are going' and you will likely get an earful – government financial cutbacks, hard-to-comprehend court rulings, disputes with union leaders, complaints by staff members that they have been maltreated by colleagues, failure to meet aspects of accreditation standards, and so on. Just as Ralph found, there are at times too many rules and at time too few. Plenty of other parallels could be established, but let us just make one. The difficulty Ralph faces is that unhelpful ideas and actions can develop very quickly. These can spread like a disease, a contagious one. By way of example, we point to a recent paper by Beck, Tubbesing, Lewey, Ji, Mendito and Robbins (2018). These authors have studied how contagion can occur on a psychiatric inpatient unit. According to their findings, episodes of violence do not occur randomly. Rather the events are triggered by definable incidents and they are more likely to be set in train by some patients more than others.

Risk Rule: An ounce of prevention is worth a pound of cure – It is sometimes difficult for staff (and patients) to deal with anti-social and unconstructive currents, some deeply entrenched, some fleeting.

20. Recovery

O Henry (1904) *The Cop and the Anthem*

Readers of this volume are accustomed to the 'recovery paradigm'. A lot hinges on assisting patients to take small, sequentially-ordered, steps. In a previous volume we ourselves have advocated for such an approach (Webster *et al,* 2014). And we stand by it. Yet. Sometimes with the best will in the world, the process does not take hold. This short story by O Henry points up the case of 'Soapy Sam'. Soapy lives in New York City. Mostly he hangs out in the park. He is what we might call 'homeless'. But Soapy is by no means to be pitied. His life on the street is just fine – that is, it is perfectly good except when, in the fall, it turns cold. That is when Soapy needs to go south in search of warmer climes. To effect this happy transition, Soapy must get himself arrested. Normally, this would not be difficult. But in this particular year it proves a challenge. He tries all his familiar ploys – dine and dash, smash and grab, a bit of light sexual opportuning, simulated drunkenness, and so on. Nothing works. So desperate is he that, outside a church, he begins to think of 'leading a better life'. He could get a job, and so on. But this 'insight' is fleeting. He remains in despair. Then, when he is doing absolutely nothing, he feels the reassuring touch of the law on his shoulder. The policeman arrests him. The judge sentences him to Rikers Island for the winter months. Soapy is free at last. He will be warm, among friends, and well fed. He has not recovered. He has had nothing to recover from. He could be made out to be a violent criminal on the basis of most of his antics, but he is no such thing. The police and the court, to Soapy's great relief, 'constructed' him to be a menace. But in reality Soapy is no menace – he is simply in need of institutional support on a periodic basis.

In this very volume there is mention (Chapter 12) of a paper by Simpson *et al* (2018) which points this out. Once patients are granted complete release from oversight, a greater proportion 'fail' than might be expected. It seems evident that some persons come to depend on the support provided by mental health and addiction services and that they are bereft when the help is discontinued. All three of us can point to cases in which former patients have committed offences precisely to regain access to services they have come to rely on. It can be, too, that the level of support is higher in parts of the forensic rather than civil mental health system. Iatrogenic effects need consideration in some instances.

Risk Rule: Cut their coat according to their cloth – Concepts of recovery personally held by patients may not always fit with conventional models of care.

21. Patient involvement

Evelyn Waugh (1957) *The Ordeal of Gilbert Pinfold*

One of us (QH, Chapter 21) makes the point that, ideally, there needs to be a close partnership between patient and those professionals charged with caring for him or her. Too often, clinicians are playing with 'only half a deck'. This gulf, especially in forensic and correctional circles, can be due to the fact that lawyers, for their own good reasons, are at work advising their clients against full disclosure in respect to the intricacies of the case. But there is more a general problem in this regard: patients themselves very often do not expound all possibly relevant information to their doctors and other professionals. In no way is this more true than with regard to their actual consumption of alcohol and other drugs. So when the doctor writes a prescription he or she often has little knowledge of the background against which the new palliative will be operating.

In *The Ordeal of Gilbert Pinfold*, the eponymous protagonist is not playing it straight. He is cast as a writer. Gilbert is married and settled in an English village. He sees the local doctor for help with sleeping. The good Dr Drake prescribes some 'grey pills'. What the doc does not know is that Gilbert is already taking a sleeping draft washed down daily with prodigious amounts of booze. Gilbert's writing being temporarily stalled and he decides he needs a change of scene. So he signs up for a cruise bound for the East via the Mediterranean. On board he starts hearing voices in his cabin and elsewhere on the ship. These are of various kinds – mostly threatening, discrediting and punishing. These voices come with characters. Waugh treats his readers to a remarkable description of how paranoia can develop. Mr Pinfold comes to be seen by the captain, the crew, and fellow passengers, as distinctly odd. Eventually, Gilbert changes cabins in an attempt to elude the voices. But they follow him. He returns early to England by air. There, his wife encourages him to see a psychologist. But by then Gilbert has figured out that he had suffered from the poisoning effects of drugs and that, recovered, he had no need of a 'looney doctor' (p154). He does agree, however, to see Dr Drake, to whom he confesses that he had had a bottle of chloral of his own (p156). The good doctor expostulates: 'That is the trouble with patients... One never knows what else they are taking on the quiet. I've known people make themselves thoroughly ill.' (p156)

*Risk Rule: Get to the nub – Genuinely helpful professionals must become adept at figuring out what they are **actually** dealing with.*

22. Transitions

Evelyn Waugh (1967) *Mr Loveday's Little Outing*

Once the present three editors have become presidents of their respective professional organisations – psychiatry, clinical criminology, social work – they plan to issue, simultaneously, an edict. Under this executive order, all members of these professions will be required to demonstrate each year that they have re-read Waugh's tale. It is simply that the story covers many sound clinical principles. Certainly two of the present editors have done their best to promulgate the tale (Webster *et al*, 2014, pp174-176). In this brief account we have extracted just one principle – be vigilant during transitions and ensure that there are securely in place adequate supports and sufficient supervision.

Lady Moping is upset. Her annual garden party was ruined by the fact that her husband chose the occasion to try to hang himself in the greenhouse. For this he is despatched to the County Home for Mental Defectives. In the Home, the good Lord is perfectly content. Much of his happiness is due to the fact that he is so well aided in his 'researches' by Mr Loveday. Mr Loveday is in fact a long-time fellow patient, though this would not be obvious to an outsider. He is a kind and thoughtful man, very devoted to the Lord and a few other well-heeled patients. Indeed, so well does Mr Loveday support the good Lord that the Lord does not actually need help from Lady Moping and her family. Lady Moping, out of pure generosity, visits once a year. Their daughter, now grown up, asks one year if she can accompany her mum on the trek to the home. Angela finds her dad to be as deranged as ever. But she cannot help but be impressed by the attentiveness of Mr Loveday. She asks the superintendent about him. The superintendent tells her that, indeed, Mr Loveday is a patient. He even tells her what crime Mr Loveday had committed long ago. And he mentions that Mr Loveday, whose services are invaluable to the home, had been perfectly sane for many a year. Angela figures that Mr Loveday, being such an all-round wonder, deserved to be released. She asks Mr Loveday whether discharge would suit him. He responds by saying it would be a wrench to leave his charges but concedes there is 'one little thing' he would like to do. And he adds that it 'wouldn't take long'. Angela inveighs with the Home Office. In due course Mr Loveday is granted his and her wish. There is a farewell tea party in the superintendent's office and Mr Loveday steps out, free at last, into the sunshine. After a couple of hours he returns and knocks at the superintendent's door. The superintendent is naturally surprised. He exclaims to Mr Loveday that 'You can hardly have enjoyed yourself at all'. To this, Mr Loveday responds by saying that he had enjoyed himself very much, and that now he can with pleasure re-assume his duties. It turns out that during his brief hours outside the home he had knocked a young woman off her bicycle and murdered her. It was this precise act that got him to the Home in the first place. The story points up the idea that being a 'model patient' in one set of circumstances does not guarantee continued commendable conduct in others.

Risk Rule: Mind the gap – Stay curious.

Related movies

These films relate, at least tangentially, to the short stories and novels discussed above.

1. Beautiful Dreamers (John Kent Harrison, Canada, 1990; or The Alienist, Jakob Verbruggen *et al*, USA, 2018)

2. To Kill a Mockingbird (Robert Mulligan, USA, 1962)

3. Dr. Fischer of Geneva (Michael Lindsay-Hogg, UK, 1984)

4. Richard III (Richard Loncraine, UK, 1995)

5. Captain Newman, M.D. (David Miller, USA, 1963) or The Best of Men (Tim Whitby, UK, 2012)

6. Elling (Peter Naess, Norway, 2001)

7. Heavenly Creatures (Peter Jackson, New Zealand, 1994)

8. The Imitation Game (Morten Tyldum, UK, 2014)

9. The Death of Mr. Lazarescu (Cristi Puiu, Romania, 2005) or Britannia Hospital (Lindsay Anderson, UK, 1982)

10. The Seven-Per-Cent Solution (Herbert Ross, USA, 1976)

11. The Fall of the Roman Empire (Anthony Mann, USA, 1964)

12. Outrageous! (Richard Benner, Canada, 1977)

13. My Brilliant Career (Gillian Armstrong, Australia, 1979) or Alice Doesn't Live Here Anymore (Martin Scorsese, USA, 1974)

14. The Kreutzer Sonata (Bernard Rose, USA, 2008)

15. Kissed (Lynne Stopkewich, Canada, 1996)

16. Boy A (John Crowley, UK, 2007) or Of Mice and Men (Gary Sinise, USA, 1982) or Little Children (Todd Field, USA, 2006) or Sling Blade (Billy Bob Thornton, USA, 1996)

17. Jeanne Dielman, 23 Commerce Quay, 1080 Brussels (Chantal Akerman, Belgium, 1975) or The Rapture (Michael Tolkin, USA, 1991)

18. Indian Horse (Stephen S. Campanelli, Canada, 2017)

19. Lord of the Flies (Harry Hook, UK, 1990)

20. The Hundred Year-Old Man Who Climbed Out of the Window and Disappeared (Felix Herngren, Sweden, 2013)

21. Requiem for a Dream (Darren Aronofsky, USA, 2000)

22. Mr. Loveday's Little Outing (Sam Hobkinson, UK, 2006) or The Ruling Class (Peter Medak, UK, 1972) or What About Bob? (Frank Oz, USA, 1991)

Literary references

Marcus Aurelius (160-180AD) *Meditations*. Penguin Classic (2006).

Eric Blair (1927) 'The Brothel Boy: A Fragment of a Manuscript'. In: Norval Morris (1982) *Madness and the Criminal Law*. University of Chicago Press.

Pat Barker (1991) *Regeneration*. Viking.

James Brussel (1968) *Casebook of a Crime Psychologist*. Bernard Geis Associates; distributed by Grove Press.

Mikhail Bulgakov (1925) Morphine. In: *A Country Doctor's Notebook*. New Directions Pearl, 2013.

Anton Chekov (1892-1895) *Ward No. 6 and Other Stories*. Penguin Classics (2002).

William Golding (1954) *Lord of the Flies*. Faber and Faber (1997)

Giles Foden (2009) *Turbulence*. Faber & Faber.

Margaret Gibson (1976) *The Butterfly Ward*. Vanguard.

Charlotte Perkins Gilman (1928) *Making a Change*.

Graham Greene (1981) *Doctor Fischer of Geneva or the Bomb Party*. Vintage (1999).

Barbara Gowdy (1992) *We so Seldom Look on Love*. Flamingo (2008).

Harper Lee (1960) *To Kill a Mockingbird* (Arrow).

Sinclair Lewis (1935) *It Can't Happen Here* (Penguin Modern Classics).

Alice Munro (2009) Child's Play. In: *Too Much Happiness* (pp188–223). Toronto: McClleland & Stewart.

Vladimir Nabakov (1972) *Transparent Things*. Penguin Modern Classics (2011)

Joyce Carol Oates (1994) Extenuating Circumstances. In: *Haunted: Tales of the grotesque*. Penguin (1995).

O Henry (1994) The Cop and the Anthem. In: *The Best Short Stories of O. Henry* (pp19–26). Originally published 1907. New York: Modern Library.

Leo Tolstoy (1890) *The Kreutzer Sonata*. Penguin Classics (2007).

Richard Wagamese (2012) *Indian Horse*. BC: Madiera Park.

Evelyn Waugh (1962) *The Ordeal of Gilbert Pinfold*. Originally published, 1957. Harmondsworth, Middlesex: Penguin.

Evelyn Waugh (1951) Mr Loveday's Little Outing. In: *Work Suspended and Other Stories*. pp 7-15.

Additional references

Beck NC, Tubbesing T, Lewey JH, Ji P, Menditto AA, & Robbins SB (2018) Contagion of violence and self-harm behaviors on a psychiatric ward. *Journal of Forensic Psychiatry and Psychology* **29** 989–1006.

Robertson Davies (1985) Murder as it looks to a literary man. In: MH Ben-Aron, SJ Hucker & CD Webster (Eds). *Clinical Criminology: The assessment and treatment of criminal behaviour* (pp299–311). Toronto, Canada: M and M Graphics.

Fyodor Dostoevsky (1866) *Crime and Punishment*. Penguin Classics (2014).

Monahan J & Steadman HJ (1996) Violent storms and violent people: How meteorology can inform risk communication in mental health law. *American Psychologist* **51** 931–938.

Simpson AIF, Chatterjee S, Duchcherer M, Ray I, Prosser A & Penney SR (2018) Short-term outcomes for forensic patients receiving an absolute discharge un the Canadian Criminal Code. *The Journal of Forensic Psychiatry & Psychology* **29** 867-881.

Webster CD & Bélisle E (2014) How Literature Can Add Value to Structured Professional Judgments of Violence Risks: An Illustrative Rare Risk Example Inspired by Alice Munro's Child's Play. *Archives of Forensic Psychology* **1** 14–26.

Webster MS (1981) Responsibility and madness in Dostoevsky's Crime and Punishment. In: CD Webster, SJ Hucker & MH Ben-Aron (Eds) *Mental Disorder and Criminal Responsibility* pp175–195. Toronto: Butterworths.

Wilson TD (2011) *Redirect: The Surprising New Science of Psychological Change*. New York: Little, Brown.

Appendix: Filmography
(compiled by Robert Menzies)

Films relevant to the study of violence and clinical risk assessment:

10 Rillington Place (Richard Fleischer, UK, 1971)

Alias Grace (Mary Harron, Canada, 2017)

Betty Blue (30 d 2 Le Matin) (Jean-Jacques Beineix, France, 1986)

Boy A (John Crowley, UK, 2007)

Devil's Knot (Atom Egoyan, Canada, 2013)
Enduring Love (Roger Michell, UK, 2004)
Extremely Wicked, Shockingly Evil and Vile (Joe Berlinger, USA, 2019)
Heavenly Creatures (Peter Jackson, New Zealand, 1994)
House of Fools (Andrey Konchalovskiy, Russia, 2002)
In Cold Blood (Richard Brooks, USA, 1967)
Lacombe, Lucien (Louis Malle, France, 1974)
L'Enfer (Claude Chabrol, France, 1994)
Legend (Brian Helgeland, UK, 2015)
Longford (Tom Hooper, UK, 2006))
Memories of a Murder (Bong Joon-ho, South Korea, 2003)
Monster (Patty Jenkins, USA, 2003)
Polytechnique (Denis Villeneuve, Canada, 2009)
Salaam Bombay! (Mira Nair, India, 1988)
Swoon (Tom Kalin, USA, 1992)
The Lesser Blessed (Anita Doron, Canada, 2012)
The Lives of Others (Florian Henckel von Donnersmarck, Germany, 2006)
The Professor and the Madman (Farhad Safinia, Ireland/Croatia, 2019)
Titus (Julie Taymor, UK, 1999)
Tyrannosaur (Paddy Considine, UK, 2011)
We Need to Talk About Kevin (Lynne Ramsey, UK, 2011)

Films depicting the human experience of psychiatric distress/disorder/madness:

A Woman Under the Influence (John Cassavetes, USA, 1974)
An Angel at My Table (Jane Campion, New Zealand, 1990)
Angel Baby (Michael Rymer, Australia, 1995)
Brain on Fire (Gerard Barrett, Canada, 2016)
Camille Claudel (Bruno Nuytten, France, 1988)
Clean (Olivier Assayas, France/Canada/USA, 2004)
Cosi (Mark Joffe, Australia, 1996)
Elling (Peter Naess, Norway, 2001)
Family Life (Ken Loach, UK, 1971)
Frances (Graeme Clifford, USA, 1982)
Jimmy P. (Arnaud Desplechin, France, 2013)
Keane (Lodge Kerrigan, USA, 2004)
Le Huitième Jour (Jaco Van Dormael, Belgium/France/Canada, 1996)
Mad to Be Normal (Robert Mullan, UK, 2017)
Man Facing Southeast (Eliseo Subiela, Argentina, 1986)

Manic (Jordon Melamed, USA, 2001))
Respiro (Emanuele Crialese, Italy, 2002)
Safe (Todd Haynes, USA, 1995)
Shine (Scott Hicks, Australia, 1996)
Sylvia (Christine Jeffs, UK, 2003)
The Private Lives of Pippa Lee (Rebecca Miller, USA, 2009)
The Virgin Suicides (Sofia Coppola, USA, 1999)
Through a Glass Darkly (Ingmar Bergman, Sweden, 1961)
Unsane (Steven Soderbergh, USA, 2018)
Vincent Wants to Sea (Ralf Huettner, Germany, 2010)

* For details on the above-listed films, refer to the Internet Movie Data Base: www.imdb.com

Afterword: Some thoughts on this volume and reflections on the future

By John Petrila

Derek Eaves was a visionary. With a handful of colleagues, he imagined and breathed into life the International Association of Forensic Mental Health Services. The annual IAFMHS conference is one of the best forensic conferences in the world, one of the only places you can find an international and truly interdisciplinary group of individuals interested not only in research but practice, not only in clinical care but policy. The Association's journal has found a place in an increasingly crowded field and provides one of the few outlets for both forensic scholars and practitioners from around the world. Derek was also, to use Henry Steadman's phrase, a 'boundary spanner' (Steadman, 1992). He could see across disciplinary lines and national boundaries, and IAFMHS and this book both reflect his vision.

The state of the field

This book is a reminder of how far the field has advanced in the last four decades. We have come from risk prediction to risk assessment, and from risk assessment to risk management, and Hart and Douglas (this volume) do a superb job summarising the evolution in our thinking.

However, the changes in the field, particularly in assessing risk, are both more profound and nuanced than the shorthand summary suggests. Four developments in particular stand out from the excellent chapters in this book.

First, the development of a research-based approach to risk assessment, with findings published in refereed journals and articulated through the creation of assessment instruments, has permitted the creation of a truly international forum in which to discuss the issues. The 'internationalisation' of the field is easy to take for granted at this time. However, without the tremendous body of research into risk assessment that has emerged over the last two decades, we would not have seen the emergence of a common language across national boundaries that permits debates about risk assessment approaches (SPJ versus purely actuarial instruments) that are not bound by the legal rules of particular jurisdictions. *Application* of the results of a risk assessment occur within the rules and processes of the specific legal system, but the debates about the basic approach can occur outside those processes because of the research captured in this book.

Second, research is essential, but not enough. Haque and Webster note (this volume), 'It is necessary to point out that, as well as providing a protocol for evaluating risks and risk management practices in individual persons, those who develop SPJ schemes *must* be able to produce data to show that the scheme possesses *reliability* and *validity*'. But beyond reliability and validity, it is also essential to consider gender, the personal experience of the individual who will be assessed, and cultural norms and distinctions. Nicholls, for example, points out that while some factors relevant to risk are not gender-specific, others (for example procriminal attitudes) may vary by degree or, as with trauma, frequency. Bloom's discussion of trauma at least implicitly suggests the limitations of a purely actuarial approach to risk assessment and reminds us of why focusing on the experience of the person is critical, not only to understand and manage future risk better, but also out of simple fairness to the individual. It is encouraging, then, to see that the HCR-20 V3 substitutes for Item H8 'History of Problems with Traumatic Experiences' for 'Early Maladjustment'. Finally, culture (whether broadly or narrowly defined) and race can affect individual and group attitudes regarding mental illness, help-seeking behavior and other factors relevant to treatment (Office of the Surgeon General, 2001) as well as the application of risk assessment measures (Shepherd & Anthony, 2018). Boer (Chapter 18, this volume) makes this point explicitly in his discussion of the unfairness of applying the HCR-20 V3 to an Aboriginal population. He stresses the necessity of working with members of affected populations to reshape risk assessment schemes so that they are culturally informed. This opens up another line of query of course: as one infuses a particular risk assessment scheme with an appropriately culturally enlightened approach, does this markedly erode the foundation of the basic device on which the approach rests? Also, does it diminish reliability and validity? These questions need to be raised, and ultimately addressed.

Third, the increased emphasis on the management of risk and prevention of future violence is a salutary development in a field that, at least in its early years, was primarily concerned with increasing the precision and accuracy of risk assessments without much regard to what then came next. The HCR-20 and the Short-Term Assessment of Risk and Treatability (START) are explicitly concerned with identifying treatment specific issues; this approach is consistent, at least generally, with the emphasis in many contemporary treatment programmes such as the Risk Need Responsivity model and Good Lives Model of treatment adopted by many criminal justice programmes today (Andrews *et al*, 2011).

In attempting to manage risk, the complexity of the individual matters: Mary-Lou Martin's insistence on the importance of assessing client strengths, and Eusterschulte's discussion of the negative effect of our failure to do our best in considering intellectual disability, illustrate this point, as does Simpson's chapter on recovery and giving individuals the skills to manage their own care. A failure to consider the person's strengths not only provides limited information but is unfair to the individual and it exaggerates the imbalance in the relationship between risk assessor and the person being assessed.

Finally, the field now benefits, at least in a limited way, from longitudinal research. As Crocker points out, Steadman pioneered the use of longitudinal studies and effectively brought social science to bear on the then embryonic field of mental health law, through his Baxstrom study (Steadman & Halfon, 1971). However, these studies are difficult to do because they require the existence of accessible databases as well as capable researchers, like Sheilagh Hodgins, to mine them. Unless these existing sources of information are cultivated, they cannot provide as much knowledge in fact as they might in principle. This kind of work, as David Farrington can attest, takes years of gruelling study. All the same, the findings of Anne Crocker's study (Chapter 27, this volume) provide the type of evidence over time that we need to understand not only violence, but attempts to assess and prevent it.

Some thoughts on where we might go

I am mindful that as an attorney who has spent the last few years immersed in health care policy rather than forensics or even mental health law, my perspective on forensic services as we contemplate the next two decades will be quite different from that of researchers and practitioners whose work is at the centre of forensic work. There have also been more in-depth attempts to identify future developments, opportunities and threats to forensic psychology than this brief afterword permits (Otto & Heilbrun, 2002; Grisso, 1987). However, reading this very fine book has provoked some reflections not only on what the field has accomplished, but also on what seems missing.

The focus on risk assessment over the last four decades resulting in the many advances captured in this volume has been appropriate, given that risk assessment had no scientific basis when controversies over its application emerged in the legal system, and given that individual liberty and community safety are at stake when risk assessment is called for, and decision-making that mediates between those two values should be as precise and rigorous as possible. At the same time, there is a danger that the field of forensic mental health services has become overly occupied with the *manner* in which risk assessment is done, with too little concern for the world in which it sits.

Three issues are worth noting. One involves definition of the field itself. The second involves the effect that developments in health care more broadly might have on risk assessment in practice. And the third is the virtual disappearance of consideration of 'the law' as something more than the set of rules governing the use of risk assessment findings.

First, how do we define the reach of the field? Otto and Heilbrun (2002, p5) defined forensic psychological assessment as 'the psychological assessment of persons for the purpose of assisting the legal fact finder'. Involuntary civil commitment is a legal process in which risk, to self or to others, is the primary issue; civil commitment results in deprivation of liberty and the 'Baxstrom' study by Steadman and Halfon (1971) introducing the use of social science research to law, emerged from a United States Supreme Court decision (Baxstrom v Herold, 1966) holding that a prisoner with mental illness could not be confined after his prison term ended unless he was civilly committed. And harm to self, not risk to others, is the dominant issue in civil commitment proceedings, something Segal (1989) noted three decades ago. Indeed, far more people die around the world from suicide than homicide (Grinshteyn & Hemenway, 2016), and depression is the leading cause of disability worldwide, and a major factor in the 800,000 deaths from suicide annually (Friedrich, 2017). Yet forensic psychology has little to say on the subject, preoccupied instead with risk to third parties, an important but less worrisome issue in public health terms than the risk of harm to self.

Second, the context in which risk assessment occurs is increasingly far from the lab in which risk assessment instruments are developed. Otto and Heilbrun (2002) described multiple examples of treatment issues relevant to 'forensic populations', such as treatment amenability of juveniles subject to transfer to adult court; treatment strategies for addressing deficits associated with incompetency to stand trial; and violence risk strategies in the context of outpatient civil commitment or community treatment orders. They noted that there had been little research or scholarly attention devoted to these issues, something that has changed very little in the nearly two decades since their article. In addition, as risk assessment has grown more structured and instructions for performing it more detailed, most people with mental illnesses are now treated, when treatment is accessible, in settings in which symptom reduction and short inpatient stays dominate (Thornicroft *et al*, 2016). Even in the context of a legal setting such as a jail, stays are often very brief. As a practical matter, there is simply not time to use sophisticated risk assessment devices, even when staff are adequately trained to do so, something that Haque and Webster note is essential both practically and ethically (Chapter 11, this volume). The result is that forensic practice and standards exist in the smaller part of a very bifurcated universe: when people are confined long enough, or the legal stakes are high enough to require risk assessment by fully trained practitioners, sophisticated forensic practice can be brought to bear. But in the much larger world beyond, the lack of time and trained staff means that risk assessment will occur repeatedly without reference to the guides and techniques discussed in this volume.

Finally, what is most striking by its absence in this book and the field of forensic mental health services more broadly is the absence of discussion of the law itself. Even Schneider's chapter is more concerned with legal process than the legal frameworks that shape forensic practice. It may also be worth reflecting in this regard that there are no attorneys among the IAFMHS Board of Directors, Members At-Large, Ex-Officio Members, and (with one exception) the Advisory Board. This is striking in a field that exists primarily (in Otto and Heilbrun's words) 'for the purpose of assisting the legal factfinder'. I think it also reflects the shrinking of the field's perspective: as it has occupied itself with research into *how* risk assessment is done, it has to an increasing degree lost contact with the world in which risk assessment actually occurs.

To a large degree, forensic psychology and the focus on risk emerged because of legal ferment. Mental health law emerged from the civil rights movement, animated in part by the elasticity of the diagnostic systems and unstructured performance of risk assessment that led to a long-term loss of liberty in both civil and criminal justice systems (Petrila, 1992). Court decisions forced governments to revamp the conditions under which involuntary confinement could occur, primarily (in the context of involuntary commitment) by requiring a finding of dangerousness. The science of risk assessment developed largely because of the need to create more precise measures in response to the demands of the legal system.

Today, the search for more precision continues, but the legal context which shapes not only practice but the conditions under which people are held as 'dangerous', appear to be taken for granted. This is despite the fact that people are held indefinitely as sexual offenders, as putative terrorists, as not guilty by reason of insanity.

None of these concluding observations should be read as discrediting this book, which stands as a worthy acknowledgement of the work of Derek Eaves – a visionary, a boundary spanner, and a giant of the field. I expect he would read it with great pleasure, give full credit for it to others, and begin talking with his colleagues about where to push the field next.

References

Andrews DA, Bonta J & Wormith JS (2011) The risk-need-responsivity (RNR) model: Does adding the Good Lives Model contribute to effective crime prevention? *Criminal Justice and Behavior* **38** 735–755.

Baxstrom v Herold, 387 U.S. 107 (1966).

Friedrich M (2017) Depression is the leading cause of disability around the world. *JAMA* **317** (15) 1517 doi:10.1001/jama.2017.3826.

Grinshteyn E & Hemenway D (2016) Violent death rates: The US compared with other high-income OECD countries, 2010. *The American Journal of Medicine* **129** 266–273.

Grisso T (1987) The economic and scientific future of forensic psychological assessment. *American Psychologist* **9** 831–839.

Otto R & Heilbrun K (2002). The practice of forensic psychology: a look to the future in light of the past. *American Psychologist* **57** (1) 5–18.

Office of the Surgeon General (US); Center for Mental Health Services (US); National Institute of Mental Health (US). Mental Health: Culture, Race, and Ethnicity: A Supplement to Mental Health: A Report of the Surgeon General. Rockville (MD): Substance Abuse and Mental Health Services Administration (US); 2001 Aug. Chapter 2 Culture Counts: The Influence of Culture and Society on Mental Health. Available from: https://www.ncbi.nlm.nih.gov/books/NBK44249/

Petrila J (1992) Redefining mental health law: thoughts on a new agenda. *Law and Human Behavior* **16** (1) 89–106.

Segal S (1989) Civil commitment standards and patient mix in England/Wales, Italy, and the United States. *American Journal of Psychiatry* **146** (2) 187–193.

Shepherd SM & Anthony T (2018) Popping the cultural bubble of violence risk assessment tools. *The Journal of Forensic Psychiatry & Psychology* **29** (2) 211–220. DOI: 10.1080/14789949.2017.1354055

Steadman HJ & Halfon A (1971) The Baxstrom patients: backgrounds and outcomes. *Seminars in Psychiatry* **3** (3) 376–385.

Steadman H (1992) Boundary spanners: a key component for the effective interactions of the justice and mental health systems. *Law and Human Behavior* **16** 1 (February 1992) 75–87.

Thornicroft G, Deb T & Henderson C (2016) Community mental health care worldwide: current status and further developments. *World Psychiatry* **15** (3) 276–286.